# Translator Self-Training Chinese

## Practical Course in Technical Translation

Morry Sofer



Schreiber Publishing
Rockville, Maryland

Second Printing



Library of Congress Control Number: 2002105647
ISBN 1-887563-70-9

Printed in the U.S.A. by Schreiber Publishing, PO Box 4193, Rockville, Maryland 20849
www.schreiberpublishing.com

# Preface

This practical course is for anyone who would like to pursue technical translation in Chinese and English, in such areas as legal, medical, financial or other kinds of non-literary documents (literary translation is a different discipline from technical).

The course is based on the practical experience of a major translation company which has been translating—routinely and successfully—Chinese-into-English and English-into-Chinese documents in all technical areas for almost twenty years. The assignments in this book are taken from real-life documents which were translated by this company, with names and other information changed in some cases to protect proprietary information.

This book grew out of a correspondence course offered about ten years ago, which became a three-ring binder program for translator's self-training five years ago. During those five years, hundreds of translators have used this program each year, and many have offered unsolicited praise for this program, letting us know that it has improved their translation skills, and in more than a few cases helped the user pass accreditation or certification tests for such organizations as the American Translators Association (ATA).

Nothing sharpens translation skills more than the actual act of translating. But one needs an entry point, either into the technical translation field in general, or into new areas of translation, if one has already been doing one kind of technical translation, such as legal. This course provides the entry point.

We at Schreiber Publishing take a personal interest in translators in all languages and subjects, and are always happy to hear from you.

Enjoy the course!

*Morry Sofer*

# Table of Contents

Appendices

# Section 1. General

## Introduction

Welcome to *Schreiber's* **Translator Self-Training Program**. We are very pleased you selected this program, which has been in use since 1992. It has helped aspiring translators around the country get their start in this exciting field while assisting practicing translators in improving their translation skills. Translation is one of the fastest growing professions in today's world, as different languages and cultures are coming closer together every day. Whether you wish to pursue translation full-time or as a sideline, you will find it to be a highly challenging and quite profitable occupation. The purpose of the following exercises is to help you improve your skills as a Chinese-into-English translator.

This program is designed to help you work at your own pace and gain experience through translation practice assignments. These assignments, excerpted from actual translation jobs, were selected to help you determine your own level of comfort and expertise, so that you may go on from there to choose the type of translation work you may like to pursue.

To derive the maximum benefit from these texts, you should carefully read the General Comments, the guidelines, and the specific notes which discuss each assignment. Every comment and every guideline represents years of experience in professional translation work. By carefully following this program, you will be able to achieve *in just a few days* what has taken others years to learn. You will be guided through many of the pitfalls of translation, taught how to avoid them, shown shortcuts in accomplishing a complex piece of translation work, and be given the benefit of comments designed to show you how to produce a translation acceptable to major clients such as government, industry, the legal world, and many more.

Before you read further, we strongly urge you to read Appendix A: Requisites for Professional Translators, and Appendix B: Translation Techniques.

The above-listed Appendices will give you a good overview of how translation work is to be approached and practiced. Try to keep the contents of these chapters in mind as you translate the following assignments.

You are presented with four different texts which, for most people, represent an increasing level of difficulty. They are:

1. **General**
2. **Legal**
3. **Chemical/Medical**
4. **Business/Finance**

At a minimum, you may want to do the first and second assignments. Those two represent a vast body of material which is being translated in the United States on a regular basis, but which does not require a highly specialized vocabulary or technical background. The third assignment requires access to chemical and medical terminology, which can be managed by any intelligent translator. The fourth assignment should be approached with caution. Here one must have an understanding of the world of finance, which not all of us do. For your own self-assessment, you may want to try it (since we provide you with the translation, you can compare the results and see for yourself how you did). But if you find it too difficult, don't be discouraged. It is clearly not for everyone.

We hope you enjoy working with these texts, and we urge you to please be patient with yourself. One does not become an accomplished translator overnight. To learn, one must make mistakes. If your heart is in it, and if you love the challenge of working with two languages you happen to know well, then you are sure to get a great deal out of this program.

**A Word about Chinese Translation**

More than 1.2 billion people speak various dialects of Chinese in the People's Republic of China. Another six million or so speak Cantonese in Hong Kong. A further 21 million or so Chinese live on Taiwan. And there are countless Chinese communities spread throughout southeast Asia and the rest of the world. Despite differences in accent and dialect, the written language has historically been the unifying element of the widely dispersed Chinese community.

The written language has split into two, however. Prior to WWII, the Chinese characters in use throughout the Chinese-speaking world were essentially the same. In the 1950s, with the avowed goal of shortening the road to literacy, the Communist government began issuing simplified characters. However, Chinese communities outside mainland China, with the exception of Singapore, have for the most part continued to use traditional characters. For instance, in the United States, the vast majority of Chinese newspapers are still published in traditional characters - including the overseas edition of the 人民日报.

In addition, there are regional differences in terminology that go beyond the distinction between simplified and traditional characters. For instance, much of China refers to a bicycle as a "自行车." A term often heard in Taiwan is "腳踏車," while people whose primary dialect is Taiwanese/Fukinese will be familiar with the terms "孔明車" and "鐵馬." And speakers of Cantonese often employ the term "單車." The fact that this list is by no means exhaustive provides some insight into the tremendous breadth of vocabulary in Chinese even for simple, everyday objects.

This diversity is reflected in the generation of modern technological vocabulary as well. A computer, even in a scientific text, might be referred to as a "计算机" or a "電腦." A hard disk is sometimes referred to as an "硬盘," and sometimes as an "硬碟." And software is known as "软件" and "軟體." The list goes on and on.

The bottom line is that, to be competitive, a Chinese-English translator needs to be able to fluently read both simplified and traditional characters and have a sensitivity to the rapid, sometimes overlapping generation of vocabulary occurring in modern Chinese.

## General Comments

The following comments are offered with two purposes in mind: the immediate purpose is to help you with the assignments. The long-term purpose is to serve as reference material for actual translation work. Keep them for future use.

A reminder:
The "source language" is the language you translate from.
The "target language" is the language you translate into.

Every language has its own "personality," so to speak. When you translate, pretend you are two different persons - a "Chinese Person" and an "English Person." The Chinese Person reads the original Chinese text, and becomes familiar with it. The Chinese Person then turns to the English Person, and says to him/her, "Okay, now it's your turn to say the same thing your way." Now the English Person takes over, and starts writing the same text in English. You will be constantly switching back and forth between the Chinese and the English Persons, as the first checks the Chinese word, phrase, sentence structure, and then the second thinks in English and comes up with the right equivalents. Here are some of the main language issues you will have to deal with:

### Clarity

We each have our own personal style of expressing ourselves - in any language. Some people make their point clearly and succinctly, while others use more words than necessary, including esoteric words, to make their point. The same holds true in translation. You can translate the phrase, " 魚與熊掌不可得兼 ," as "You can't have your cake and eat it, too," or you could also translate it correctly as, "You can't have it both ways." In the first instance, nine words were used; in the second, only six. Most of the time, the second translation is better, because it is simpler and shorter. Make it your point to pursue simplicity whenever possible.

### Consistency

Most of the time, if you start out translating the Chinese word "大樓" as "house," stick to "house," and don't start suddenly shifting to "building," or vice versa. The reader may become confused, wondering why the word suddenly changed. Generally in English, building is bigger than house, and one may wonder whether the dimensions of that particular structure might have changed. If you are familiar with word-processing you know how easy it is to do a "global search and replace" throughout the text, so that if halfway into the document you decide that "building" is better than "house," then go back to the beginning and do a global change, replacing the word "house" with "building."

## Sentence Structure

It is difficult, yet very important, to ensure that sentence structure is correct and makes sense, yet still retains the flavor of the original text, particularly if this is written in a flowery, elaborate, or otherwise unique style. This fine line is achieved mainly through practice, but it is definitely helpful to read the original several times before even beginning the translation process in order to gain a good idea of the author's style.

It is not necessary to follow the structure of a sentence literally. A run-on sentence which may make sense in one language may not make sense in the other, and therefore should be divided into two sentences (or more). The converse is also true. You should also avoid being too literal when it comes to word order, or your text will sound stilted, awkward, and artificial. You will need to rely on your own good writing skills in determining the most sensible word order and punctuation so that your translation flows smoothly.

## Format

Format should be followed as closely as possible. Ideally, every page of translation should look exactly like the corresponding page of the original, except, of course, for the language. There is a very practical reason for this. It helps the reader, who may or may not know the source language, compare the two texts, make sure all the parts are there, and check a particular word or phrase in the source text. This, however, is not always possible, since a page of translation at times is longer than the same page in the source language. Nevertheless, every effort should be made to keep the format as similar as possible to the original.

## Terminology

The use of the right terminology is critical in any translation, especially in any technical subject. Here the right kind of dictionaries and reference literature becomes very critical. Keep in mind, however, that dictionaries, no matter how good, are never complete, and do not provide all the answers. The other source of information is people who work in the field the particular translation covers. Their input is often more valuable than that of the dictionary, since they are the ones who work in the field and represent the potential readers of your translation.

The first thing to keep in mind about terminology - as was discussed before - is consistency. If you translate a word a certain way, do not change in the middle of the text to another synonym of the same word, even though it may be accurate. This will throw the reader off. The second thing is to make sure you are using the right terms, rather than trying to approximate them. Keep a list of those terms to maintain consistency throughout the document, and also for future use. If you continue to translate in the same technical field, these lists will become your most valuable translation tool.

### Numbers

Always remember when translating large Chinese numbers to carefully convert units (萬 =10 thousand; 億=100 million; 兆=trillion).

### Errors in the Source Text

Sometimes you will find that the original has errors, such as an incorrect character where it is clear by the context that the author intended to say " 務必 " and not " 勿必 ," or the sequence in a series of numbered clauses is wrong. You can do a number of things in situations such as these. You can go ahead and make the correction and leave it at that. You can translate the text as is, and use the term [sic] after the error, to alert the reader. Or you can make a translator's note on a separate sheet of paper. Ultimately, the client will have to decide what to do with it.

### Untranslatable Words or Terms

You may run into a word, a term or a phrase which cannot be translated, or which should be rendered phonetically (such as:" 功夫," rendered as "Kungfu"). If there is a need to explain it, it can be done in a footnote or in parentheses (or brackets, which makes it clearer that the bracketed text is not part of the original). As a general rule, however, it is best not to burden your translation with footnotes or parenthetic or bracketed text.

### Specific Chinese Translation Points

#### 1) The Chinese Writing System

Chinese is written in characters. Given the great complexity of the writing system, it is doubtlessly the most intricate written language in use in the world today, and arguably one of the most beautiful. However, reading requires the knowledge of a large number of characters - a minimum of somewhere around three to five thousand. Translating technical Chinese into English, given the specialized vocabulary, requires even more. And making money translating Chinese requires the ability to read fast and accurately. Thus, any native speaker of English who is seriously attempting Chinese-English translation will have invested a substantial number of years in cultivating the skill of reading Chinese.

#### 2) Sentences and Paragraphs

Ideas about the internal organization of written text can be quite different in Chinese and English. One Chinese writer has described English paragraphs as "linear," with individual sentences moving a central idea forward one step at a time. Chinese writers who have not been influenced by Western notions of writing, however, sometimes adopt a "spiral" approach. They repeat what has already been said as they gradually converge on their target, like a moth to a flame. This can result in an extended paragraph with only one period and countless commas. The task of the translator, then, is to grasp what the target is, organize the paragraph into segments of suitable length, knock out redundant portions, and render what is left into English. This skill is not limited to translating prose; it is often necessary in technical translation as well.

3) Word Order

Luckily, the usual word order of a Chinese sentence is S-V-O, just as in English. Unlike English, however, the subject can be omitted when understood. Thus, it is sometimes necessary to fill in the subject in English when it has been omitted in a Chinese sentence. Long clauses introduced by "that," "which," "who," and the like in English, come before the noun in Chinese. For this reason, it is often necessary to rearrange Chinese sentences containing long clauses modifying nouns. (The "held-last-Saturday-at-two-soccer match" just doesn't "make it" in English!)

4) Filling in the Missing Pieces

Chinese and English convey information somewhat differently. Thus, what can be omitted in one is sometimes required in the other. As mentioned above, you will sometimes have to complete the subject when it has been left out of a Chinese sentence. Additionally, since Chinese nouns rarely reflect number, you will have to fill in the gap. Definite and indefinite articles are yet another area where little guidance will be forthcoming from the source text. And the reconstruction of appropriate verb tenses will require careful attention as you polish your finished product.

## In Conclusion

The above notes are by no means exhaustive. They do not cover all the issues facing a translator. Language is not mathematics. Keep this in mind, and do the best translation job you possibly can.

## Guidelines for Translating the Assignments

1. We are providing you with a Chinese text and an English translation of that same text. Pretend you don't have the English translation. If you read it before you do the assignment, you will not be able to do an honest job, and you will not derive the benefit of learning from your own mistakes.

2. Read the Chinese text once for general comprehension. Underline any difficult words or passages.

3. As you start the translation process by reading the text for the first time (see 2., above), keep track of time, so that when you finish you will know how long it took you to translate the text. This is very critical, because you want to increase your translation speed as you go along. The rule is simple: The more words you translate per hour, the more money you will make. A very low hourly word-count can earn you less than minimum wage, which is not at all desirable. (Note: The hours indicated at the top right hand corner for each assignment include two numbers. The first is for beginners while the second number is for an experienced translator. Therefore, an assignment that would take a beginner 5-7 hours to complete might take an experienced translator 2 hours. The timeframe includes research, draft, and final copy.)

4. Read it again. This time make a list of difficult words, and make any notes regarding things you need to clarify about the text (e.g., look up something in an encyclopedia to better understand some concept or piece of information).

5. Try to determine which dictionaries and reference books you need for this assignment, get hold of them, and keep them nearby.

6. Now you are ready to start translating. Preferably, you will be using a computer. If this is too intimidating, write it out the first time. It will take longer, but you will have more time to think. Remember, your objective is to translate on computer, not in longhand. These days, if you want to earn money translating, you have to submit text on disk. There are hardly any exceptions to this requirement.

7. Do a draft translation. Go over the draft. Do the best you can to make the English sound like good, clear, correct English, which does not sound like Chinese, and does not retain any Chinese forms in either style, format, or any technical points. Be sure you did not omit anything. Ask yourself if you succeeded in conveying the correct sense of every idea and every word in the source text. Be sure you are comfortable with every single word you chose in English, and that you have no doubts or hesitations. If, after all this, you do have some questions, do not worry. No one expects you to do perfect work the first time around. You will do better next time.

8. Now that you have accomplished your translation, figure out the time it took you to reach your final version (including all the previous steps, namely first reading, research, draft, and final copy).

9. Make a list of the words, passages, and concepts in the text where you encountered difficulty, and keep for future reference. This kind of record keeping will help you improve your performance, and serve as a reminder not to repeat the same mistake twice.

10. Print out your corrected and edited text.

## Guides for Self-Evaluation

1. Turn to the English translation in Section 3, and compare it to yours. Next read the notes concerning the pitfalls and salient points of this text very carefully, and see how they compare to your own experience with the text. They may not necessarily coincide with everything you experienced personally, but they do provide you with some tips on the do's and don'ts of technical translation.

2. The most important thing for you to keep in mind as you compare your translation to the one in Section 3, is that there is no one absolutely correct way of translating a text. Many words can be translated in more than one way. Many sentences can be structured in more than one way. Many ideas can be conveyed in different words. In fact, your translation may turn out to be just as good, and in some spots even better than the one in the book.

3. Keep track of the shortcomings of your translation. The areas you are interested in are the following:

   **Omissions** - did you fail to translate any particular word or phrase, or even paragraph?

   **Format** - does your format follow the original (breaking into paragraphs, for instance)?

   **Mistranslations** - did you mistranslate any particular word?

   **Unknown words** - were there any words you were not able to translate?

   **Meaning** - did you miss the meaning of any particular phrase or sentence?

   **Spelling** - did you misspell a word?

   **Grammar** - did you make any grammatical mistakes?

   **Punctuation** - did you mispunctuate or miss any punctuation marks?

   **Clarity** - did you fail to clearly convey the meaning of any particular part of the text?

   **Consistency** - did you call something by one name, and then by another without good reason?

   **Style** - are you satisfied with the way your translation reflects the style of the original (for example, the original is written in a clear, direct style, while the translation sounds more complex and indirect)?
   These are some of the questions you have to ask yourself. As you go on to translate other

texts, always keep these questions in mind as you self-assess your translation. By improving your performance in the above areas, you are on your way to becoming an accomplished translator.

# Part One

# Translation: Chinese into English

## Section 2. Assignments

## Assignment 1: General

**4-5/2 hours**

### 专栏 1.2　基础设施对于经济发展的重要性：中国的例证

当瓶颈现象发生时，基础设施可以对经济增长提供重要的支持这一事实是显而易见的。最引人注目的例子莫过于中国城市间的交通系统，以及它与原料、煤炭和电力供应的联系。

中国城市间的交通网络是世界上最稀疏的交通网络之一：人均道路长度或单位可耕地拥有道路长度——公路或铁路——等同于或低于巴西、印度和俄罗斯的水平。这主要是长期以来对交通基础设施的投资过低的结果。在对交通的需求迅速增长的1981至1990年期间，中国对交通的投资每年大约只相当于GNP的1.3%。

自从中国于1979年实行对外开放政策以来，每年平均9%的经济增长率导致城市间运输空前的扩展——每年的货运量平均增长8%，客运量平均增长12%。运输量的增长造成交通基础设施供应极度紧张，表现在铁路运输网瓶颈现象加剧，对铁路线运输能力实行严格的限额管理，航运和铁路客运为旅客提供的服务质量很差。

交通运输能力不足特别对煤炭供应产生了不利影响。煤炭占中国商品能源来源的73%，占铁路货运总吨位的43%。煤炭短缺又对电力供应产生了不利影响，大约76%的电力是热电厂生产的。1989年，中国有20%的工业用电供应不足。中央和地方政府管理部门实行配额用电制度，限制新的用户进网，但是，停电现象仍然很频繁。

一项保守的估计认为，在过去的几年间，每年因交通基础设施不足而增加的成本大约相当于GNP的1%。

### 专栏 4.4　马来西亚集权型与分权型的基础设施建设计划

马来西亚的基础设施建设计划模式结合了分权制与集权制两种方式。首先，在中央政府一级，国家经济委员会（由总理担任主席的部级机构）和国家发展计划委员会（由联邦政府各部部长组成）决定发展目标。除这两个机构外，经济计划小组（隶属总理办公室）负责协调和中间联系，但不作为行业计划的制订者。

在经两个计划机构反复研究后，联邦政府的发展计划及各行业的发展重点计划被发送到各部、立法机构及州政府。然后，这些机构应上报下一个五年的发展规划。第二阶段是分权化的计划过程。在向相应联邦机构上报计划前，各州的联邦机构应与州发展计划单位讨论自己的发展方案。这一做法能够保证州政府了解联邦发展计划在它们各自管辖范围内的运作构想。在确定五年规划财政支出方案时，国家发展计划委员会有最终决定权。

马来西亚的基础设施发展的体制框架有效地保证了基础设施由政府提供，以反映国家重点和地方需要。直至90年代以前，基础设施足以支撑强劲的经济持续增长。

然而，80年代以后，强大的私人部门产生了。这使马来西亚政府认为不必继续直接参与某些部门的活动。马来西亚政府认为，为了消除日益严重的基础设施瓶颈现象，应采取新的方式，而对新情况，政府采取了灵活的态度。基础设施在私有化进程中被列为优先私有化的对象。迄今为止，85个项目部分地或全部地被私有化，其中包括900公里长的南北线公路、巴生港的集装箱集散站、马来西亚电话公司和国家电力局。1985年颁布的《私有化纲要》以及1989年制定的《私有化总体方案》明确表示，以基础设施私有化为实现现行发展战略的手段之一。

## 专栏 4.5　评估一个项目的影响：加德满都供水项目

至少应当说基础设施项目评估是一项困难的工作。应当找出项目对环境的不利影响，确定人们将对既定服务支付的价格，还应评估该项服务对其他基础设施的影响。给水、排水、卫生设施、固体废弃物处理和邻近地区水质等问题都交叉相关。其中一个因素存在缺陷都会影响到其他基础设施的设计要求。

在尼泊尔首都加德满都，政府官员们用传统的成本–效益分析法的扩展模式——"服务水平法"评估供水改进工程的效益。这一方法认为，不同的用户对环境保护的重视程度不同，并试图测算供水的间接影响。

加德满都有 110 万居民。完全按照标准的项目评估方法，该项耗资 1.5 亿美元的新投资项目每年可节省 50 万美元维修费，此外还有大量的年度收益（按照支付意愿，根据不同用户，大约每个水站用户每年交 10 美元，商业用户每年交 250 美元）。总收益约为 1910 万美元。按 12% 的贴现率，该项目可获得 520 万净边际收益。

然而，如果采用更加详细的服务水平评估法，在某些地区，从减少因水污染而造成腹泻的角度看，获得的每一单位服务所带来的健康收益可达 1000 美元。关于改进用水方法的宣传教育计划可以进一步增强居民体质、降低运输成本。如果考虑到这些间接收益，此项目的总收益可达 2.75 亿美元左右。

*word count*: 1515

## 专栏4.6　妇女能否受益于基础设施取决于是否有周密的事先计划

人们普遍认识到供水和卫生设施可以改善家庭成员的身体健康状况，使妇女可以支配更多的时间。然而事实上基础设施给妇女带来的好处往往远不止这些。不过，若要想确保妇女受益于基础设施，必须在项目计划阶段就预先周密考虑如何使妇女受益的问题。

在许多非洲国家，妇女是主要的食品生产者和销售者。农村公路为她们前往市场提供了便利。但是除非她们有钱用卡车运送农产品，否则她们还是得自己把农产品搬运到市场去，公路的作用也就因此大大下降了。中间（非机动）运输工具，例如自行车和手推车，与用头顶运载相比较，不失是一种颇具吸引力的选择，不过初始投资成本相当高。在加纳的改善运输状况二期工程里，一个由非官方机构组织的试点计划将劳动密集型公路工程的部分工资收入引入为分期付款购买中间运输工具融资。

在很多国家中，一贫如洗的妇女们渴望参与能够给她们带来赚钱机会的公路建设工程。在孟加拉国的一个主要养路计划中，妇女是主要劳动力。然而在肯尼亚的农村支线公路计划（非洲同类计划中历史最悠久、最为成功者之一）中，妇女劳工占总劳动力的比重不足 20%。在其他非洲国家中也存在类似的妇女参与率低的问题。有些时候，人们认为非洲妇女参与率低是由于她们已经不堪家务劳动和自给性农业劳动的重负。然而不同国家（包括博茨瓦纳、肯尼亚、莱索托、马达加斯加和坦桑尼亚）的情况表明，妇女欢迎这类就业机会，而且有能力与男工同酬同工。为了使妇女更多地参与到这类项目中来，应放宽招工条件并广泛宣传就业机会。此外，妇女应有晋升为监工的机会。当对养路工程实行承包时，应鼓励妇女团体竞标。

预先估计基础设施对妇女的影响相当困难。应对妇女活动、机遇和限制性因素的细节有深刻的认识。在冈比亚中部，存在着公社制和家庭制并存的农村体制。传统上男子与妇女共同从事农业劳动。男人负责公社的高地谷物种植，而妇女则承担起家庭水稻的种植和销售的全部责任。实施了一项水稻种植计划，将 1500 公顷水田分给农户。这项计划的明显意图是，通过提高水稻产量增加收入，达到改善女性种植者经济地位的目标。可是，男性农民也开始对水稻种植的商业价值感兴趣，要求分掉公社土地中的水田部分。妇女的确从水稻种植计划中受益，增加了家庭收入，然而她们作为水稻专门种植者和销售者的地位却遭到削弱。

*word count*: 1100

(1)

# 宣誓书

我，郝敬舫，为免被控作假证供，谨此宣誓如下：

1、根据本人所知作此宣誓声明。

2、我是中华人民共和国公民，所持中国居民身份证号码为：510212550101031。我目前是海南南亚国际投资有限公司总经理，海南筑本工程材料科技有限公司董事及海南豪城房地产有限公司董事长。

3、我于八十年代末认识朱步杨先生。1993年3月，我邀请朱先生担任我在中国海南省海口市创办的一间名为海南豪城房地产有限公司的董事长，并得到他的接受。我绝对相信朱先生的公正与诚实，因此我们之间的合作是愉快的，我亦将他介绍给多位海南省政府高级官员。

郝敬舫 4、1993年12月，在香港九龙富豪酒店，朱先生介绍我认识了赵先生和吴小姐，按我的理解，他们是朱先生的商业合作伙伴。后来，当三人来海口访问期间，我会见了他们，并在海口宾馆就餐。从他们之间的谈话看，赵先生和吴小姐与朱先生一起在海南发展电厂项目，尽管当时他们的项目都未成功。

5、1994年4月，得知赵先生和吴小姐不适当地把朱先生排除在伙伴关系之外，我非常吃惊。赵先生和吴小姐竟然如此对待商业伙伴，尤其是朱先生曾长期为他们的商业活动提供经济支持。在与朱先生商讨事后，我了解了事实，并确信，为了保障朱先生、我本人以及我公司的利益，朱先生有必要把事实向海南省政府汇报。我非常支持朱先生这样做，并知道他已接受了我的建议致函总商会。

郝敬舫

于一九九五年 2 月二十2 日

在见证人面前宣誓　郝敬舫

[见证人] 兹证明郝敬舫在我面前签署，但对内容不负任何责任。

[盖印] 林青律師

(2)

# 中华人民共和国

## 企业法人

# 营业执照

## （副本）

注册号 工商企独琼副字193989号

该公司经核准登记注册，具有法人资格，准予开业。

(3)

编号№ 0023682

企业名称：（中文） 海南宗城房地产有限公司

（外文）

住 所： 海南省海口市机场西路杭州大厦首层

企业类别： 外商独资

经营范围： 房地产开发经营、园林工程；兼营：建筑材料、装修材料的省内贸易。＊＊＊

注册资本： 贰仟万港元

董 事 长： 郝敬舫

副董事长： 朱步杨

总 经 理： 郝敬舫

副总经理： 吴建军 包振生 朱征

分支机构：

本执照正本有效期限自 1993年 03月 17日至 2013年 03月 16日

中华人民共和国
国家工商行政管理局 局长 王众孚

中华人民共和国国家工商行政管理局

1995 年 日

本副本有效期至 1996 年03 月 17 日

22 Chinese into English

(4)

# 中华人民共和国

## 企业法人

# 营业执照

（副本）

中华人民共和国国家工商行政管理局

(5)

一九四九五年度第 号

兹证明前面的复印件与原件相符。

中华人民共和[illegible]公证处

# 公 证 书

(95)琼证字第2005号

兹证明前面的复印件与原件相符。

中华人民共和国海南省公证处

公证员：

一九九五年[illegible]月[illegible]五日

*word count*: 400

表1　镰刀菌素C诱发DAB小鼠食管与前胃癌

| 实验天数 (总剂量) | 大鼠数 | 食管-前胃损伤 | | | |
|---|---|---|---|---|---|
| | | 增生 | 不典型增生 | 乳头瘤 | 癌 |
| 9～27(3.5～3mg) | 14 | 12 | 0 | 0 | 0 |
| 122～130(3.25～5mg) | 9 | 5 | 1 | 1 | 0 |
| 299(10.1mg) | 1 | 0 | 0 | 1 | 0 |
| 469～502(8.2～12.0mg) | 3 | 1 | 0 | 1 | 2 |
| 655(14.2mg) | 2 | 0 | 1 | 0 | 1 |
| 总计 | 29 | 18 | 2 | 3 | 3 |
| 对照组 | 29 | 0 | 0 | 0 | 0 |

对照组小鼠中，食管与前胃未见有癌前病变及癌的发生。

二、Fc诱发大鼠食管癌与前胃癌：

40只大鼠中可作病理组织学检查的有20只，其中食管与前胃的乳头瘤和癌各5例（表2）。一只大鼠（742天）食管上皮全长亦呈不

表2　镰刀菌素C诱发Wistar大鼠食管与前胃癌

| 实验天数 (总剂量) | 大鼠数 | 食管-前胃损伤 | | | |
|---|---|---|---|---|---|
| | | 增生 | 不典型增生 | 乳头瘤 | 癌 |
| 408～488(214～264mg) | 4 | 3 | 0 | 1 | 0 |
| 531～596(294～354mg) | 4 | 0 | 0 | 0 | 1 |
| 601～675(357～447mg) | 5 | 2 | 1 | 1 | 1 |
| 742～814(477～537mg) | 7 | 0 | 0 | 3 | 3 |
| 总计 | 20 | 5 | 1 | 5 | 5 |
| 对照组 | 25 | 0 | 0 | 0 | 0 |

同程度的不典型增生及鳞癌（图4，5）。前胃发生乳头瘤。其他四只大鼠（实验590、609、813和817天）前胃有鳞癌，癌细胞团来源于乳头瘤，形成不同长度下伸的乳头状生长（图6～8）。还有一些经Fc处理的大鼠，食管与前胃上皮有不典型增生与乳头状瘤的癌前病变，除一例乳腺瘤外，肝及肺等无肿瘤形成。25只不经Fc处理的对照组大鼠，其上消化道未见有病变。

## 讨　论

镰刀菌素C有一定的毒性，特别是对小

层析处理为Fc粗提物，供大鼠试验用[…]。Fc应用时避光，先经微量乙醇溶解，后加蒸馏水至所需浓度。

实验用小鼠和大鼠，40只DBA雄性小鼠

鼠，因此在实验过程中，需要调整灌喂Fc的剂量。大鼠对Fc有较强耐受力，在体重增加后，给予Fc的剂量亦加大。但与一般使用多环芳烃类致癌物或亚硝胺类致癌物相比，Fc诱癌为实验时间较长。

作为一种化学致癌物，按其结构在Fc的$C_{13}$与$C_{14}$之间有环氧基团，可能有直接致癌作用（图9）。我们在小鼠与大鼠各看到一只

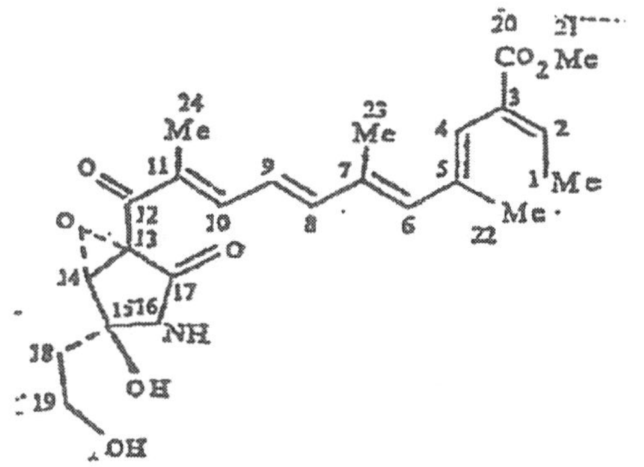

图9　镰刀菌素C构造式

食管全长与前胃上端发生癌变的现象，似表明Fc的灌喂可能有直接致癌作用。在过去给予S-9混合物的体外代谢实验中，虽能加强Fc的致突变作用，特别在沙门氏菌TA 100株，以及对$V_{79}$细胞的SCE、微核、染色体畸变与6-TG抗性突变等[6]，但是延长Fc作用到24小时后，虽不加肝微粒体酶制备，也可能有一定的作用[7]。在代谢激活下，Fc能增加细菌DNA的断裂数及引起多瘤病毒转化的大鼠成纤维细胞病毒DNA序列的非同步化复制[8]。我们证明在大鼠食管组织培养中，$^3$H-Fc能与DNA共价结合。此外，我们建立的大鼠食管上皮细胞株（RE-525），经Fc处理后发生恶性转化特征，能在无血清、无生长因子的选择培养基中继续生长，并能在半固体琼脂上形成集落；染色体核型发生变化，数目增多，结构畸变；N-ras、C-myc和V-erb-B三种癌基因mRNA表达水平增高；失去对TPA调节C-myc基因表达的反应；经Fc作用的RE-525细胞接种裸鼠后，可以形成鳞癌[…]

变、细胞增大与核深染，但未形成肝癌。20只

* 国家科委资助的"七・五"攻关课题
* 邮政编码 100021

表 1 镰刀菌素C诱发DAB小鼠食管与前胃癌

| 实验天数 (总剂量) | 大鼠数 | 食管-前胃损伤 | | | |
|---|---|---|---|---|---|
| | | 增生 | 不典型增生 | 乳头瘤 | 癌 |
| 9～27(1.5～3mg) | 14 | 12 | 0 | 0 | 0 |
| 122～130(3.25～5mg) | 9 | 5 | 1 | 1 | 0 |
| 299(10.1mg) | 1 | 0 | 0 | 1 | 0 |
| 469～502(8.2～12.0mg) | 3 | 1 | 0 | 1 | 2 |
| 655(14.2mg) | 2 | 0 | 1 | 0 | 1 |
| 总 计 | 29 | 18 | 2 | 3 | 3 |
| 对 照 组 | 29 | 0 | 0 | 0 | 0 |

对照组小鼠中，食管与前胃未见有癌前病变及癌的发生。

二、Fc 诱发大鼠食管癌与前胃癌：

40 只大鼠中可作病理组织学检查的有 20 只，其中食管与前胃的乳头瘤和癌各 5 例（表 2）。一只大鼠（742 天）食管上皮全长亦呈不同程度的不典型增生及鳞癌（图 4，5）。前胃发生乳头瘤。其他四只大鼠（实验 590、609、813 和 817 天）前胃有鳞癌，癌细胞团来源于乳头瘤，形成不同长度下伸的乳头状生长（图 6～8）。还有一些经 Fc处理的大鼠，食管与前胃上皮有不典型增生与乳头状瘤的癌前病变。除一例乳腺瘤外，肝及肺等无肿瘤形成。25只不经 Fc 处理的对照组大鼠，其上消化道未见有病变。

表 2 镰刀菌素C诱发Wistar大鼠食管与前胃癌

| 实验天数 (总剂量) | 大鼠数 | 食管-前胃损伤 | | | |
|---|---|---|---|---|---|
| | | 增生 | 不典型增生 | 乳头瘤 | 癌 |
| 408～488(214～264mg) | 4 | 3 | 0 | 1 | 0 |
| 531～596(294～354mg) | 4 | 0 | 0 | 0 | 1 |
| 601～675(357～447mg) | 5 | 2 | 1 | 1 | 1 |
| 742～814(477～537mg) | 7 | 0 | 0 | 3 | 3 |
| 总 计 | 20 | 5 | 1 | 5 | 5 |
| 对 照 组 | 25 | 0 | 0 | 0 | 0 |

## 讨 论

镰刀菌素C有一定的毒性，特别是对小鼠，因此在实验过程中，需要调整灌喂 Fc 的剂量。大鼠对 Fc 有较强耐受力，在体重增加后，给予 Fc 的剂量亦加大。但与一般使用多环芳烃类致癌物或亚硝胺类致癌物相比，Fc 诱癌为实验时间较长。

作为一种化学致癌物，按其结构在 Fc 的 $C_{13}$ 与 $C_{14}$ 之间有环氧基团，可能有直接致癌作用（图 9）。我们在小鼠与大鼠各看到一只

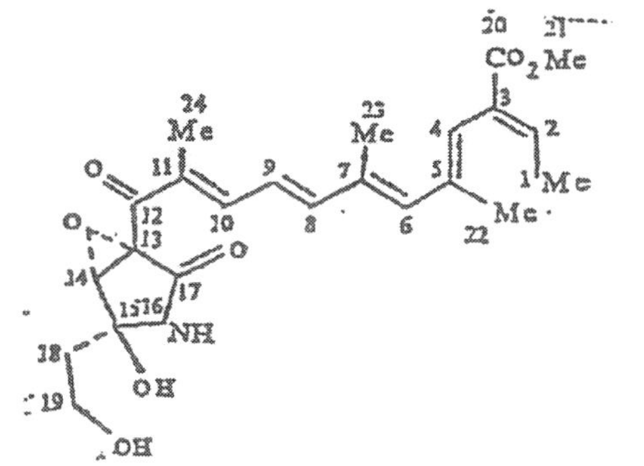

图 9 镰刀菌素 C 构造式

食管全长与前胃上端发生癌变的现象，似表明 Fc 的灌喂可能有直接致癌作用。在过去给予 S-9 混合物的体外代谢实验中，虽能加强 Fc的致突变作用，特别在沙门氏菌 TA 100 株，以及对 $V_{79}$ 细胞的 SCE、微核、染色体畸变与6-TG 抗性突变等[6]，但是延长 Fc 作用到 24 小时后，虽不加肝微粒体酶制备，也可能有一定的作用[7]。在代谢激活下，Fc 能增加细菌 DNA 的断裂并及引起多瘤病毒转化的大鼠成纤维细胞病毒 DNA 序列的非同步化复制[8]。我们证明在大鼠食管组织培养中，$^3$H-Fc 能与 DNA 共价结合。此外，我们建立的大鼠食管上皮细胞株（RE-525），经 Fc 处理后发生恶性转化特征，能在无血清、无生长因子的选择培养基中继续生长，并能在半固体琼脂上形成集落；染色体核型发生变化，数目增多，结构畸变；N-ras、C-myc 和 V-erb-B 三种癌基因 mRNA 表达水平增高；失去对 TPA 调节 C-myc 基因表达的反应；经 Fc 作用的 RE-525 细胞接种裸鼠后，可以形成鳞癌[9]。

本实验研究的结果表明，经TLC纯化或不经纯化的Fc处理，均能诱发动物的食管和前胃发生肿瘤，证明其有致癌作用。至于对接受不同纯度的Fc有何影响，还需作更进一步的研究。然而，南非工作者用串珠镰刀菌培养物喂大鼠，认为Fc可能不是镰刀菌中的致癌物[10]。

（本文图1～8见插页图第1页）

## 参 考 文 献


1. Li MH. et al. Experimental studies on the carcinogenicity of funguscontaminated food from Linxian county. In: Gelboin HV, eds. Genetic and Environmental Factors in Exp. and Human Cancer. Tokyo: Japan Spe Press 1980:139.
2. Maresas WF, et al. Incidence of Fusarium species and the mycotoxins, deoxynalenol and zearalenone, in corn produced in esophageal cancer areas in Transkei. Agric Food Chem 1979; 27:1108.
3. 李铭新，等。串珠镰刀菌接种的玉米面诱发大鼠前胃癌。中华肿瘤杂志 1982；4:241.
4. [illegible]，等。林县串珠镰刀菌致突物——镰刀菌素C的分离和提纯 中华肿瘤杂志 1985；7(增刊):62.
5. Weibe LA. et al. Fusarin C, a mutagen from Fusarium moniliforme grown on corn. J Food Sci 1983; 46:1424.
6. Cheng SJ, et al. A mutagenic metabolite produced by Fusarium moniliforme isolated from Linxian county, China. Carcinogenesis 1985; 6:903.
7. 王跃凤。两种镰刀菌毒素——T-2和Fusarin C的基因毒性作用。中国协和医科大学研究生论文 1986.
8. Lu SJ, et al. Fusarium moniliforme metabolites: genotoxicity of culture extracts. Carcinogenesis 1988; 9:1523.
9. [illegible]，等。镰刀菌素C体外诱发人胚食管上皮细胞转化的研究。中国科学 1990；12:1293.
10. Jaskiewicz K, et al. Carcinogenicity of Fusarium moniliforme culture material in rats. JNCI 1987; 78:321.


（1990年3月1日收稿 3月23日修回）

*word count*: **1050**

# Assignment 4: Economic/Business

## 专栏 5.2 挖掘国际资本市场

在挖掘利用国际资本市场方面存在着几个渠道。一些较大的私人企业已直接进人债务和股票市场。1993 年 10 月阿根廷电信公司向美国和亚洲的投资者发行 5 亿美元 7 年期的债券。阿根廷的电话公司也利用债券市场贷款来筹集扩建资金。

外国直接投资打开了进人国际股本市场的又一条途径。通用电力公司是一家国际性的大企业，对在发展中国家开发基础设施项目非常感兴趣。它的子公司，通用电力资本公司（GECC）在美国和欧洲市场上发行股票，并将资金投放到选好的项目上。例如，GECC 作为股本投资者参与了菲律宾北棉兰老岛的功率为 108 兆瓦的柴油发电项目。由于得到集团所有企业的支持，由 GECC 发行股票比只为发展中国家的电力项目发行要容易。

最近采取了两种方法以利用美国资本市场上的资源——美国的预托证券（ADRs）和 144a 条款下的申请。ADRs 是存款的证明，能够使外国公司在没有复杂的结算和转让机制的条件下，在美国市场上筹集股本。证券由一家美国预托银行发行，公司的主要股份是由所在国的保管银行托管。1990 年，智利电话公司在纽约证券交易所以 ADRs 形式发行股票筹集了 9200 万美元的资金。这是 30 年来拉丁美洲国家第一次在美国市场上大量发行股票。

1990 年 4 月，美国证券交易委员会通过了 144a 条款，允许外国公司在美国申请发行私有股票。在那以前，合格购买者（财产至少为 1 亿美元的机构）所持有的私人发行的股票只有在持有 2 至 3 年后才可进行交易。假使新的购买者合格，144a 条款允许可以立刻进行交易。除此之外，3 年后，证券可以卖给任何人。1992 年，使用 144a 条款为墨西哥市 Toluca 收费道路发行了 20750 万美元的国际债券。自那以来，墨西哥的其他收费道路和菲律宾的苏比克湾电厂也利用 144a 条款筹集了资金。

## 专栏 5.3　19 世纪的警告信号

在 19 世纪基础设施都掌握在私人手里。当时人们抱怨由于资金短缺，很多有价值的项目被忽略了。一些抱怨反映了资助创业性的交通（特别是铁路）项目的困难。其他抱怨则为自己辩护，想把所有风险转嫁到政府预算上。在很多情况下，企业的财务破产对政府的财政造成了严重的后果。

全世界的政府都以不同的形式对私营基础设施项目提供援助，包括直接补贴。当时使用了两种至今人们仍感兴趣的方法——财政担保和土地赠与。

担保。在印度，如果一个铁路公司不能获得最小的投资收益率，例如 5%，政府以其税收权力为后盾保证补偿其不足部分。这种担保在加拿大的铁路建设中也起了至关重要的作用。但是，担保不仅消除了投资者监督管理的积极性，而且为项目发起人与施工和供应公司洽谈“好心”契约打开了方便之门。由于许多基础设施项目性质不同，可以不费力地掩盖不当的做法。现在看来，债券担保会导致建设费用增加。

土地赠与。19 世纪时，联接铁路和运河的土地经常割让给项目发起人，允许他们从投资周围发展起来的多项副业活动中受益。土地赠与提供的是可用来支持债券债务的附属担保，如同利率担保一样，使资本市场不尽完善。加拿大在 19 世纪 50 年代和 60 年代，担保债券的拖欠耗尽了政府的收入。因而在 1871 年，加拿大下院通过了一项土地赠与政策——即在不用增加税率的前提下，补助铁路的建设。在诸如印度铁路和美国横贯大陆的铁路这样的大型冒险项目上，土地赠与被证明是最有效的。

## 专栏 5.5　土地赠与和征用

土地赠与对新项目来说是一种很有用的附属担保，否则由于借贷人对类似项目没有经验，这些项目得不到资金。但是贯彻土地赠与政策时有风险，那就是如果把土地给了无论如何都要建设的项目，那么赠与的土地就浪费了。

然而，总的来说，由于土地赠与代表着资源的一次性注入，而不影响经营一个项目的积极性，因此与利息担保相比具有更多的优越性。土地赠与可能是适应风险性较大的项目，例如，工业国的高速铁路或发展中国家的高风险交通投资。

赠与土地带来了征地程序和对地主赔偿的复杂问题。征地可能要花几年时间，并使基础设施项目大大推迟。曼谷二期高速公路遇到了与这些延误有关的一些困难。不仅需要一个恰当的征用法来确定政府可以征收土地的条款，而且正如东京成田机场事例所表明的那样，在执行过程中缺乏敏感性会由于争论而导致经济损失惨重的延误。

在期待土地被征用时，地主具有过度开发它们财产的刺激力，或采取其他手段过高估价他们的土地。一个可行的解决方式是以现有的市场价格和社区土地开发标准作为标准。一个更难的问题是如何赔偿那些随着新基础设施开发和商业活动产生变化而带来的其不动产价值降低的人们。在一般情况下，政府对这类损失不作补偿。

*word count*: 970

# Section 3. Translation of Assignments and Notes

## Assignment 1: Translation

### Box 1.2 The importance of infrastructure to economic development: an example from China

The fact that infrastructure provides critical support to the growth of an economy can be clearly seen when bottlenecks arise. One of the most striking examples is that of China's intercity transport system, with its links to the supply of raw materials, coal, and electricity.

The coverage of China's intercity transport networks is one of the thinnest in the world: the total route length per capita or per unit of arable land—for highways or railways—is similar to, or lower than, that in Brazil, India, and Russia. This has resulted mainly from chronic underinvestment in China's transport infrastructure. China's transport investments amounted to only 1.3 percent of GNP annually during 1981–90, a period of rapid growth in transport demand.

Since the onset of China's open door policy in 1979, economic growth averaging 9 percent a year has resulted in an unprecedented expansion in intercity traffic—with growth averaging 8 percent a year for freight and 12 percent a year for passengers. This traffic growth has imposed tremendous strains on the transport infrastructure, as manifested by the growth of bottlenecks in the railway network, the severe rationing of transport capacity on railway lines, and the poor quality of service experienced by shippers and passengers.

Transport shortages have adversely affected the supply of coal in particular. Coal is the source of some 73 percent of China's commercial energy and represents about 43 percent of the total tonnage of freight handled by the railways. The shortage of coal has in turn adversely affected supplies of electricity, about 76 percent of which is generated by thermal plants. In 1989, China was experiencing a shortfall in available power of about 20 percent of industrial electricity requirements. Central and local authorities established quotas for allocating electricity and rationed new connections, but power cuts have nevertheless been frequent.

A conservative estimate is that the annual economic costs of not having adequate transport infrastructure in China during the past several years amount to about 1 percent of China's GNP.

### Box 4.4 Centralized and decentralized infrastructure planning in Malaysia

The Malaysian approach to infrastructure planning blends centralized and decentralized forms. First, at the central level, national development objectives and targets are formulated by the National Economic Council (a ministerial council chaired by the prime minister) and the National Development Planning Committee (composed of top civil servants from federal ministries). Alongside these two groups, the Economic Planning Unit, located in the prime minister's department, acts as a coordinating and integrating agency rather than an initiator of sectoral plans.

Following deliberation by these two groups, the federal government's development policies and sectoral priorities are conveyed to ministries, statutory bodies, and state governments, which are then invited to submit their programs for the next five-year plan. This second stage constitutes the decentralized approach to planning. Agencies that are located in the states are required to discuss their development programs with the appropriate State Economic Planning Unit before submitting them to the relevant federal ministry. This ensures that the state governments are aware of the development proposals of the federal agencies operating within their boundaries. The National Development Planning Committee has ultimate jurisdiction over the selection of expenditure programs for the five-year plans.

The institutional framework for infrastructure development in Malaysia has been effective in ensuring that public provision of infrastructure has reflected both broad national priorities and local needs. Infrastructure provision was sufficient to sustain strong economic growth up to the 1980s.

By that time, however, the emergence of strong private sector capacity convinced the government that its direct involvement in some sectors and activities was no longer necessary. Fresh approaches were also perceived to be desirable in dealing with growing infrastructure bottlenecks. The government responded flexibly to these changing circumstances, placing infrastructure sectors at the forefront of its privatization program. To date, eighty-five projects have been partly or completely privatized, including the 900-kilometer North-South Highway, the container terminal in Port Kelang, Telekom Malaysia, and the National Electricity Board. The government's "Guidelines on Privatization" issued in 1985 and "Privatization Master Plan" formulated in 1989 clearly confirm its view of infrastructure privatization as yet another means to achieve its underlying development strategies.

## Box 4.5 Assessing a project's reach: water in Kathmandu

Evaluating infrastructure projects is difficult at best. Environmental costs must be identified and valued, the amount that individuals will pay for service determined, and the effect that service will have on other infrastructure sectors assessed. Water supply, sewage treatment, sanitation, solid and hazardous waste handling, and ambient water quality are all interrelated. A weakness in any one will affect infrastructure requirements elsewhere.

In the Nepalese capital of Kathmandu, officials assessed the effects of improving the water service using an extension of traditional cost-benefit analysis—the "service-level" approach to valuation. This approach recognizes that environmental services are valued differently by different users and also attempts to assess indirect effects of water provision.

Kathmandu has 1.1 million inhabitants. Based on estimates using narrowly defined project appraisal techniques, benefits from the city's new $150 million water distribution system included a direct financial savings of $500,000 annually from lower maintenance costs, plus substantial annual benefits (based on willingness-to-pay estimates for different users ranging from a low of $10 for standpipe users to a high of $250 for business users). Total benefits were estimated to be $19.1 million per year. At a 12 percent discount rate, the project showed a marginally positive net benefit of $5.2 million.

Using the more detailed service-level approach to project appraisal, however, it was determined that in some cases health benefits from a reduction in coliform contamination of the water approached $1,000 per unit serviced. An education program that improved water use led to further reductions in health and transport costs. After these indirect benefits were factored in, the project showed a positive net benefit of about $275 million.

## Box 4.6 Women can benefit from infrastructure, but success lies in the details

The beneficial impacts of infrastructure on women can be profound, often extending beyond the commonly cited impacts of water and sanitation infrastructure on household health or women's time allocation. But ensuring such outcomes requires foresight and attention to detail during project planning.

Women, as principal producers and marketers of food in many African countries, benefit from the improved access to markets that rural roads bring. Yet unless they can afford to transport their produce by truck, goods must be carried to markets by the farmers themselves. This sharply diminishes benefits from road infrastructure. Intermediate (nonmotorized) means of transport, such as bicycles and carts, can be attractive alternatives to head portage but involve high initial investment costs. In Ghana a pilot component administered by NGOs in the Second Transport Rehabilitation Project channels part of the wage earnings from labor-intensive road works to finance hire-purchase programs for intermediate means of transport.

In many countries, destitute women are eager to participate in road works programs that offer them opportunities to earn cash. In one of Bangladesh's main road maintenance programs, women comprise the bulk of the workforce, but in Kenya's Rural Access Roads Program, one of the oldest and most successful of such programs in Africa, less than 20 percent of the workforce are women. Similarly low participation rates for women have been observed in other African countries. Although it is sometimes argued that low participation by African women is due to their already oppressive burden of domestic duties and subsistence agriculture, evidence from various countries, including Botswana, Kenya, Lesotho, Madagascar, and Tanzania, reveals that many poor women welcome such employment opportunities and are able to perform the same tasks as men for similar wages. To expand women's participation in these projects, eligibility conditions must be extended, and job opportunities must be advertised more widely. In addition there should be scope for advancement by women to supervisory positions. Where maintenance is contracted out, women's groups should be encouraged to bid for contracts.

Predicting the impact of infrastructure on women can be difficult and requires a close understanding of the details of their activities, opportunities, and constraints. In central Gambia, agriculture traditionally involved both women and men within a system of coexisting communal and individual cultivation. Men were responsible for organizing the communal subsistence cultivation of upland cereals, with both men and women contributing labor, while women alone were responsible for cultivating and marketing rice from individual plots. A rice irrigation project was introduced, distributing 1,500 hectares of irrigated land to farming households. An explicit intention of the project was to improve the economic status of the female cultivators by raising their incomes from higher rice yields. However, male farmers became interested in rice cultivation for commercial purposes and laid claim to the irrigated land for their communally farmed plots. While women did benefit from the project through the higher incomes accruing at the household level, their position as producers and marketers of rice was undermined.

# Assignment 1: Notes

Box 1.2

1. 经济增长率 (line 14) 货运量 (line 15) - Rendered by the translator as "economic growth" and "freight," respectively. Terms ending with the suffix "率" are normally rendered in English as rates, proportions, ratios, or moduli. Here, the word "rate" has been omitted in the English translation. Terms ending with the suffix "量" are normally rendered in English as quantities, amounts, volumes, or levels. Here the word "volume" has also been omitted.

2. 质量 (line 19) - If you translate a fair amount of traditional Chinese text, care is necessary in distinguishing between "质量" in simplified characters, which normally means "quality," and "質量" in traditional characters, which can denote both quality and quantity in some contexts. ("品質" is normally used to denote "quality" in traditional characters).

3. 相当于 (line 28) - Rendered by the translator as "amount to." This term has a wide variety of possible translations in English, including: "corresponding to," "equivalent to," "equal to," "analogous to," and "commensurate with."

Box 4.4

1. 在…时 (line 16) - Means "when" or "at the time of." Notice that the translator has elected to leave out these words entirely from the English translation. Part of good translation is knowing what needs to be rendered from the source language into the target language and what does not.

2. 被列为[优先私有化]的对象 (line 27) - Means "has been made a [priority] target for [privatization]." Thus construction has not been adopted by the translator, who has translated the entire phrase as "placing...at the forefront of its privatization program."

Box 4.5

1. 该项服务 (line 4) - Rendered by the translator as "that service." "该" is often used in more formal texts to mean "that," "the above-mentioned" or "said." Its use should be distinguished from that of "本," which is often used in more formal texts to mean "this," "the present," or "the current."

2. 关于… (line 24) - Means "as regards" or "with regard to." Sentences beginning with "As regards..." are common in Chinese; this structure is not usually necessary in English, as is the case here.

Box 4.6

1. 不足20% (line 23) - Rendered by the translator as "less than 20 percent." Note that the similar phrase "20%以下" means "20 percent or less." The first phrase covers everything up to, but excluding, 20 percent, while the second covers everything up to, and including, 20 percent.

2. 人们认为 (line 24) - Rendered by the translator as "it is...argued." Note that the dummy subject "people" in Chinese has been rendered by a passive construction in English.

## Assignment 2: Translation

[page 1]

AFFIDAVIT

I, Hao Jingfang, to avoid being accused of offering false testimony, do solemnly swear:

1) The following declarations are made based on my personal knowledge.

2) I am a citizen of the People's Republic of China. The number of my Chinese Resident Identity Card is 510212550101031. I am currently the general manager of Hainan Nanye Guoji Touzi Co., Ltd., a director of Hainan Zhuben Gongcheng Cailiao Keji Co., Ltd., and chairman of the board of Hainan Haocheng Fangdichan Co., Ltd.

3) I met Mr. Zhu in the late 1980's. In March, 1993, I invited Mr. Zhu to serve as chairman of the board of a company I established in Haikou City, Hainan Province, China, named Hainan Haocheng Fangdichan Co., Ltd., and obtained his acceptance. I absolutely believed in the fair-mindedness and honesty of Mr. Zhu. Thus, our cooperation was pleasant, and I introduced him to a number of high-level officials in the Hainan Provincial Government.

4) In December, 1993, at the Regal Hotel in Kowloon, Hong Kong, Mr. Zhu introduced a Mr. Zhao and a Miss Wu to me. It was my understanding that they were business partners of Mr. Zhu's. Afterward, while the three were visiting Haikou, I met with them and attended a dinner at the Haikou Guesthouse. Judging from their conversation, Mr. Zhao and Miss Wu were developing an electrical generation project in Hainan with Mr. Zhu, although at the time their project had not been successful.

5) In April, 1994, I learned that Mr. Zhao and Miss Wu had improperly excluded Mr. Zhu from the partnership; I was greatly surprised. How could Mr. Zhao and Miss Wu treat a business partner in this way — especially when Mr. Zhu had provided long-term economic support for their business venture? After discussing affairs with Mr. Zhu, I understood the truth. I firmly believe that, to safeguard Mr. Zhu, myself, and the interests of my companies, Mr. Zhu must report the truth to the Hainan Provincial Government. I strongly support Mr. Zhu in doing so, and know that he has already accepted my advice and written a letter to the Chamber of Commerce.

Hao Jingfang

May 25, 1995
Sworn before a witness [signed: Hao Jingfang]
[Witness] This certifies that Hao Jingfang made this sworn statement before me; however, I do not attest to the truth of its contents.
[Seal] Lin Qing, Attorney

[seal: Haikou City Law Office]

[page 2]

The People's Republic of China
Business Corporation

**Business License**

(Copy)

Registration No.: Gongshangqiduqiong Fu-Zi No. 193989

This company has been approved for registration, has the status of a corporation, and is hereby permitted to begin business.

[page 3]

No. 0023682

| | |
|---|---|
| Name of enterprise: | (Chinese) Hainan Haocheng Fangdichan Youxian Gongsi<br>(Foreign language) |
| Address: | First floor, Hangzhou Building, Jichang West Road, Haikou City, Hainan Province |
| Enterprise classification: | Foreign proprietorship |
| Business scope: | Real estate development and management, garden and park projects; also, trading of construction materials and decoration materials within the province. |
| Registered capital: | 20 million Hong Kong dollars |
| Board chairman: | Hao Jingfang |
| Assistant board chairman: | Zhu Buyang |
| General manager: | Hao Jingfang |
| Assistant general managers: | Wu Jianjun, Bao Zhensheng, Zhu Zheng |
| Branch organizations: | |

This original license valid from March 17, 1993 to March 16, 2013.

National Industry and Commerce
Administration Bureau
of the People's Republic of China,
Bureau Chief [signed: Wang Zhonghou]

[seal: National Industry and Commerce Administration Bureau of the People's Republic of China]
[date partially obscured by seal], 1995

This copy valid through March 17, 1996.

[seal][seal]

[page 4]

The People's Republic of China
Business Corporation

**Business License**

(Copy)

National Industry and Commerce Administration Bureau of the People's Republic of China

[page 5]

Fiscal 1994, 1995 [partially obscured by seal]

[seal: Industry and Commerce Administration Bureau of Hainan Province, Business Corporation Seal [illegible]]

This certifies that the above copy and the original are identical.

[page 6]

## Notarization

(95) Qiong Zheng-Zi No. 2005

This certifies that the above copy and the original are identical.

Office of Notary, Hainan Province, The People's Republic of China

Notary: [signed: Jia Gouyou]

[seal: Office of Notary, Hainan Prefecture]
[Month obscured by seal] 15, 1995

III01475750

## Assignment 2: Notes

1. Seals: Translate seals when they are legible. Often, not only will a seal will be illegible, but it may obscure the text under it, as well. An illegible seal can be dealt with by placing the word "illegible" in brackets in the English translation: "[seal illegible]." In a legal document, the translator wants to include everything possible in the translation.

2. Proper nouns: Since this document is in simplified characters, the pinyin system of romanization is appropriate for the names of persons. Thus, the name "郝敬舫" occurring in line 2 is rendered as Hao Jingfang, not Hao Chingfang as it would be in the Wade-Giles system (used primarily in Taiwan and in scholarly publications in the U.S.). Here, the surname comes before the given name, as is normal in Chinese. In some cases, a client may prefer the given name to come first. Some people prefer to have their given names hyphenated when there are two characters (in which case "Hao Jingfang" would be rendered "Hao Jing-fang"). Such questions of personal preference, sometimes carrying legal consequences, are best resolved by the client if the client is Chinese.

Note that in paragraph four, the translator has rendered "香港九龙富豪酒店" as the "Regal Hotel in Kowloon, Hong Kong." Whether to use a romanization of the Chinese term or an alternate English rendition is a judgment call the translator must learn to make.

3. Handwritten texts: Handwritten texts that have been faxed three or four times can be quite difficult to make out. Here, at the bottom of the affidavit, there are some handwritten corrections ("公证人 " is corrected to "见证人") and a line of handwritten text. Fortunately, everything is legible. However, this is not always the case. Remember to factor in extra time for deciphering large blocks of hard-to-read handwritten text if you receive such a document to translate.

4. Punctuation: It is desirable in legal documents to remain as faithful to the original punctuation as possible. There are, however, limits to this notion. Note that the first paragraph in the affidavit, two sentences in Chinese, has been broken into three sentences in English.

5. Numbers: Be careful with the larger numerical units. On page 3, line 8, "贰仟万" is correctly rendered as 20 million. Remember to keep track of the zeroes when dealing with numbers given in units of 亿 (hundred million) and 兆 (billion).

6. Filing designations: The term "工商企独琼副字193989号" on page 2, line 5, is the filing designation under which the document of page 2 is recorded in the Chinese administrative filing system. Employing extensive abbreviation even in Chinese (note the use of "琼" for Hainan Province), such designations typically follow the format of [designation] + "正／副" + "字" + [number], and are best transliterated. Thus, the translator has rendered this designation as "Gongshangqiduqiong Fu-Zi No. 193989." Compare this rendition with that of the designation appearing on page 6, line 2.

## Assignment 3: Translation

# Fusarin C Induced Esophageal and Forestomach Carcinoma In Mice and Rats[1]

Chinese Academy of Medical Sciences, Tumor Research Institute[2]: *Li Mingxin, Jiang Yuanzhou, Han Naijun, Fan Weiguo, Ma Jilin, L. E. Bjeldanes* from the University of California, USA

**Abstract** Fusarium moniliforme sheldon is the most commonly occurring contaminating fungus seen in food in Linxian County in China whose carcinogenicity has already been reported on. The principal fungal virus of Fusarium moniliforme sheldon is Fusarin C and has a mutagenic effect on Salmonella typhimurium in ectosomatic experiments and in Mammalia cells ($V_{79}$). In addition, it can induce malignant transformations following subcutaneous inoculation of nude mice with the esophageal epithelium rat cell strain (RE-525). This study is the first report on the capacity of Fusarin C, when administered by irrigation, to induce esophageal cancer and cancer of the forestomach in DBA mice and Wistar rats.

**Key words:** Fusarin C Esophageal tumors

Fusarium moniliforme sheldon is one of the most commonly occurring fungi which is found throughout the world in contaminated maize, millet and other grains, particularly in regions with a high incidence of esophageal cancer such as Linxian County in the Henan Province in China, in the South African Transkei and other places[1,2]. We have already proven that it is possible to induce squamous carcinoma of the forestomach in rats which have been fed and raised on cornmeal with fusarium moniliforme sheldon[3]. In recent years, we have been able to obtain a new type of toxin - Fusarin C (Fusarin C, Fc) from fusarium moniliforme sheldon cultures, and Fc also was found in contaminated maize from Linxian County[4]. Therefore, finding out whether or not Fc can induce esophageal tumors is worthy of special attention. We are the first to report that long-term administration of Fc can induce esophageal and forestomach cancer in mice and rats thus proving that Fc has carcinogenicity.

### Materials and Methods

Fc is a yellow amorphous compound which was first prepared by Prof. L.F. Bjeldanes in the laboratory, where he carried out tests on mice and which we ourselves have also prepared in the laboratory. [Alternative translation: Fc is a yellow amorphous compound which was first prepared by Prof. L.F. Bjeldanes for us to carry out tests on mice, and which we ourselves have also prepared.] After we had cultured the Fusarium moniliforme sheldon for four weeks, we immersed it in methyl alcohol. We extracted it and filtered it and then

---

[1] "5·7" key problem under grant by the State Committee on Science

[2] Postal code 100021

extracted it with n-hexane; the methyl alcohol layer concentrated solution was then subjected to silica gel column layer chromatography. We used 9:1 chloroform:methyl alcohol to cleanse it. We subjected the cleansed solution to thin layer chromatography (TLC), purified it, obtained pure Fc and continued to use it in the experiments on the mice. After we concentrated the cleansed solution, we used that part which had not been subjected to thin layer chromatography as the Fc coarse product which we used for tests on the rats[4,5]. Whenever we used the Fc, we kept it away from the light. First we dissolved it in a small amount of ethanol, then we added distilled water and obtained the desired concentration.

We used mice and rats for the experiments. We used 40 DBA female mice. When we began the experiments, their body weight ranged from 18 g to 25 g. Twice a week we used stomach tube irrigation to administer 0.5 to 0.05 mg Fc per ml. Since a repeated administration of Fc produced a toxic reaction, we gradually lowered the dose. We used another 20 DBA female mice as a contrast group. 40 female Wistar rats, which weighed 80 g to 120 g when we started the experiments, were administered a coarse Fc extract twice a week via stomach tube irrigation in the amount of 2 mg per each ml. As the body weight increased, we increased the dose to 3 mg per each ml. The contrast group consisted of 25 female Wistar rats.

## Results

### 1. Fc-Induced Esophageal and Forestomach Cancer in Mice

As a result of the Fc treatment, there were 3 cases showing both esophageal and forestomach papilloma and cancer in the 20 DBA mice which we were able to observe (see Table 1). One of the mice on which we had experimented for 655 days showed canceration along the entire length of the esophagus as well as the top end of the forestomach (Figures 1 and 2). Another (469 days) showed partial forestomach epithelial cancer and papilloma with the cancer occurring near the crest of stomachus glandularis (Figure 3). In the third case (469 days), cancer was also observable at the crest of the forestomach. The animals which had been treated with the Fc showed other pathological changes, such as epithelial hyperplasias, atypical hyperplasias, papillomas and other precancerous pathological changes. In some we found liver cell hyperplastic pathological changes with cell metaplasia and nucleus deep contamination, however liver cancer had not yet been formed. In a contrast group consisting of 20 mice, we did not observe any occurrences of pre-cancerous lesions or cancer in the esophagus and the forestomach.

Table 1

Fusarin C Induced Esophageal and Forestomach Cancer in DBA Rats

| Number of days in experiment (total dose) | Number of rats [sic] (mice) | Esophageal and forestomach lesions | | | |
|---|---|---|---|---|---|
| | | Hyperplasias | Atypical hyperplasias | Papillomas | Cancer |
| 9~27 (1.5~3 mg) | 14 | 12 | 0 | 0 | 0 |
| 123~150 (3.25~5 mg) | 9 | 5 | 1 | 1 | 0 |
| 299 (10.1 mg) | 1 | 0 | 0 | 1 | 0 |
| 469~502 (8.2~12.0 mg) | 3 | 1 | 0 | 1 | 2 |
| 655 (14.2 mg) | 2 | 0 | 1 | 0 | 1 |
| Total | 29 | 18 | 2 | 3 | 3 |
| Contrast group | 20 | 0 | 0 | 0 | 0 |

## 2. Fc-Induced Esophageal Cancer and Forestomach Cancer in Rats

We were able to carry out pathological histological tests on 20 of the 40 rats, among which there were 5 cases of esophageal cancer and forestomach papilloma (Table 2). One of these rats (742 days) also presented various degrees of atypical hyperplasias and squamous carcinoma all along the length of the esophageal epithelium (Figure 4 and Figure 5). The

Table 2
Fusarin C Induced Esophageal and Forestomach Cancer in Wistar Rats

| Number of days in experiment (total dose) | Number of rats | Esophageal and forestomach lesions | | | |
|---|---|---|---|---|---|
| | | Hyperplasias | Atypical hyperplasias | Papillomas | Cancer |
| 408~488 (214~264 mg) | 4 | 3 | 0 | 1 | 0 |
| 531~596 (294~354 mg) | 4 | 0 | 0 | 0 | 1 |
| 601~675 (357~447 mg) | 5 | 2 | 1 | 1 | 1 |
| 742~814 (477~537 mg) | 7 | 0 | 0 | 3 | 3 |
| Total | 20 | 5 | 1 | 5 | 5 |
| Contrast group | 25 | 0 | 0 | 0 | 0 |

forestomach showed occurrence of papilloma. The other four rats (experiments carried out for 590, 609, 813 and 817 days) presented squamous carcinoma of the forestomach with cancerous cell groups originating in the papilloma, forming papillose growths of different lengths stretched below (Figures 6 through 8). There were still other rats which had been treated with the Fc whose esophagus and forestomach epithelium displayed atypical hyperplasias and papillomatous pre-cancerous lesions. Except for one case of mammary gland cancer, the liver and the lungs [of the other rats] showed no tumorous formation. We did not observe any pathological changes in the upper digestive tracts of the 25 rats in the contrast group which had not been treated with Fc.

## Discussion

Fusarin C certainly possesses toxicity, particularly for mice, so that the dose of the Fc administered by irrigation had to be adjusted in the course of experiments. Rats have a comparatively high resistance to Fc and we further increased the dose of Fc administered after their body weight had increased. However, compared to the generally used polycyclic aromatic hydrocarbon carcinogens and the nitrosamine carcinogens, the experiment time for Fc induced cancer was longer.

As a chemical carcinogen, based on the presence of an epoxy group between the $C_{13}$ and $C_{14}$ in Fc, it can have a direct carcinogenic effect (Figure 9). In both mice and rats we

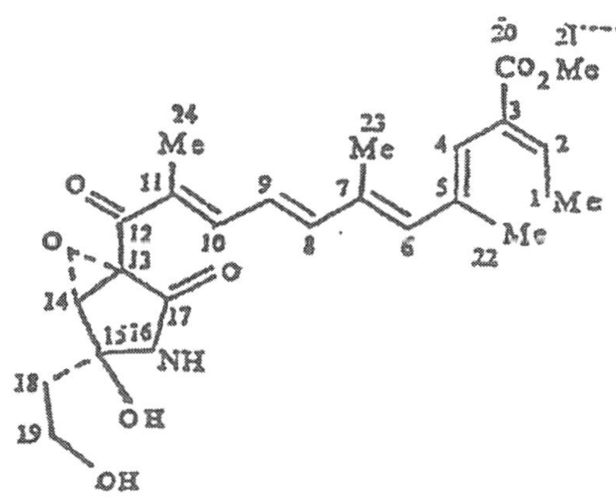


**Figure 9 Structural Formula of Fusarin C**

observed one animal which had a canceration phenomenon along the entire length of the esophagus and at the top of the forestomach which seems to prove that Fc administered by dropper can have a direct carcinogenic effect. In previous experiments on ectosomatic metabolism involving administering an S-9 mixture, although the mutagenic effect of Fc could be strengthened, particularly in the TA 100 Salmonella strain, as well as the cell SCE, microkaryo- and chromosome aberrations, 6-TG resistant mutations etc. of the $V_{79}$[6], still, if the Fc action was extended beyond 24 hours, even without adding a liver microsome enzyme preparation, it could have a certain effect[7]. Under conditions of metabolic activity, Fc can increase the number of bacterial DNA splits and cause asynchronized replications of the rat fibroblast virus DNA sequence transformed from polyoma virus[8]. We proved that $^3$H-Fc can form a covalent bond with the DNA in the rats' esophageal tissue culture. Moreover, after the rats' esophageal epithelial cell strains (RE-525), which we had grown, had been treated with Fc, they develop the following characteristics of malignant transformation: continued growth in selected culture media without serum or growth factors and ability to form colonies in semisolid agar-agar; changes, increased number, and structural aberrations of the chromosome karyotype; an increased mRNA expression level of three types of cancer genes---N-ras, C-myc and V-erb-B; loss of reaction to the expression of TPA-adjusted C-myc gene. Additionally, after nude mice had been inoculated with RE-525 cells treated with Fc, they could develop squamous carcinoma.

The results of these experiments and studies indicate that treatment with TLC purified or unpurified Fc, could equally induce squamous carcinoma of the esophagus and the forestomach in animals, proving that it has a carcinogenic effect. Further research is required to determine the effect of Fc with different degrees of purity. However, researchers in South Africa who have fed Fusarium moniliforme culture to rats, believe that Fc is not necessarily the carcinogen in the Fusarium moniliforme sheldon. (Please see the first page of the insert for Figures 1 through 8 in this text.)

## References

1. Li MH, et al. Experimental studies on the carcinogenicity of fungus contaminated food from Linxian county. In: Gelboin HV, eds. Genetic and Environmental Factors in Exp. and Human Cancer. Tokyo: Japan Spc. Press 1980:139.
2. Marasas WF, et al. Incidence of Fusarium species and the mycotoxins, deoxynalenol and zearanlenone, in corn produced in esophageal cancer areas in Transkei, Agric Food Chem. 1979; 27:1108.
3. Li, Gongxin, et al., "Squamous Carcinoma of the Forestomach induced in Rats by Feeding Cornmeal Inoculated with Fusarium moniliforme sheldon", Chinese Journal of Oncology, 1982, 4:241.
4. Jiang Yuanzhou, et al., "Fusarium moniliforme Mutagen in Linxian County--Isolation and Purification of Fusarin C," Chinese Journal of Oncology, 1985: 7 (supplementary issue): 42.
5. Weibe LA, et al. Fusarin C, a mutagen from Fusarium moniliforme grown on corn. J. Food Sci. 1981; 46:1424.
6. Cheng SJ, et al. a mutagenic metabolite produced by fusarium moniliforme isolated from Linxian county, China, Carcinogenesis 1985; 6:903.

7. Ju, Gefeng, "Genotoxicity of Two Types of Fusarin - T-2 and Fusarin C", graduate student thesis at Chinese Joint Medical College, 1986.
8. Lu SJ, et al. Fusarium moniliforme metabolites: genotoxicity of culture extracts. Carcinogenesis 1988; 9:1523.
9. Lu Fuxiong, et al., "Research on Fusarin C Ectosomatically Induced Epithelial Cell Transformations in Rats", Scientia Sinica, 1990, 12:1293.
10. Jaskiewicz K, et al. Carcinogenicity on Fusarium moniliforme culture material in rats. NCI 1987; 78:321

## Assignment 3: Notes

1. 皮下 (page 1, line 7) - This term, meaning "under the skin" in Chinese, comes up as "subcutaneous" in good Chinese-English medical dictionaries. Such terms, often appearing quite simple in Chinese, can be deceptively difficult to render appropriately in English. For instance, take the term "体外" appearing on page 1, line 6. In one C-E medical dictionary, you will encounter the possibilities of "*in vitro*," "extrinsic," "extrasomatic," and "extraneous" in addition to the "ectosomatic" rendition adopted here by the translator. One way to narrow down these alternatives is to cross check them in an English-language medical dictionary.

2. wistar 大鼠 (page 1, line 8) - What do you do as a translator when English appearing in a Chinese text has been incorrectly rendered (misspelled, wrong case, etc.)? Here, you are fortunate in that the term "Wistar" appears several times correctly capitalized elsewhere in the document, allowing him/her to make the correction in the English translation. Were this the only place the term appeared in the document, you would have the choice of researching the term to make the necessary correction (more desirable) or leaving the term as it appeared in the Chinese text (far less desirable). Where you are fairly sure that there is a mistake in the original but have no ground on which to base a correction, a "[sic]" can be placed after the term in the English translation. Creating a translator footnote is another possibility.

3. L.F. Beldanes 教授 (page 1, line 23) - Fortunately, the name of this professor has been given in English in the Chinese text. You will not always be so fortunate. When what is clearly a Western proper noun is rendered phonetically in a Chinese text, look around to see if it is not given in English elsewhere. For instance, the term "特兰斯开," appearing on page 1, line 14 in the original, appears in English in the second entry under References at the end of the article as "Transkei."

4. 甲醇 and 正已烷 (page 1, line 26) - When tackling a medical/chemical text, the translator will require a good Chinese-English dictionary of chemical terminology. Just as for taxonomic terms (*Fusarium moniliforme* sheldon), pay attention to what is, and what is not, italicized in chemical terminology (methyl alcohol, *n*-hexane).

5. 对照组 (page 1, line 37) - The translator has rendered this term as "contrast group" in the English translation. Another commonly encountered rendering of this term in medical contexts is "control group."

6. 可观察的 (page 1, line 44) - This has been rendered by the translator as "We were able to observe." Notice that the pronoun "We," although not appearing in this sentence in the Chinese, has been filled in by the translator. He/she is justified in doing this, first, because the pronoun "we" is employed elsewhere by the Chinese author (for example, page 1, line 14), and second, because the use of a pronoun is appropriate in such medical papers published in English. (It would not be appropriate in a patent, for example.)

## Assignment 4: Translation

Tapping international capital markets

Several channels exist for tapping international capital markets. The larger private utilities in developing countries have direct access to debt and equity markets. In October 1993 Telecom Argentina placed much of its $500 million, seven-year bond issue with U.S. and Asian investors; Argentina's Telefonika has also used bond market placements to raise expansion funds.

Foreign direct investment opens another route into international equity markets. General Electric Corporation, an international conglomerate, has an active interest in developing infrastructure projects in developing countries. Its subsidiary, the General Electric Capital Corporation (GECC), issues securities on U.S. and European markets and invests the funds in selected projects. GECC has participated as an equity investor, for instance, in the Northern Mindanao power project - a 108-megawatt diesel-fired power project in the Philippines. Backed by the group's total operations, the placement of securities issued by GECC is easier than it would be for developing country power projects alone.

An instrument widely used to tap resources in the U.S. capital market is the American depositary receipt (ADR). ADRs are certificates of deposit that enable foreign companies to raise equity on U.S. markets without the need for a listing on a U.S. stock exchange and without complex settlement and transfer mechanisms. They are issued by a U.S. depository bank, and the underlying shares of the company are held in trust by a custodian bank in the home country. In 1990 Compañía de Teléfonos de Chile (CTC) raised $92 million on the New York Stock Exchange through an issue of equity in the form of ADRs - the first major equity issue from Latin America in three decades.

In April 1990 the U.S. Securities and Exchange Commission approved rule 144a, facilitating private placement of securities, including those placed as ADRs. Before then, privately placed securities held by qualified buyers (institutions that manage assets worth at least $100 million) could be traded only after a two- or three-year holding period. Rule 144a allows trading to occur immediately, provided that the new buyer is also qualified. Moreover, after three years the securities can be sold to all buyers. Rule 144a was used in 1992 to enable a $207.5 million international bond issue for the Mexico City-Toluca Toll Road. Since then, other Mexican toll roads and the Subic Bay power plant in the Philippines have raised funds using rule 144a.

**Warning signs from the nineteenth century**

Throughout the nineteenth century, when infrastructure was largely in private hands, contemporaries complained that many worthwhile projects were neglected for lack of financing. Some of the complaints reflected the difficulties of financing pioneering transportation (especially railway) projects. Other complaints were self-serving efforts to shift all risk on to government budgets, and in many cases the financial bankruptcy of enterprises had severe consequences for government finances.

Governments all over the world provided aid to private infrastructure projects in various forms, including direct subsidies. Two instruments in use then and of current interest as well are financial guarantees and land grants.

*Guarantees*. In India, if a railway company did not attain a minimum rate of return of, for example, 5 percent, the government made up the difference under the terms of a guarantee backed by its full powers of taxation. Such guarantees were also critical in the construction of the Canadian railways. But guarantees removed incentives for investors to monitor management performance while opening the way for promoters to negotiate so-called "sweetheart" deals with construction and supply companies. Because many infrastructure projects were one of a kind, the practice could be readily disguised. It now appears that bond guarantees led to higher construction costs.

*Land grants*. During the nineteenth century, lands adjoining railways and canals were often ceded to promoters, allowing them to profit from the many side businesses that grew up around their investments. By providing collateral that could be used to back bonded debt, land grants - like interest guarantees - corrected for capital market imperfections. In Canada during the 1850s and 1860s, defaults on guaranteed bonds drained government revenues. In 1871, therefore, the Canadian House of Commons adopted a policy of land grants as a way to subsidize railway construction without having to raise the rate of taxation. Land grants proved most effective in such large speculative ventures as the Indian railroads and the transcontinental lines in the United States.

**Land grants and eminent domain**

Land grants have proved to be a valuable form of collateral for innovative projects that might otherwise not have been financed because lenders had little experience with similar projects. But in implementing a policy of land grants, there is a risk that the grants might be wasted if they are given to projects that would be built in any case.

Overall, however, land grants have greater merit than interest guarantees because they represent a one-time infusion of resources and do not reduce the incentives for efficient operation of the project. They may be especially suited for more speculative projects - such as high-speed rail in industrial countries or high-risk transport investment in developing countries.

## Assignment 4: Notes

Box 5.2

1. 国际股本市场 (line 8) - Rendered by the translator as "international equity markets." When tackling economic and financial texts, you will need good Chinese-English references to properly translate such terms. Since the term "股本" can also be rendered as "capital stock," a good English-language dictionary of financial terms is also necessary for cross checking.

2. 和144a条款下的申请 (line 19) - Notice that this portion of the Chinese text has not been translated into English. Carefully check your work once you have finished a translation to make sure that you haven't omitted anything!

Box 5.3

1. 把所有风险转嫁到政府预算上 (line 6) - Rendered by the translator as "shift all risk on to government budgets." Note how the term "转嫁," originally meaning to remarry, has come to mean to transfer something undesirable (here, the risk) on to someone else.

2. 使资本市场不尽完善 (line 26) - Rendered by the translator as "corrected for capital market imperfections." The translator seems not to have captured the original meaning. What do you think?

3. ...50年代 (line 27) - Rendered by the translator as the "[18]50s." You can also expect to encounter a decade to be written out in Chinese as "五十年代".

4. 大型冒险项目上 (line 31) - Rendered by the translator as "in such large speculative ventures." Does the use of the word "speculative" for "冒险" go beyond what the original text is conveying?

Box 5.5

1. 土地赠与和征用 (line 1) - Rendered by the translator as "Land grants and eminent domain." The term "地主" (landowner) also appears in this text (line 21). Note that you may also occasionally require a Chinese-English legal dictionary to handle legal terms appearing in an economic/financial text.

2. 积极性 (line 8) 刺激力 (line 22) - Both rendered by the translator as "incentive(s)." In some cases, a single English word has to do double duty for Chinese terms with highly different meanings.

# Part Two

# Translation: English into Chinese

**Box 1.4 Infrastructure´s direct and indirect effects in rural India**

A study of two villages in rural Karnataka state, Southern India, offers a glimpse of the full impact that infrastructure can have on rural living standards. The researcher, who studied the Wangala and Dalena villages in the 1950s and 1970s, described how the two villages had been similarly poor and backward until a large-scale irrigation project brought Wangala into a canal network while Dalena´s high elevation left it unirrigated.

Although canal irrigation directly promoted rapid intensification of cultivation in Wangala, institutions and the villagers´way of life were relatively unaffected otherwise. In contrast, Dalena did not benefit directly from the canal. Its villagers were compelled to adjust their way of life significantly in order to capture the indirect economic benefits from the irrigation project. The villagers purchased land outside Dalena, sought positions in the Public Works Department and a nearby sugar mill, and became involved in the transport of irrigated villages´sugarcane to the mill. Dalena quickly established itself as a service center in the region, and its residents integrated themselves into a much wider economic sphere than did those in Wangala.

The research emphasized how many Dalena villagers traveled daily between their homes in the village and their places of work in nearby towns. This observation, echoed in other studies, suggests that the development process need not entail migration from rural areas to urban centers. In the Uttar Pradesh village of Palanpur, per capita living standards rose between 1957 and 1993 in the face of population growth, in part because of expanding nonfarm employment. Residents of Palanpur commute daily to the towns of Chandausi and Moradabad, largely by rail. This type of rural commuting more commonly occurs along roads by foot, bicycle, motorcycle, bus, or car.

**Box 2.3 It took ten years to corporatize Indonesia's main ports**

In Indonesia, there are three formal stages in the adoption of commercial principles. First, the government department is transformed into a government enterprise. Then the enterprise becomes a corporation that still has a combination of commercial and noncommercial goals. Finally, the corporation is turned into a profit-oriented entity whose ownership can be shared with the private sector. Ports have just reached this third stage.

of all 300 ports was centralized in the Directorate General of Sea Communications, a government department. Most of these ports had obsolete equipment and failed to meet regional needs. In mid-1983 the government decided to decentralize management for ninety of its ports by creating four new public port corporations, headquartered at the four largest ports.

Two years elapsed before the government addressed the overregulation that remained a major impediment to the success of the new corporations. Moreover, managers did not yet have a clear understanding of their responsibilities and accountability and lacked the autonomy to implement reforms they thought were needed. These problems had been addressed by 1988, when an effective cost control program lowered expenses by 5 percent and increased revenue by 20 percent for the largest port corporation. Between 1987 and 1992, revenue grew almost twice as fast as expenses.

Ten years after the reform process started, the port corporations face the market test. Competition promises to be tough: a recent survey of foreign investors ranked Indonesia's port infrastructure at about the same level as Australia's but below others in the region, such as Hong Kong, Malaysia, and Singapore.

**Box 3.8 Regulation and privatization: which comes first? The case of Malaysia**

Privatization of the infrastructure sector has progressed rapidly in Malaysia since the mid-1980s. In all cases, the government department or statutory body that was previously supplying the services has assumed the statutory role of regulating the privatized supplier. For example, the Kelang Port Authority is now the regulatory agency supervising the two private operating companies at the port, and the Telecommunications Department is the regulator of the telecommunications sector. (The change in the function of the government department or statutory body has, in each case, necessitated new empowering legislation.)

Significant government equity ownership in formerly privatized enterprises and the mechanism of the "golden share" also play a role akin to regulation. (The golden share, which gives the government veto powers on major policy matters of the privatized firm, was first introduced in the privatization of Malaysian Airline Systems and the Malaysian International Shipping Corporation.) Equity ownership by the government and the golden share are intended to ensure that the policies of the privatized firm are in conformity with government policies and national objectives.

Regulation in Malaysia has really meant the supervision of tariffs and the maintenance of service standards. The scope of regulatory action in Malaysia, however, is fairly rudimentary. For instance, no clear link exists between the functions of the regulatory agencies and the creation of incentives for the privatized supplier of infrastructure services to achieve efficiency. Although regulatory agencies exist, the respective ministers still appear to have considerable influence over the policies of the privatized suppliers of infrastructure services. Rate revisions, for example, are not completely a matter for the regulatory agency to decide and almost always appear to require ministerial sanction. There is also a distinct possibility that industry might "capture" the regulatory agency in some cases. At present, considerable ambiguity exists about the independence of the regulatory agencies from ministerial or political interference.

Although still evolving, the regulatory mechanism does not appear to have limited new entry and investment. The lesson from the Malaysian experience is that moves toward privatization and private sector provision of infrastructure services need not wait for the formal creation of a comprehensive regulatory framework.

*word count*: 947

# Resident Rights and Responsibilities

**U.S. Department of Housing and Urban Development**
Office of Multifamily Housing Programs

**You, as a resident, play an important role in helping to make your HUD-assisted housing a home for you and your family.**

Along with your management agent, you can participate in making your place of residence - the unit, the grounds, and other common areas - a better place to live, and also create a community of which you are proud.

The U.S. Department of Housing and Urban Development (HUD) administers several affordable housing programs. This brochure is being provided to you because HUD has provided some form of financing in this apartment building.

As a team member in this effort, your HUD Field Office encourages and supports:

- Communication between residents and management agents and owners of the property.
- Prompt consideration and resolution of valid resident complaints by owners and managers.
- Residents organizing and participating in the decisions regarding the apartment building that affect the well-being of their home.

As a resident you have rights and responsibilities. This brochure briefly lists some of your most important rights and responsibilities.

# Your Rights . . .

HUD wants you to know your rights as a resident in HUD's multifamily housing. These rights include:

- The right to live in decent, safe, and sanitary housing with timely repairs and quality maintenance.
- The right to organize as residents without obstruction, harassment, or retaliation from property owners, management agents, or their representatives.
- The right to use appropriate common space or meeting facilities to either organize or to consider any issue affecting the management of the property.

- The right to timely response to requests and complaints made to the management without harassment or intimidation.
- The right to request to review HUD files on your building and its management.
- The right to  be given reasonable notice, in writing, of any inspection or other entry to your apartment.
- The right of confidentiality of information provided to you by management in accordance with State and local privacy laws.
- The right to be recognized by property owners and managers as having a voice in residential community affairs.
- The right to equal and fair treatment and use of your building's services and facilities without regard to race, color, religion, gender, disability, familial status (children under 18), national origin (ethnicity or language), or age.

In addition, different HUD programs provide for specific rights for residents. To find out if the apartment building you live in is covered by one of the following categories, talk to your management agent.

**If you live in an apartment building which is eligible under the Low-Income Housing Preservation and Resident Home Ownership Act or the Emergency Low=Income Housing Preservation Act for prepayment of its HUD-insured mortgage, and the owner has filed a notice to either sell the building or stay on as the owner, you have additional rights including:**

- The right of notification of the submission of an initial Notice of Intent.
- The right to timely written notice of the Preservation Capital Needs Assessment inspection to identify all needed repairs.

- The right to be represented at the inspection review meeting, called the Exit Conference.
- The right to comment on the plan for the future of the building called the Plan of Action, including discussing proposed rents, utility allowances, and repairs and renovation.
- The right to offer to buy the building or pick a nonprofit organization to buy it, if the owner chooses to sell.

## If you live in an apartment building that has a HUD-insured mortgage subject to Section 250(a) of the National Housing Act, the mortgage may be prepaid only with the Secretary's consent. For such buildings, the primary rights of residents regarding prepayment include:

- The right of notification of submission of a request for prepayment.
- The right to provide comments to be considered by the Secretary when reviewing such requests.

## If you live in an apartment building that is owned by HUD and is being sold:

Residents are notified when a HUD-owned building will be sold. In addition, residents have the right to comment on HUD's plans for disposing of the building before the building is sold. HUD will directly negotiate the sale of HUD-owned multifamily housing to resident organizations that meet certain criteria such as demonstrating capacity and commitment. Resident organizations should contact the HUD Field Office nearest to you.

**If you live in an apartment building where HUD provided a subsidy under certain programs (known as Section 236 and 221(d)(3) below-market interest rate and rent supplement programs):**

Residents have the right to receive written notice of , participate in, and comment on the following issues:

- A request to HUD for approval of an increase in maximum permissible rent.
- A request to HUD for approval of a conversion from project-paid utilities to resident-paid utilities, or of a reduction in the resident utility allowance.
- A request to HUD for approval of a conversion of residential units to non-residential use or to cooperative housing or condominiums.
- A request to HUD for approval of major physical improvements.

## . . . and Responsibilities

By signing your lease, you have entered into a legal, enforceable contract. Therefore, you are responsible for complying with the rules and guidelines governing your lease. Other responsibilities you have include, but are not limited to, the following:

- Giving the management agent prompt notice of any defects in plumbing, fixtures, appliances, or other parts of the unit or related facilities.
- Not engaging in criminal activity in the unit, common areas, or community grounds.
- Paying the correct rent amount on a timely basis each month.

- Providing accurate information to the owner at the certification or recertification interview that is necessary for determining eligibility for assistance.
- Consenting to the release of information by a third party and HUD computer matching, so that the owner can verify the information provided on the application.

Your management agent/owner of the property is also responsible for certain activities that are stipulated in the lease. Be sure to read your lease carefully and understand all of the terms so you can be a responsible resident. If you have any questions about your lease or do not have a copy, contact your management agent or your local HUD Field Office.

## If you need help or more information, you may contact:

- The Resident Initiatives Specialist in the Multifamily Housing Division at your local HUD Field Office.
- The housing counseling agency in your community (for assistance, call the HUD Housing Counseling Service Locator at 1-800-569-4287).
- HUD's National Multifamily Housing Clearinghouse at 1-800-685-8470.

Your local government tenant/landlord affairs office, legal services, and tenant organizations may also provide you with information on additional rights you have under local or State law.

This brochure about your rights and responsibilities as a resident of HUD multifamily housing is also available in Chinese, Korean, Russian, Spanish, and Vietnamese. Contact your local HUD Field Office or HUD's National Multifamily Housing Clearinghouse at 1-800-685-8470.

*word count*: 1162

**05-03 PENICILLINS**

## PENICILLINS (Oral)

---

The information that follows is about a group of medicines known as penicillins. This group includes the following drugs which are listed by their generic names, with common brand names shown in parentheses:

| | |
|---|---|
| **Amoxicillin (Amoxil, Trimox)** | **Dicloxacillin (Dynapen)** |
| **Amoxicillin and Clavulanate (Augmentin)** | **Penicillin V (V-cillin K)** |
| **Ampicillin (Polycillin)** | **Other________________** |

---

**PLEASE READ CAREFULLY**

---

## ABOUT YOUR MEDICINE

**Penicillins** (pen-i-SILL-ins) are used to treat infections caused by bacteria. They will not work for colds, flu, or other virus infections. Some penicillins are also used to prevent "strep" infections in patients with a history of rheumatic heart disease.

If any of the information in this leaflet causes you special concern or if you want additional information about your medicine and its use, check with your doctor, nurse, or pharmacist. **Remember, keep this and all other medicines out of the reach of children and never share your medicines with others.**

---

### BEFORE USING THIS MEDICINE

Tell Your Doctor, Nurse, and Pharmacist If You . . .

- are allergic to any medicine, either prescription or nonprescription (OTC);
- are pregnant or intent to become pregnant while using this medicine;
- are breast-feeding;
- are taking any other prescription or nonprescription (OTC) medicine, especially birth control pills containing estrogen, cholestyramine, colestipol, or probenecid;
- have any other medical problems, especially infectious mononucleosis ("mono") or history of stomach or intestinal disease, such as colitis, including colitis caused by antibiotics, or enteritis.

## PROPER USE OF THIS MEDICINE

Most penicillins are best taken with a full glass (8 ounces) of water on an empty stomach; however, some are best taken with a snack or meal. Follow your doctor's or pharmacist's directions on how to take your medicine.

If you are taking a penicillin G, do not take acidic fruit juices (for example, orange or grapefruit juice) or other acidic beverages within 1 hour of the time you take penicillin G. To do so may keep the medicine from working properly.

**Keep taking this medicine for the full time of treatment** even if you begin to feel better after a few days, **do not miss any doses. This is especially important if you have a "strep" infection since serious heart problems could develop later** if your infection is not cleared up completely.

**If you do miss a dose of this medicine**, take it as soon as possible. However, if it is almost time for your next dose, skip the missed dose and go back to your regular dosing schedule. Do not double doses.

## PRECAUTIONS WHILE USING THIS MEDICINE

If your symptoms do not improve within a few days, or if they become worse, check with your doctor.

In some patients, penicillins may cause diarrhea. Severe diarrhea may be a sign of a serious side effect. **Do not take any diarrhea medicine without first checking with your doctor.**

**Oral contraceptives (birth control pills) containing estrogen may not work properly if you take them while you are taking ampicillin, bacampicillin, or penicillin V. unplanned pregnancies may occur. Use a different or additional means of birth control while taking any of these penicillins.**

**Diabetics - Some penicillins may cause false test results with some urine sugar tests.** Check with your doctor before changing your diet or the dosage of your diabetes medicine.

**This medicine must not be given to other people or used for other infections** unless you are otherwise directed by your doctor.

## POSSIBLE SIDE EFFECTS OF THIS MEDICINE

*Side Effects That Should Be reported To Your Doctor Immediately*

**Stop taking this medicine and get emergency help immediately** if you notice:

*Rare (may be less common with some penicillins)* - Difficulty in breathing; lightheadedness; skin rash, hives, itching, or wheezing.

*Rare (may be more common with some penicillins)* - Abdominal bloating; blood in urine; convulsions (seizures); decreased amount of urine; diarrhea (watery and severe) which may also be bloody; fever; joint pain; sore throat and fever; stomach or abdominal cramps and pain (severe; unusual bleeding or bruising.

Some of the above side effects may occur up to several weeks after you stop taking this medicine.

***Side Effects That Usually Do Not Require Medical Attention***

These possible side effects may go away during treatment; however, if they continue or are bothersome, check with your doctor, nurse, or pharmacist.

*More common (may be less common with some penicillins)* - Diarrhea (mild); nausea or vomiting; sore mouth or tongue.

Other side effects not listed above may also occur in some patients. If you notice any other effects, check with your doctor, nurse, or pharmacist.

*word count*: 746

## Assignment 4: Business/Economics

THE NEED FOR NEW APPROACHES. In the coming decade, demand for infrastructure investments will simultaneously increase in two different sets of countries: those that have undertaken macroeconomic adjustment with consequent low investment levels and, at the other extreme, those whose rapid growth is now placing a heavy burden on infrastructure. Infrastructure investments in developing countries represent, on average, 4 percent of GDP, but they often need to be substantially higher. Where telecommunications or power-supply networks are expanding rapidly, annual investments in either sector can be as high as 2 percent of GDP. A special factor increasing investment demand in many countries is the rapid pace of urbanization, requiring investments in water supply as well as waste treatment and disposal.

In Asia, the share of infrastructure investment in GDP is expected to rise from 4 percent today to more than 7 percent by the turn of the century, with transport and energy likely to demand the most resources, followed by telecommunications and environmental infrastructure. Some of the planned investments are without precedent. China, for example, has set a target of installing at least 5 million telephone lines annually up to 1995 and at least 8 million lines per year thereafter, to more than triple its 1992 base of 18 million lines by the year 2000.

*Private entrepreneurship: trends and opportunities*

Current efforts to secure increased private sponsorship and risktaking in infrastructure projects reflect these various challenges. After decades of severe regulatory restriction, private entrepreneurship in infrastructure bounce back in two ways during the late 1980s: through the privatization of state-owned utilities and through policy reform that made possible the construction of new facilities in competition with, or as a complement to, existing enterprises.

The principal new infrastructure entrepreneurs are international firms seeking business in developing countries and operating often in association with local companies. These firms bring to bear not only their management expertise and technical skills, but also their credit standing and ability to finance investments in developing countries. Major electric, telecommunications, and water utilities in industrial countries face slowly growing demand and increased competition (following deregulation) in their home markets. As a result, they are vigorously seeking high-yielding investments in developing countries. Construction conglomerates are active in toll-road construction and in power projects, where they sometimes take an equity interest. Some companies or groups of companies also specialize in stand-alone infrastructure projects, putting together financing packages and overseeing project development and operation.

Most indicators of infrastructure investment under private sponsorship reveal rapid growth. Privatized telecommunications and electricity utilities in Latin America and Asia are undertaking large and growing new investments. The number of these so-called greenfield projects - especially in the road and electric power sectors - has grown rapidly (as discussed below). Infrastructure investments by the International Finance Corporation (IFC), a World Bank affiliate that invests only in private entities, have experienced a surge, from modest amounts in the late 1980s to $330 million in fiscal 1993. The amount invested by the IFC was leveraged more than ten times, so that, in 1993, IFC participated in private investments of $3.5 billion.

The most important development during the past four years has been the explosion in international flows of long-term private capital to developing countries, especially in the form of foreign direct investment and portfolio flows. Aggregate flows stood at more than $80 billion in 1992 and were projected to reach $112 billion in 1993 (Table 5.1). Infrastructure has been a significant beneficiary of such flows (Box 5.2).

Aggregate private investment in infrastructure in developing countries is currently about $15 billion a year, or roughly 7 percent of the $200 billion being spent annually on infrastructure in these countries. Although small, the fraction of private investment in infrastructure investment is much larger than it was some years ago, and there is a strong likelihood that private investment will continue to grow, possibly doubling its share of the total by the year 2000. One indication is the IFC's current infrastructure pipeline, which is almost as large as all the projects financed to date.

The small overall share of private finance in infrastructure obscures large regional and sectoral disparities. Private finance is proportionately greater in Latin America than in other regions, and larger in telecommunications and electric power generation than in other sectors. The diffusion of current experience across regions and sectors will raise the global share of private sponsorship and finance. For example, telecommunications privatization and independent power generation are under discussion in all regions, including Sub-Saharan Africa. And continuing technological and financial innovations will undoubtedly make private financing more attractive. As an example, electronic methods of identifying vehicles and charging tolls could make roads more like a public utility service, and boost the share of private finance in the highway sector.

Even with the rising share of privately financed infrastructure, governments will continue to be an important source of financing. Often, they will need to be partners with private entrepreneurs. Public-private partnerships in some ways represent a return to the nineteenth century, when infrastructure projects were privately financed in much of the world while government support acted as a stimulant. But the nineteenth century experience also offers important warning signs (Box 5.3)

**Table 5.1 Portfolio and foreign direct investment in developing countries, 1990–93**
*(net inflows in billions of dollars)*

| *Type* | *1990* | *1991* | *1992* | *1993*[a] |
|---|---|---|---|---|
| Foreign equity securities | 3.78 | 7.55 | 13.07 | 13.1 |
| Closed-end funds[b] | 2.78 | 1.20 | 1.34 | 2.7 |
| ADRs and GDRs[c] | 0.14 | 4.90 | 5.93 | 7.2 |
| Direct equity | 0.77 | 1.45 | 5.80 | 3.2 |
| Debt instruments | 5.56 | 12.72 | 23.73 | 42.6 |
| Bonds | 4.68 | 10.19 | 21.24 | 39.1 |
| Commercial paper | 0.23 | 1.38 | 0.85 | 1.6 |
| Certificates of deposit | 0.65 | 1.15 | 1.64 | 1.8 |
| Total portfolio[d] | 9.34 | 20.27 | 36.80 | 55.7 |
| Foreign direct investment | 26.30 | 36.90 | 47.30 | 56.3 |
| Total | 35.64 | 57.17 | 84.10 | 112.0 |

*Note:* This table records all portfolio and direct investment flows. Separate figures for infrastructure are not available.
a. 1993 figures are estimated or projected.
b. A closed-end fund has a predetermined amount of funding and sometimes a fixed life.
c. ADR = American depositary receipts; GDR = global depositary receipts. An ADR is an instrument used by an offshore company to raise equity in the United States without formal listing on a U.S. stock exchange. GDRs are similar instruments used in Europe and elsewhere.
d. Portfolio investment is the sum of equity and debt.
*Source:* World Bank 1993i, pp. 10, 21.

*word count*: 1005

# Section 2. Translation of the Assignments and Notes

## Assignment 1: Translation

### 专栏 1.4 基础设施对印度农村的直接和间接影响

有关印度南部农业省份卡那塔克邦的两个村庄的一份研究报告提供了有关基础设施对农村生活水平的全面影响的概况。研究人员对 50 年代和 70 年代的旺加拉村和达赖那村进行了研究，他描述了这两个村庄如何一样的贫穷落后，直到大面积的灌溉工程使旺加拉村加入了一个灌渠网这种现象才中止，而达赖那村则因地势较高而无法得到灌溉。

尽管水渠灌溉直接促进了旺加拉村耕作密度的增加，但是，这个村庄的体制和人们的生活方式并没有受到多少影响。相比之下，达赖那村并没有直接从灌渠得到好处。但是，为了从灌渠获得间接的经济利益，这个村的村民们被迫调整了自己的生活方式。村民们购买了达赖那村以外的土地，在公共工作部和附近的一家榨糖厂中找到一席之地，并参与了将得到灌溉的村庄生产的甘蔗运往糖厂的运输。达赖那村很快成为当地的服务业中心，与旺加拉村相比，其居民投身的经济环境更加广阔。

这份研究报告强调有大量的达赖那的居民每天往返于住家和其工作的周围城镇之间。这项考察指出（其他研究也有同感），经济发展过程不需要使人口从农村地区转移到中心城市。在北方邦的巴伦布尔村，从 1957—1993 年间，尽管人口增加，其人均生活水平依然提高，其中部分原因就是因为非农业就业的扩大。巴伦布尔村的居民每日出入金道西和莫拉达巴德的城镇，主要是乘坐火车。但更经常的是沿途步行或骑自行车、摩托车、乘公共汽车或小轿车。

### 专栏 2.3 印度尼西亚主要港口长达十年之久的公司化

在印度尼西亚，国有企业转为按商业原则经营需经历三个正式阶段。首先，政府机关转变成为政府企业。然后实行公司化，兼有商业性和非商业性经营目标。最后，公司变为以盈利为目的的实体，可与私人共同拥有所有权。目前，印度尼西亚的港口管理体制改革刚刚完成第三步骤。

印度尼西亚的港口管理体制改革于 1983 年起步。在此之前，全部 300 个港口都由一个政府部门（海洋运输总理事会）统管。多数港口设备陈旧，不能满足当地需要。1983 年中，政府决定分权，建立了四个新的国有港口公司，管理 90 个港口，总部分别设在四大港口。

两年之后政府才着手解决繁项的规章制度，它们是新公司成功的主要障碍。而且管理人员对其责任不甚了了，缺少经营自主权，无法推行它们认为必须进行的改革。到 1988 年，这些问题得到解决。印度尼西亚最大的一家港口公司通过一项有效的成本控制措施将开支减少了 5%，并将收入提高了 10%。从 1987 到 1992 年，收入增长速度几乎是开支增长速度的两倍。

改革措施启动十年之后，港口公司又面临新的市场考验。竞争看来会十分激烈。一项外国投资者的调查排列表明，印度尼西亚港口设施与澳大利亚处于同一水平，但低于该地区其他港口，如香港、马来西亚及新加坡等。

## 专栏3.8　规章制度与私有化：孰前孰后？马来西亚的例子

自从80年代中期以来，基础设施部门的私有化在马来西亚迅速地进行。在所有情况下，以前提供服务的政府部门或制订规章的机构承担了对私有化的供应商实施管理的责任。比如，克朗港务局目前是监督该港两家私营公司的管理机构，而电信部则是电信部门的管理机构。（政府部门或立法机构职能的变化，往往要求制订新的立法。）

政府在前私有化企业中占有重要的财产所有权以及"金股"机制，也可起到类似于管理的作用。（金股使政府对于私有化企业的重大政策问题拥有否决权，它首先应用于马来西亚航空公司和马来西亚国际航运公司的私有化中。）使用政府对资产的所有权和金股的目的，是保证私有化企业的政策符合政府政策与国家目标。

马来西亚的管理实际上意味着对价格和保持服务标准进行监督。不过，在马来西亚，管理行使的范围还是非常不完善的。例如，在管理机构的职能与为基础设施服务的私人供应商提高效率而建立激励机制方面，还不存在明确的联系。

虽然存在着制订规章制度的机构，但对于基础设施的私人提供者的政策，相应的部长们似乎仍有相当的影响。例如，对价格的评估就并不完全是由制订规章的机构决定的，它几乎都需要由部长来核准。此外还有一种可能性，在某些情况下，该部会"抓住"立法机构不放。在目前，制订规章的机构如何独立于部委或政治性的干预，还存在着许多模糊不清之处。

虽然马来西亚制订规章制度的机制仍在发展之中，它似乎没有限制新企业的参与和投资。从马来西亚的经验中可以总结出的教训就是，向私有化以及由私营部门提供基础设施服务的转变，不必等到正式建立了全面的规章制度框架以后才能进行。

## Assignment 1: Notes

### Box 1.4

*This observation, echoed in other studies . . . (line 20)* - Rendered by the translator as "这项考察指出(其他研究也有同感)" Here, the grammatical subject of the sentence in parentheses is the "other studies." In the Chinese translation, the verb "echoed" is translated by " 有同感, " meaning, to have the same feeling or impression. Thus, the Chinese seems to imply that reports have feelings. An alternative possibility which avoids this awkward construction is " 这项考察(其他研究也同样)指出 . . ."

*along roads by foot, bicycle, motorcycle, bus, or car (line 25)* - Rendered by the translator as "沿途步行或骑自行车、摩托车、乘公共汽车或小轿车。 " Notice that to make the Chinese work, the translator has had to add the verb "乘 " before bus. It is often necessary to creatively add fine details to render what is a simple list of items in English into a workable list in Chinese. Changing of the order in Chinese might even have been necessary had the English list been presented as "by foot, bus, bicycle, motorcycle, or car."

### Box 2.3

*In Indonesia, there ar three formal stages in the adoption of commercial principles (line 28)* - Rendered by the translator as " 在印度尼西亚，国有企业转为按商业原则经营需经历三个正式阶段." Here, the translator has added several terms to the Chinese that do not correspond directly to the English, such as " 国有企业 " and " 经营 " (this goes beyond the simple addition of a verb in the previous text). On the positive side, this adds clarity to the Chinese when the additions are accurate. on the negative side, the additions might be incorrect. Normally, unless your client has expressly told you to go ahead and rewrite a text to make it sound good in the target language, it is best to stick as close to the source language as possible in your translation.

*managers did not yet have a clear understanding of their responsibilities and accountability (page 2, line 11)* - "管理人员对其责任不甚了了 " The translator has not taken pains to capture the full content of the English sentence. The term "accountability" does not seem to have been rendered into Chinese. Additionally, the phrase " 不甚了了 " may be a little too vernacular for an article of this type. Perhaps there is a typographical error, and the Chinese text should read "不甚了解 ?"

Box 3.8

*. . .the Telecommunications Department is the regulator of the telecommunications sector. (line 26)* - Rendered by the translator as "电信部则是电信部门的管理机构." The word "sector" can be rendered in many ways in Chinese depending on the context. In line 22, the translator has rendered "sector" as "部门." The translator has then consistently rendered "sector" this way throughout the text. The problem is that "部门" can also mean a department, such as a government department. In line 26, both possible meanings of "部门" come head to head (both the term "电信部" and the term "电信部门" sound like Telecommunications Department," so at first glance the Chinese translation appears to read "the Telecommunications Department is the regulator of the Telecommunications Department"). In such cases, the translator has to make a tough choice: maintain consistency or avoid confusion. Here, he/she has chosen consistency over clarity. A way of avoiding this problem would be to translate this passage as "电信部门则是电信业的管理机构."

*regulatory agency (lines 25,38-39 and page 3, line 6)* - Consistency is highly important in translation. However, as we have seen, there are times when it may be sacrificed for clarity. In line 25, the translator has rendered "regulatory agency" as "管理机构," in lines 38-39 as "规章制度的机构," and on page 3, line 6 as "立法机构." Since there is no substantial difference in the meaning of "regulatory agency" as employed in English in these three places in the text, no clarity is gained by using three different terms. Consistency, however, has been greatly compromised.

# 居民的權利與義務

美國住宅與都市發展部
多家庭住宅計劃局

身為居民的您能扮演好一個重要的角色，來幫助住宅與都市發展部提供一個更好的居住環境給您及您的家人。

與您的管理人員一同參與能使您的住處——居住單位、草坪和其它共同空間——成爲一個更好的居住地方且成爲您引以爲傲的社區。

美國住宅與都市發展部(以下簡稱爲HUD)提供一些居民住得起的房屋計劃。因爲HUD對這棟公寓大廈提供了某種融資，因此提供這本小冊子給您做參考。

身爲這項計劃的組員，您的HUD當地辦事處鼓勵與支持：

- 居民與管理人員及房東之間相互的溝通。
- 對於居民的正當抱怨，房東和管理人員迅速與以重視並解決。
- 居民組織並參與會影響到居民住屋福利的有關公寓大廈的決定。

做爲一位居民，您有權利也有義務。這本小冊子簡單地列出一些您最重要的權利與義務。

## 您的權利…

HUD希望您能知道身爲一名HUD多家庭住宅的居民所擁有的權利。這些權利包括：

- 有權住在一個像樣、安全和清潔的房屋裡，並且適時地得到適當地修護與維修。
- 有權組織居民免於受到來自房東、管理人員或他們的代表的阻撓、騷擾或報復。
- 有權使用適當的共同空間或聚會設施來組織或討論任何會影響此公寓大廈管理的問題。

・有權要管理單位對於您的要求與抱怨做出適時地回應而不受騷擾或恐嚇。

・有權調閱有關您的大廈及其管理細則的HUD檔案。

・有權在因任何檢查或因其它理由而需進入您的公寓之前接到合理的書面通知。

・有權由管理單位基於州與地方的隱私權法，對於您提供給他們的資料予以保密。

・有權由房東和管理人員認可您對住屋社區事務的發言權。

・有權得到平等與公平的對待以及使用大樓的服務與設備，不可因人種、膚色、宗教、性別、殘障、家庭狀況(18歲以下的孩子)、祖籍(種族或語言)或年齡而有差別。

另外，不同的HUD計劃提供居民特別的權利。如果您居住的公寓大廈是屬於下列的任何一種類別，請與您的管理人員接洽。

如果在低收入住屋預留與住者有其屋法或緊急低收入住屋預留法之下，您所居住的公寓大廈的房東有資格預先付清由HUD做擔保的抵押貸款，並且房東已經提出求售大廈或決定留下來當房東的公告，此時您另外的權利包括：

・有權得到初次計劃公告的提交通知。

・有權適時地得到爲了查出需要修復之處而進行的預留資金估計調查的書面通知。

・當您與房東做資格證明或再次證明面談時，必須提供正確的資料給房東來做爲決定是否有資格得到補助。

・同意從第三者取得資料並且用HUD電腦查對，讓房東能夠查證您所提出的申請資料。

您的管理人員／房東有責任履行契約中列明的一些活動。請仔細閱讀您的契約且了解所有的條款，因而能使您成爲一個有責任的居民。如果您對契約內容有任何疑問或您沒有一份副本的話，請向您的管理人員或地方HUD當地辦事處洽詢。

如果您需要協助或更多的資料，請洽：

・您的地方HUD當地辦事處多家庭房屋組裡針對居民提出計劃的專家。

・您社區的房屋評議機構（需要幫助的，請撥HUD房屋評議服務專線：1-800-569-4287）

・HUD國家多家庭房屋票據交換所：1-800-685-8470。

您地方政府的房客／房東事務處法律服務組及房客組織團體也可以提供您在地方或州的法律之下您所能享有額外權利的資料。

這本小冊子的內容是攸關做爲一名HUD多家庭住宅居民所應有的權利與義務，同時也備有中文、韓文、俄文、西班牙文和越南文版本；需要者請向您的地方HUD當地辦事處或HUD國家多家庭住宅票據交換所洽詢：1-800-685-8470。

・有權有人代表您參與審核調查結果的會議，稱爲清查會議。

・有權對此棟大廈未來的計劃——稱爲行動計劃——表示意見，內容則包括討論適當的房租、公用設施費津貼、維修費以及更新費。

・有權在房東選擇求售時，提出購買計劃或挑選非營利機構來購買此棟大廈。

## 如果您所居住的公寓大廈是由HUD做擔保的抵押貸款，依照國家住宅法第250(a)條，只在部長的同意下才能提前付清抵押貸款；像這類關於提前付清抵押貸款的大廈，居民主要的權利包括：

・有權得到當房東請求提前付清抵押貸款時的提交通知。

・有權就評估這項請求提供意見給部長做參考。

## 如果您所居住的公寓大廈是屬於HUD，但準備出售：

當HUD的公寓大廈要出售時，居民會得到通知。另外，居民有權在大廈出售前就HUD的大廈轉讓計劃發表意見。HUD會直接與能夠證實其有能力與承諾購買HUD多家庭住宅的居民組織團體進行價格商談。
居民組織團體應就近與HUD當地辦事處洽談。

如果您所居住的公寓大廈是由HUD基於某項計劃(稱為第236條及第221(d)(3)條低於市場利率與租金補助計劃)而有提供補助金的情形：

居民有權對於下列問題得到書面通知書、參與及表達意見：

- 當房東要求HUD批准增加最高容許房租時。
- 當房東要求HUD對此項計劃中支付公用設施費轉移到居民需支付公用設施費，或要求減少居民公用設施費津貼時。
- 當房東要求HUD批准把住宅單位轉爲非住宅用或共同住宅或分戶出售的公寓大樓時。
- 當房東要求HUD批准房屋的重大改良工程時。

## …與義務

當您簽下租約時，您已經在進行一項依法的強制性契約，因此您有義務照您契約的規則及準則來行事。您其它的義務包括下列各項，但不限於此。

- 如果鉛管、固定物、器具設備或住宅單位的其它部份或相關的設施發生問題時，一定要立刻通知管理人員。
- 不可在住家單位、共同空間或戶外草坪上從事非法活動。
- 每個月要適時地繳付正確金額的房租。

## Assignment 2: Notes

*U.S. Department of Housing and Urban Development (line 4)* - Rendered by the translator as "美國住宅與都市發展部. " A dictionary with extensive coverage of U.S. Government branches is one possibility for locating the names of government departments. If not found, the Chinese newspaper is another place where such terms are commonly encountered. However, greater care must be exercised when using the newspaper to confirm terms because of differences in how such terms are translated in China, Taiwan, and Hong Kong.

*Multifamily Housing Programs (line 5)* - Rendered by the translator as "多家庭住宅計劃" Since this document is intended for Chinese residing in the United States, the translator has used the term "多家庭. " A region-specific term might be used if the document were intended for use abroad. For instance, the term "國民住宅 " might be used were the document bound for Taiwan.

*Your rights . . .(page 2, line 20)* - Rendered by the translator as "您的權利. " Note the use of the polite form "您." This term is appropriately employed here.

*Exit Conference (page 4, lines 5-6)* - Rendered by the translator as "清查會" In Chinese, the word "exit" has a variety of meanings, such as "出境, " "走出, " and "離開. "
None of these quite fits here. The translator has thus adopted a term intended to convey the meaning of what is done at the meeting rather than attempting to stick slavishly to the original English word.

*Section 250(a) (line 13)* - Rendered by the translator as " 第250(a)條 " A possible alternative translation is "第250條(a)款. "

## Assignment 3: Translation

05-03 Penicillins

# 青黴素(口服)

下面是有關青黴素藥品系列的資料。這一藥品系列包括下面以俗名所列的藥品，括號內是其常見的商標名：

Amoxicillin (Amoxil, Trimox)
Amoxicillin 和
Clavulanate (Augmentin)
Ampicillin (Polycillin)
Dicloxacillin (Dynapen)
Penicillin V (V-Cillin K)
其它__________

## 請謹慎閱讀

### 有關您的藥品

青黴素(盤尼西林)是用來治療因細菌導致的感染，對於感冒、流行性感冒或其它病毒引起的感染則無效。有些青黴素也可讓曾患過風濕性心臟病的患者用來防止"鏈球菌"的感染。

如果本說明書上的任何資料引起您特別的關心，或有關您的藥品及其用法上您想多知道一些相關訊息，請教您的醫生、護士或藥劑師。切記，將此藥物及其它藥物放在孩子拿不到的地方，並且絕對不要將您的藥給別人服用。

### 服用此藥物之前

如果您有下列的情況……，告訴您的醫生、護士及藥劑師。

- 對於任何藥物有過敏現象，無論是處方藥或非處方藥(在櫃台即可買到)；
- 當使用此藥物時懷孕或打算懷孕；
- 餵母奶；
- 正服用任何其它處方藥或非處方藥(在櫃台即可買到)，特別是那些含有雌激素的避孕丸、消膽胺(cholestyramine)、降血脂藥(colestipol)或丙磺舒(probenecid)；
- 有任何其它健康方面的問題，特別是傳染性單核血球病("mono")或曾患過腸胃性疾病，如結腸炎，包括由抗生素所導致的結腸炎，或腸炎。

## 此藥物的適當服用法

大部份的青黴素在服用時最好是空腹配一滿杯水(8盎司)，但有些則最好與餐點一起服用。按照您的醫生或藥劑師的指示服藥。

如果您服用的是青黴素G，在服用後的一個小時內不要飲用酸性果汁(如柳橙汁或葡萄柚汁)或其它酸性飲料。如此才不會失去藥效。

即使服用幾天後您已開始感覺比較舒服，也不能在治療期間停止服用此藥，不要漏了任何一服藥。這一點是非常重要的，因為如果您感染了"鏈球菌"，而您的感染沒有完全康復，這之後可能引發嚴重的心臟問題。

如果您漏了一服藥，儘快服用，但是如果慢到幾乎已是吃下一服藥的時間，則不要補吃，回到正常的吃藥時間，千萬不要一次吃兩服。

---

## 服用此藥需注意的事項

服藥的幾天內若您的症狀沒有改善，或情況變得更嚴重，請教您的醫生。

對某些患者，青黴素可能會造成腹瀉；嚴重的腹瀉可能是某種嚴重副作用的徵兆；沒有請教過您的醫生之前不可吃任何的腹瀉藥品。

當您服用安必西林(ampicillin)、巴肯必西林(bacampicillin)或青黴素V時，如果同時也吃含有雌激素的口服避孕藥(避孕丸)，則避孕藥可能失效而導致懷孕。因此當您在服用這些青黴素時，應該使用不同的或加上另外的避孕方法。

糖尿病患者——有些青黴素可能導致不正確的尿糖測試結果。在您改變飲食或糖尿病藥物的服用量之前，先請教您的醫生。

除非經過您醫生的其它指示，否則不可將此藥物給別人服用或用來治療其它的感染。

---

## 此藥物可能產生的副作用

### 應立即告訴您的醫生的副作用

如果您發現下列的情況……，請停止服用此藥並立即請求緊急救助。

罕見(可能不常見於某些青黴素)——呼吸困難、輕微的頭暈、皮膚疹、蕁麻疹、瘀或哮鳴

其它應立即告訴您的醫生的副作用

罕見(可能較常見於某些青黴素)——腹脹、尿液中有血、痙攣(發作)、尿量減少、腹瀉(水狀及劇烈的)也可能帶血、發燒、關節痛、喉嚨痛及發燒、胃或腹部痙攣及疼痛(劇烈的)、異常的出血或瘀傷

上述有些副作用可能會在您停藥的幾星期後才出現。

通常不需要就醫的副作用

在治療期間這些可能出現的副作用將會消失，但是如果副作用持續或讓您不舒服時，請教您的醫生、護士或藥劑師。

較常見(可能不常見於某些青黴素)——腹瀉(輕微的)、惡心或嘔吐、口腔或舌頭痛

有些病患可能會出現一些上面沒提到的副作用。所以如果您發現任何其它的副作用，請教您的醫生、護士或藥劑師。

# Assignment 3: Notes

*Penicillins (line 3)* - When it comes to the names of pharmaceutical drugs, the translator may have a choice of several possible renditions in Chinese. There are, at maximum, three possibilities. The first is the popular name by which a drug is known in Chinese ("青黴素" for penicillin). The second is a Chinese transliteration of the English name ("盤尼西林" for penicillin). The third is the name indicating the chemical composition of the drug (an example of which would be "羧苯磺丙胺" for probenecid). Here, the translator has opted for the common name for penicillin, "青黴素"

*medicine . . .prescription or nonprescription (OTC) (line 29)* - Rendered by the translator as "非處方藥(在櫃台即可買到)." Another possibility for nonprescription medicine is "成藥." Note that "(OTC)" has been translated in its expanded form of "over the counter."

*Birth control pills containing estrogen, cholestyramine, colestipol, or probenecid (line 33)* - Rendered by the translator as "含有雌激素的避孕丸、消膽胺、降血脂藥或丙磺舒." Care is required here. Sometimes the English itself can be quite difficult to understand, even for a native speaker. Note the difference between the correct translation given by the translator and the following (seemingly plausible from the English on its face, but incorrect) "含有雌激素、消膽胺、降血脂藥或丙磺舒的避孕丸."

Note that throughout the document, the translator has used "細明體" for the main text and "仿宋體" to set off text bolded in English. Do you think this is effective? (Good sets of bold characters are difficult to come by for Chinese. You may have to be creative in finding ways of making characters stand out if the bold set you have does not provide enough emphasis.

所需的新方法。在未来的10年里，基础设施投资需求在两类不同的国家均会同时增长。一类是经历了宏观经济调整痛苦过程和保持低水平投资的国家；另一类是经济迅速增长正给基础设施增加了沉重负担的国家。在发展中国家，基础设施投资平均占GDP的4%，但实际上往往在大超过这个比例。在电信业和供电迅速发展的国家，这两个部门每年的投资

高达占GDP的2%。许多国家增加基础设施投资的特殊原因是城市化步伐的加快，因此需要在供水和废弃物处理方面进行投资。

在亚洲，基础设施投资占GDP的比例预计从今天的4%将增加到本世纪末的7%多，其中大部分用于交通和能源部门，其次是电信业和环保基础设施。一些已经规划的投资是没有先例的。例如，中国制定了1995年之前每年至少安装500万门电话的目标，1995年后每年至少安装800万门电话。到2000年将是1992年的1800万门的3倍。

私人企业：趋势与机会

目前在鼓励私人企业参与并承担基础设施项目风险方面的工作，反映了所面临的各种不同的挑战。经过几十年的严格限制之后，80年代后期，通过两种途径参与基础设施建设的私人企业重新活跃起来：通过国有公用事业私有化；通过政府制度改革使私人企业能在新设施的建设方面与现有企业进行竞争，或作为现有企业的补充。

资迅猛发展的阶段。从80年代后期的少量投资上升到1993财政年度的3.3亿美元，国际金融公司的投资额增加了10多倍。1993年的投资总量达35亿美元。

过去的4年中，最重要的发展是国际上流入发展中国家的长期私有资本的急剧增加，尤其是在外国直接投资和有价证券的流动方面。1992年这些资金的流量达800亿美元，1993年预计达到1120亿美元（表5.1）。基础设施是这些资金流入的主要的受益部门（专栏5. 2）。

目前私人企业在基础设施方面的投资总额一年约为150亿美元，相当于发展中国家每年投入基础设施建设的2000亿美元的7%。虽然私人企业在基础设施方面的投资较少，但与几年前相比已经增加了很多，而且将会继续增加，到2000年可能增加一倍：国际金融公司目前在基础设施方面的资金投入几乎相当于迄今为止的投资总量，就是一个例证。

私人企业在基础设施融资方面所占的总额

主要的新型基础设施企业是一些在发展中国家寻求商业机会的国际性公司。这些公司不仅带来了先进的管理和技术，而且可以提供信贷，并具有为发展中国家的投资项目融资的能力。工业国的电力、电信和供水公司正面临着国内市场增长缓慢和竞争愈发激烈的局面。因而他们积极在发展中国家寻找高收益的投资项目。建筑大公司积极从事收费公路和电力项目的建设，他们有时也投资参股。一些公司或公司集团擅长于建设能独立运营的基础设施项目，把融资和项目开发及经营的监督结合在一起。

许多私人企业资助下的基础设施投资指标表明这一领域在迅速增长。拉丁美洲和亚洲的私有化的通讯和电力公司正在承担越来越多的大规模投资项目。所谓的绿地项目的数量——特别是公路和电力部门——增长非常迅速（如下所述）。世界银行所属的只给私人实体投资的国际金融公司（IFC），已经经历了一个投

较小掩盖了较大的地区间和部门间的差别。拉丁美洲国家的私人投资相应地大于其他地区，电信和发电部门大于其他部门。现有跨地区和跨部门的经验的推广将增加全球私人企业的参与和融资份额。例如在所有地区，包括撒哈拉以南非洲国家在内，都在讨论电信业私有化和电力企业自负盈亏的问题。技术和融资的持续革新无疑将使私人筹资更加具有吸引力。例如，鉴定车辆和收费的电子方法会使公路更象一种公共服务设施，从而增加私人企业在公路部门的投资比例。

尽管私人企业基础设施投资方面的份额不断增加，但政府部门仍将是基础设施投资的重要来源。通常政府想与私人企业家建立起伙伴关系。公私式合作的伙伴关系可追溯到19世纪。那时基础设施项目在世界的很多地区均是私人投资的，而政府起的是催化推动作用。但是19世纪的经验也有深刻的教训值得借鉴。

**表 5.1　1990—1993 年发展中国家的有价证券和外国直接投资**

*（10亿美元净流入额）*

| 类　型 | 1990 | 1991 | 1992 | 1993[a] |
|---|---|---|---|---|
| 外国股份 | 3.78 | 7.55 | 13.07 | 13.1 |
| 限额基金[b] | 2.78 | 1.20 | 1.34 | 2.7 |
| 美国预托证券和全球预托证券[c] | 0.14 | 4.90 | 5.93 | 7.2 |
| 直接股份 | 0.77 | 1.45 | 5.80 | 3.2 |
| 债务证券 | 5.56 | 12.72 | 23.73 | 42.6 |
| 债券 | 4.68 | 10.19 | 21.24 | 39.1 |
| 商业票据 | 0.23 | 1.38 | 0.85 | 1.6 |
| 存单 | 0.65 | 1.15 | 1.64 | 1.8 |
| 有价证券总计[d] | 9.34 | 20.27 | 36.80 | 55.7 |
| 外资直接投资 | 26.30 | 36.90 | 47.30 | 56.3 |
| 总　计 | 35.64 | 57.17 | 84.10 | 112.0 |

注：本表记录了所有有价证券和直接投资的流动情况，并未提供有关基础设施方面的数据。

a. 1993 年的数字为估计数或预测数。

b. 限额基金有一个预先的基金数额，有时是固定的。

c. ADR 为美国预托证券；GDR 为全球预托证券。ADR 是 offshore 公司在美国发行的另一种增加的有价证券，这种证券不包括在美国证券交易所正式上市的证券之列。GDRs 是在欧洲和其他地方使用的类似的有价证券。

d. 有价证券投资为证券与债务的数额。

资料来源：世界银行 1993i，pp.10，21。

## Assignment 4: Notes

*GDP (line 10)* - It is often a good idea to provide the translation of the expanded form of a term the first time it appears. This would give "国内生产毛额(GDP)."

*they often need to be substantially higher (line 10)* - Rendered by the translator as "往往在大超过这个比例." The meaning rendered in Chinese does not seem to make sense, so there may be a typographical error. Check your work carefully once you have completed a translation to try and avoid such problems. The translator probably intended something along the lines of "往往需远超过这个比例."

*take an equity interest (line 37)* - Rendered by the translator as "投资参股;" *direct equity (Table)* is rendered as "直接股份." The English word "equity" is a slippery one. Notice how the translator has handled it in these different contexts.

*greenfield projects (page 2, line 9)* - Rendered by the translator as "绿地项目." It is always a challenge to translate newly coined terms whose use is restricted to highly specialized fields such as finance and economics. As a translator, you ideally want to find out exactly what a newly coined term is intended to mean and translate it accordingly. If you think a translator's note is necessary for a reader in the target language to understand your rendition, provide one. Do you think the Chinese reader will know what this term is intended to convey from the translation?

*the International Finance Corporation (IFC), a World Bank affiliate that invests only in private entities, . . . (lines 10-11)* - Rendered by the translator as "世界银行所属的只给私人实体投资的国际金融公司(IFC)." The second term between the commas is known as an appositive and modifies the first term. (A simple example would be: "Ruth, a woman from Montana, has experience in . . .") Notice how the translator has rendered this construction in Chinese. This is a valuable technique to employ in English-to-Chinese translation.

*closed-end funds (Table)* - Rendered by the translator as "限额基金." Technical, economic and financial terms require good dictionaries to translate correctly. Good dictionaries may be expensive, but they are well worth the cost!

# Section 3

## Where Do I Go from Here?

After you have completed all the assignments, or at least those you have chosen to do, you have to make a major decision. If you have never translated for profit before, you have to ask yourself if you are ready to try your hand at soliciting for-profit translation work. If the answer is yes, contact one or two of the enclosed work sources (Appendix E) and apply for a test or a short assignment. If you have translated for profit before in a specific area, such as legal documents, and you feel you are now ready to venture into another area, such as medical translation, first try out some short assignments in that field, until you become comfortable with it.

It is important that you develop a relationship with one or more translation companies in your own geographical area. There is absolutely no reason in this day and age for a translator, say, in Wisconsin, not to develop a profitable relationship with a translation company in Florida, and in time you may indeed find out that a certain company on the other side of the continent is your best source of work. But as a beginner, there are many advantages to interfacing personally with the staff of a translation company close to home. They can give you a great deal of practical advice, help you with the hardware and the software, and share other kinds of experience with you. There is an old saying: "A good neighbor is better than a distant relative."

If, on the other hand, you feel you are not ready to take the plunge, you may want to consider a translation course or study program. Refer to Appendix 4 in the book, and see if there is a program close to home you can sign up for. Or you may decide to continue practicing on your own.

Whatever you decide to do, don't give up too easily. If you do enjoy the challenge of translation, continue to improve you skills. Remember: Translation can be a full-time career or a very fulfilling and profitable sideline. It is definitely the kind of expertise worth having, no matter what else you choose to do with your time.

# Appendices

# Appendix A. Requisites for Professional Translators

Any person who knows more than one language has the ability to explain a word or a sentence in what translators call "the source language" (the language you translate from) by using an equivalent word or sentence in what they call "the target language" (the language you translate into). This, in effect, is the beginning of translation. But it is only the beginning. It does not automatically turn a person into an accomplished translator. Along with the knowledge of the source and the target language, a translator must have an aptitude for translation. Some people are endowed with a talent for translation. It is not an acquired skill, like riding a bicycle. It is rather a talent, like playing the violin. Some people have it and some don't. It is not necessarily an indication of a lower or higher IQ. Nor is it an indication of how linguistically gifted one is. It is an inborn skill that enables a person to change a text from one language into another quickly and accurately, or, if you will, think in more than one language at the same time. If you possess this skill, then it behooves you to develop it and make use of it, because there is never an overabundance of good translators, and it is almost axiomatic that the good ones can always find either full-time or part-time work.

The **first** requisite for the working translator is a thorough knowledge of both the source and the target languages. There is no point in billing oneself as a translator if one is not fully familiar with both languages, or does not possess a vocabulary in both equal to that of a speaker of those languages who has a university education or its equivalent.

The **second** requisite is thorough "at-homeness" in both cultures. A language is a living phenomenon. It does not exist apart from the culture where it is spoken and written. It communicates not only the names of objects and different kinds of action, but also feelings, attitudes, beliefs, and so on. To be fully familiar with a language, one must also be familiar with the culture in which the language is used, indeed, with the people who use it, their ways, manners, beliefs and all that goes into making a culture.

**Third**, one must keep up with the growth and change of the language, and be up-to-date in all of its nuances and neologisms. Languages are in a constant state of flux, and words change meaning from year to year. A pejorative term can become laudatory, and a neutral term can become loaded with meaning. Thirty years ago the English word "gay" simply meant "joyous." Now it is used to define an entire segment of society. We once spoke of the "almighty dollar." Now as we travel abroad we may find out the dollar is not necessarily everyone's preferred currency.

**Fourth**, a distinction must be made between the languages one translates from and into. Generally speaking, one translates from another language into one's own native language. This is because one is usually intimately familiar with one's own language, while even years of study and experience do not necessarily enable one to be completely at home with an acquired language. The exceptions to this rule are usually those people who have lived in more than one culture, and have spoken more than one language on a regular basis. Those may be able to translate in both directions. There are also rare gifted individuals who have mastered another language to such a degree that they can go both ways. They are indeed extremely rare. Given all of this, one should allow for the fact that while the ability of the accomplished translator to write and speak in the target language (i.e., one's native tongue) may be flawless, that person may not necessarily be able to write excellent prose or give great speeches in the source language (i.e., the language from which one translates). Then again, it is not necessary to be able to write and speak well in the language one translates from, while it is to be expected that a good translator is also a good writer and speaker in his or her native language.

**Fifth**, a professional translator has to be able to translate in more than one area of knowledge. Most professional translators are called upon to translate in a variety of fields. It is not uncommon for a translator to cover as many as twenty or thirty fields of knowledge in one year, including such areas as political subjects, economics, law, medicine, communications and so on. Obviously, it would be hard to find a translator who is an economist, a lawyer, a medical doctor, and an engineer all wrapped into one. In fact, such a person probably does not exist. One does not have to be a lawyer to translate legal documents. Many a professional translator has been able to gain enough knowledge and acquire a vocabulary in a variety of technical fields to be able to produce perfectly accurate and well-written translations in those fields. This is not nearly as difficult as it may seem, since most technical fields utilize a well-defined number of terms which keep repeating themselves, and as one keeps translating the same subject, they become more and more familiar to the translator. One must, however, have a natural curiosity about many different areas of human knowledge and activity, and an interest in increasing one's vocabulary in a variety of related as well as unrelated fields.

**Sixth**, an effective translator must have a facility for writing or speaking (depending on whether the method used is writing, speaking, or dictation), and the ability to articulate quickly and accurately, either orally or in writing. Like a reporter, a translator must be able to transmit ideas in real time, and in good understandable language. Translation is a form of writing and speech-making, and a translator is, in a sense, a writer and an orator.

**Seventh**, a professional translator must develop a good speed of translation. There are two reasons for this: First, most clients wait until the last minute to assign a translation job. As a result, they turn to a translator or a translation service with what is perhaps the most typical question in this business: "How soon can you have this job ready for me?" The professional translator has to be prepared to accept that long job with the short turnaround time, or there will be no repeat business from that particular client or from most other clients, for that matter. Secondly, translation is generally paid by the word. The more words one can translate per hour, the more income one will generate. Translating 50 words per hour can land a translator in the poorhouse. Serious translation starts at 250 words per hour, and can reach as high as 1000 words per hour using word processing, and close to 3000 words per hour using dictation (the author actually knows such a translator). High volume translators are the ones who will be the most successful.

**Eighth**, a translator must develop research skills, and be able to acquire reference sources which are essential for producing high quality translation. Without such sources even the best of translators cannot hope to be able to handle a large variety of subjects in many unrelated fields. Dedicated translators are the ones who are always on the lookout for new reference sources, and over time develop a data bank which can be used in their work.

**Ninth**, today's translator cannot be a stranger to hardware, software, fax, modem, the Internet, and the latest developments in all those media. Translation has become completely dependent on electronic tools. Gone are the days of handwriting, the typewriter, and all the other "prehistoric" means of communication. The more one becomes involved in translation, the more one finds oneself caught up in the latest high-tech developments.

**Tenth**, a translator who wishes to be busy on a fairly regular basis doing translation work must carefully consider the fact that certain languages are in high demand, say, in Washington or in Los Angeles, while others are not. Thus, for example, there is high demand for Japanese, German, Spanish, French, Chinese, Arabic, Russian and Italian in both Washington and Los Angeles, but not nearly as much for Bulgarian, Farsi, Czech, or Afrikaans. If your language falls within the second group, it is extremely advisable to also have language expertise in one of the languages of the first group, or to seriously consider whether your particular language has enough of a demand to warrant a major investment of time and effort on your part. One should always check and see what kind of a potential one's language specialty has in a given geographic area.

The above ten points are the essential criteria for developing a translation career. There are many other considerations, but none as important as these. If you feel that you can meet all of the above criteria, then you should continue reading this handbook and putting it to good use.

**The Well-Rounded Translator**

The main division in the translation field is between literary and technical translation. Literary translation, which covers such areas as fiction, poetry, drama, and the humanities in general, is often done by writers of the same genre who actually author works of the same kind in the target language, or at least by translators with the required literary aptitude. For practical reasons, this handbook will not cover literary translation, but will instead focus on the other major area of translation, namely, technical translation. High quality literary translation has always been the domain of the few, and is hardly lucrative (don't even think of doing literary translation if your motive is money), while technical translation is done by a much greater number of practitioners, and is an ever-growing and expanding field with excellent earning opportunities. This chapter discusses the characteristics of the well-rounded technical translator.

The term "technical" is extremely broad. In the translation business it covers much more than technical subjects in the narrow sense of the word. In fact, there is an overlap between literary and technical translation when it comes to such areas as social sciences, political subjects, and many others.

One way of defining technical translation is by asking the question, does the subject being translated require a specialized vocabulary, or is the language non-specialized? If the text being translated includes specialized terms in a given field, then the translation is technical.

The more areas (and languages) a translator can cover, the greater the opportunity for developing a successful translation career. Furthermore, as one becomes proficient in several areas, it becomes easier to add more. Besides, many technical areas are interrelated, and proficiency in one increases proficiency in another. In addition, every area breaks down into many subareas, each with its own vocabulary and its own linguistic idiosyncrasies. Thus, for example, translating in Arabic does not make one an expert in all spoken Arabic dialects, yet a knowledge of several of those dialects is very beneficial for the professional Arabic translator.

How does one become a well-rounded translator? The answer can be summed up in one word—experience. The key to effective translation is practice. Since human knowledge grows day by day, and since language keeps growing and changing, the well-rounded translator must keep in touch with knowledge and language on a regular basis. The worst thing that can happen to a translator is to be out of touch with the source language for more than a couple of years. What the rusty translator may find out is that new words, new concepts and new ways of using those words and applying those concepts have come into being during that period of "hibernation," and one's old expertise is no longer reliable.

Translation, therefore, is a commitment one makes not for a limited period of time, but rather long-term. It is to be assumed that anyone who becomes a translator is the kind of person who loves words and loves the challenge of using words effectively and correctly. Such a person will not become an occasional translator, but will make translation a lifelong practice.

## Good and Bad Translation Habits

The accomplished translator can develop good as well as bad habits. Starting with the bad, we have already pointed out oneClosing touch with the source language for long periods of time. Another bad habit is taking illegitimate shortcuts while translating. There are several types of such shortcuts. The most typical is failing to look up a word one is really not sure how to translate. Being ninety percent sure of a word's meaning is not good enough in professional translation. If one is not sure of a word's meaning, even after all available means have been exhausted, then one must put in a translator's note to that effect, or make it known in some other way that there is a problem with translating that particular word. Anything less would be deceptive.

Another illegitimate shortcut is summarizing a paragraph instead of providing a *full* translation. There is such a thing as summary translation of a paragraph or a document. If a summary is called for, then this is precisely what the translator is expected to provide. But the most common form of translation is what=s known in the business as a verbatim translation, which is a full and complete rendition of the source text. When verbatim translation is ordered, anything less than a full translation is an illegitimate shortcut. Unfortunately, some translators tend to overlook this from time to time, especially when they undertake more work than they can accomplish by a given deadline, and decide to summarize rather than miss that deadline.

Perhaps the worst habit for a translator is to decide at a certain point in time that his or her knowledge of either the source or the target language is so good that it cannot possibly stand any improvement. The moment one stops growing linguistically, one is no longer on the cutting edge of one's profession. The good translator is a perennial language student, always eager and willing to learn more and to keep up with the latest.

As for good habits, the most important, perhaps, are the ones we obtain by reversing the above-mentioned bad habits. But there are many more. One excellent habit is to read professional literature in the field one will be called upon to translate in with reasonable frequency. One good example is *Scientific American*, which can help anyone who translates subjects of science and technology to learn the style or styles used in scientific writing. People who work in the field of translating business documents should definitely read business periodicals, not the least of which is *The Wall Street Journal*. One does not have to be a scientist to translate scientific articles, or have a business degree to translate business documents, but a general understanding of the subject goes a long way towards providing an accurate translation of the subject.

Another excellent habit is to translate not only for profit but also for enjoyment and experience. Most people, unfortunately, are not so taken with their daily work that they would want to continue doing it after hours for fun or practice. But an accomplished translator is someone who will on occasion translate simply for the sake of sharpening his or her skill, or accept a very small fee because of personal commitment to the subject matter, or because of a personal interest. This writer, for example, enjoys translating poetry because of the challenge of doing what is perhaps the most difficult type of translation, and, quite simply, because of the enjoyment of poetry.

Yet another good habit is always to be on the lookout for dictionaries. Many dictionaries are hard to find, and are available in few places. This writer in all his travels across the United States and abroad always stops in bookstores to look for dictionaries. One can also order dictionaries from bookstores and from publishers, but then one has to know what to order and from whom.

The last good habit I would like to mention is the practice of compiling word lists and building a reference library. Dictionaries do not have all the words and terms a translator needs, nor do they contain all the information which specialized references may have. There are aids for translators put out by certain organizations, and there is professional literature in every field. In recent years there has been a growing awareness of the need for terminology management, and with the constant advances in computer technology databases have been proliferating, making the work of the translator much easier than ever before. Good references are worth their weight in gold when they are needed for a specific translation, and over time the experienced translator develops an extensive library of glossaries which become essential for any translation assignment.

## Appendix B. Translation Techniques

### Preliminary Considerations

You are given a text to translate. Before you commit yourself to doing any work on it, you must ask yourself a few preliminary questions. They are:

1. Is the text legible?
2. Am I familiar enough with the subject to tackle it?
3. Do I have the linguistic resources (dictionaries, human contacts) to decipher unfamiliar words?
4. Is the text complete, or are there any missing parts?
5. Can I do it within the requested timeframe?
6. Do I have a good reason for doing it (doing it as a learning experience, or because you enjoy it, or to help a friend, or because you are properly compensated for doing it)?

Once you have answered all the above questions to your own satisfaction, you are ready to proceed with the translation.

### Effective Approaches

There is no single effective approach to translation, and over time translators develop personal techniques which enhance the quality and the speed of their translation. No one set of rules applies equally to everyone, but there are certain methods and means of translation which can help almost any translator achieve greater accuracy and output. The following is a review of some of the key techniques which are becoming almost universal among professional translators.

The first and foremost question a translator must deal with today is what kind of equipment to use in the process of translating. In the days of the pen and the typewriter this question was much less crucial. Today, however, translation has become almost totally dependent on computers, for several good reasons: (a) Word processing allows far greater flexibility in producing text than any other contemporary means. The output of most translators has been tripled and quadrupled through the use of computers; (b) Computers allow text to be stored on a disk and reprinted or modified later on, a function which is invaluable in the translation field, (c) Clients nowadays are getting used to asking for translation on disk, since it allows them to edit, reprint, modify and enhance the physical appearance of a document; (d) If more than one translator is involved in a given translation project, the text from the various translators can be entered by an editor on one disk and equalized or manipulated as necessary, without having to redo any particular portion thereof.

In addition, it is becoming more common every day to use electronic means such as a modem, fax or e-mail to transmit and receive text. These tools are no longer a luxury. Their cost has been coming down, and more and more translators are acquiring them. Many people today are saying they cannot imagine how translators were ever able to manage without them. The answer is very simple: manage we did, but it took us ten days to two weeks to do what we can now receive, translate and deliver in two or three days.

The next question when approaching a translation assignment is: Am I qualified to do this particular translation? Only an honest answer will do. If one is not sure, then chances are one should not tackle that particular task. One must feel confident about a particular assignment if the results are to be satisfactory. The exception to this rule is a case where a client cannot find anyone else to do that particular job, and for some good reason is either willing to take a chance or to receive less than a complete and fully accurate rendition. In such a case it should be made clear between translator and client that the translation is not legally binding.

Once the commitment is made to proceed with the job, the translator will spend some time going over the entire document—even if it is book-length—and do a realistic assessment of the following points:

a. How long will it take to translate the document?
b. What reference tools are needed to get it done?
c. What kind of preliminary steps are needed prior to the actual work of translating?
d. What special problems are related to the document, such as legibility of blurred or poorly copied text or difficult handwriting?
e. Does the document contain text in a language or languages other than the main source language, and, if so, can the translator handle that language?

Regarding the question of time, one can do a quick estimate of the length of the document by averaging words per line, times lines per page, times number of pages. An experienced translator has a pretty good idea of the number of words per hour he or she can translate. This is an essential feature of undertaking a professional translation job, since most clients have tight deadlines and tend to give repeat business to those translators known for keeping to their deadlines.

As for reference tools, if, for example, one is given a document about telecommunications, one should make use of on'=s own resources in that field and/or borrow from other sources whatever one needs to accomplish the task.

Preliminary steps prior to actual translation can include a consultation with an expert in a specialized technical field regarding a difficult term, phrase, paragraph or concept which the translator does not feel comfortable with. Having access to such experts is one of the translator's most cherished assets. It can make all the difference in the world between a correct and effective translation and one that misses the main point of the entire text. Another preliminary step is a trip to the local, regional or even specialized library to do some research on the subject.

The problem of legibility should be identified *before* one begins the task, not after. Sometimes the problem may start in the middle of the document and be so severe as to render the translation of the first part useless. In that case, the translator may have wasted a great deal of time. Sometimes the problem is minor, and does not affect the overall outcome of the translation. In other cases, the client may decide to proceed with the translation and simply put the designation [illegible] (between brackets rather than parentheses) wherever a word or part of the text cannot be deciphered.

Unbeknownst to client and translator, when a translation job is first assigned, there may be portions of text inside the source document in a language other than the main language of the document. This can happen in commercial, scientific and scholarly documents. It even happens in Tolstoy's novel *War and Peace,* when the author starts using French instead of Russian. This too should be detected prior to commencing the translation work, and a decision has to be made as to: (a) Does that text need to be translated? (b) Can the translator handle it? (c) Is it necessary to assign it to another translator?

Once all this preliminary work has been done, one is ready to proceed with the actual translation work.

Depending on the particular text, one should either start translating at this point, or, in the case of a text containing highly specialized terminology which may send the translator on frequent trips to the dictionary, one should first go through the document and make a list of as many unknown or uncertain terms as possible, and then spend some time looking them up and making a word list. This technique saves a great deal of time, since once a list is completed it is much easier to sail through the text, and the time spent initially on making the list is very short compared to the time wasted on repeated interruptions to look up words. Moreover, by first mastering the more difficult terminology of the text, one gains a much better understanding of the subject and is certain to produce a better translation. From the very start, make it a habit to compile word lists and glossaries of subjectspecific terminologies, and keep it in a computer database program for future reference. In time, these lists will become your most valuable translation tool.

One should also follow good work habits. Some translators, particularly those engaged in freelance work, tend to overdo it, especially during their "busy season," when they can generate a large income during a relatively short period of time. They will go for twelve or more hours a day, and before they know it they will start complaining of stiffness in the neck and shoulders, blurred vision, and fatigue. One should not translate more than eight hours a day. Six is ideal. Eight is tolerable, provided one takes a few short ten to fifteen minute breaks. Ten is pushing it. Over ten is definitely hazardous to your health.

Before you get ready to submit your translation go over it again, using the following checklist:

**Omissions**—did you fail to translate any particular word or phrase, or even paragraph?
**Format**—does your format follow the original (breaking into paragraphs, for instance)?
**Mistranslations**—did you mistranslate any particular word?
**Unknown words**—were there words you were not able to translate which you would like to explore further?
**Meaning**—did you miss the meaning of any phrase or sentence?
**Spelling**—did you misspell any word which the spell-check function on your computer did not catch?
**Grammar**—did you make any grammatical mistakes?
**Punctuation**—did you mispunctuate or miss any punctuation marks?
**Clarity**—did you fail to clearly convey the meaning of any particular part of the text?
**Consistency**—did you call something by one name and then by another without any good reason?
**"Sound-alike" words**—did you mistranslate a word because it looks or sounds like the word in your target language but in reality has a different meaning?
**Style**—are you satisfied with the way your translation reflects the style of the original text (for example, the original is written in a clear, direct style, while the translation sounds more complex and indirect?)

This checklist is by no means exhaustive, but it does cover the main areas a translator must pay attention to.

As was already explained, your personal computer is your best friend when it comes to translating, editing, and producing a final copy. One can learn a few basic commands, say, in WordPerfect or Microsoft Word, and start using the computer. But there is much more to software than entering, deleting and inserting text. The better acquainted with software you become, the more it will help you with translation. Learn how to do columns and tables, how to use special technical and scientific symbols, do graphic functions, use the spell-check and the thesaurus, create data bases for glossaries and for your own administrative records, and you will tackle a great variety of technical text in many fields at a speed that will amaze you. Remember: speed in translation is the most important thing next to language proficiency. Without it you will not be profitable, and you will be overrun by the competition. With an established record of fast accurate translation you can write your own ticket.

After a few years of using the computer you may want to consider dictation. Personally, I prefer a mix of PC and dictation. When I have an unusually long job and not enough time to do it in, I may revert to dictation. Otherwise, I prefer word-processing. One could argue that by dictating one gets more done and earns more, but there are other things to consider, such as the cost of transcription, the need to edit transcription, and the better control one has over writing than speaking. Some of us are natural speakers; others are writers.

One continues to develop translation techniques over time. One of the most wonderful things about translation, in my opinion, is the fact that your mind is never idle, never in a rut, but rather always being challenged by new tasks, new subjects, new knowledge, and the need to keep up with new developments in language, with different fields of human knowledge, and with the events of the world. As a translator in the Washington area since the late seventies, I have found myself in the middle of world events, beginning with the peace treaty between Egypt and Israel in 1979, when I met Begin, Sadat and Carter, and, more recently, in my daily dealings with events in post-Cold War Eastern Europe, with a strife-torn Middle East, the famine in Somalia, the new North American Free Trade Agreement (NAFTA) between the United States, Canada and Mexico, and the growing involvement of the U.S. space program with the space programs of other nations. Very few people cover as broad an area as a translator. Every day we in the translation business find new challenges, and have to solve new problems. As a result, we are always developing new techniques and finding new answers.

# APPENDIX C: TRANSLATOR'S SELF-EVALUATION

The following criteria were developed some years ago by a U.S. Government agency for determining the skill level of a potential translator whom that agency might have liked to hire. You may want to read this chapter carefully to try to make an honest determination as to where on this scale you find yourself at this time. If you are below Level 2+, you need to keep practicing. If you are at Level 3 or higher, you can start doing some professional translating. After Level 4 you are ready for some serious translating, and at Level 5 you can start making a living as a translator.

**Translator Skill Levels**

**Level 0**

No functional ability to translate the language. Consistently misunderstanding or cannot comprehend at all.

**Level 0+**

Can translate all or some place names (i.e., street or city designations), corporate names, numbers and isolated words and phrases,
often translating these inaccurately.

In rendering translations, writes using only memorized material and set expressions. Spelling and representation of symbols (letters, syllables, characters) are frequently incorrect.

**Level 1**

Sufficient skill to translate the simplest connected written material in a form equivalent to usual printing or typescript. Can translate either representations of familiar formulaic verbal exchanges or simple language containing only the highest-frequency grammatical patterns and vocabulary items, including cognates when appropriate. Translated texts include simple narratives of routine behavior; concrete descriptions of persons, places and things; and explanations of geography and government such as those simplified for tourists. Mistranslations common.

In rendering translations, writes in simple sentences (or clauses), making continual errors in spelling, grammar and punctuation, but translation can be read and understood by a native reader used to dealing with foreigners attempting to translate his/her language.

**Level 1+**

Sufficient skill to translate simple discourse for informative social purposes in printed form. Can translate material such as announcements or public events, popular advertising notes containing biographical information or narration of events and straightforward newspaper headlines. Has some difficulty with the cohesive factors in discourse, such as matching pronouns with referents. In rendering translations, writing shows good control of elementary vocabulary and some control of basic syntactic patterns, but major errors still occur when expressing more complex thoughts. Dictionary usage may still yield incorrect vocabulary of forms, although can use a dictionary to advantage to translate simple ideas. Translations, though faulty, are comprehensible to native readers used to dealing with foreigners.

**Level 2**

Sufficient skill to translate simple authentic written material in a form equivalent to usual printing. Can translate uncomplicated, but authentic prose on familiar subjects that are normally present in a predictable sequence, which aids the translator in his/her work. Texts may include description and narration in context, such as news items describing frequently occurring events, simple biographical information, social notices, formatted business letters and simple technical material written for the general reader. The prose is predominantly in familiar sentence patterns. Some mistranslations.

In rendering translations, has written vocabulary sufficient to perform simple translations with some circumlocutions. Still makes common errors in spelling and punctuation, but shows some control of the most common formats and punctuation conventions. Good control of morphology of language (in inflected languages) and of the most frequently used syntactic structures. Elementary constructions are usually handled quite accurately, and translations are understandable to a native reader *not* used to reading the translations of foreigners.

**Level 2+**

Sufficient skill to translate most factual material in nontechnical prose as well as some discussions on concrete topics related to special professional interests. Has begun to make sensible guesses about unfamiliar words by using linguistic context and prior knowledge. May react personally to material, but does not yet detect subjective attitudes, values or judgments in the material to be translated.

In rendering translations, often shows surprising fluency and ease of expression, but under time constraints and pressure language may be inaccurate and/or incomprehensible. Generally strong in either grammar or vocabulary, but not in both. Weaknesses or unevenness in one of the foregoing or in spelling results in occasional mistranslations. Areas of weakness range from simple constructions, such as plurals, articles, prepositions and negatives, to more complex structures, word order and relative clauses. Normally controls general vocabulary, with some misuse of everyday vocabulary still evident. Shows a limited ability to use circumlocutions. Uses dictionary to advantage to supply unknown words. Translations are understandable to native readers not used to dealing with foreigner=s attempts to translate the language, though style is obviously foreign.

**Level 3**

Able to translate authentic prose on unfamiliar subjects. Translating ability is not dependent on subject matter knowledge. Texts will include news stories similar to wire service reports, routine correspondence, general reports and technical material in his/her professional field, all of which include hypothesis, argumentation and supported opinions. Such texts typically include grammatical patterns and vocabulary ordinarily encountered in professional reading. Mistranslations rare. Almost always able to correctly translate material, relate ideas and make inferences. Rarely has to pause over or reread general vocabulary. However, may experience some difficulty with unusually complex structures and low-frequency idioms.

In preparing translations, control of structure, spelling, and general vocabulary is adequate to convey his/her message accurately, but style may be obviously foreign. Errors virtually never interfere with comprehension and rarely disturb the native reader. Punctuation generally controlled. Employs a full range of structures. Control of grammar good, with only sporadic errors in basic structures, occasional errors in the most complex frequent structures and somewhat more frequent errors in low-frequency complex structures.

Consistent control of compound and complex sentences. Relationship of ideas presented in original material is consistently clear.

**Level 3+**

Increased ability to translate a variety of styles and forms of language pertinent to professional needs. Rarely mistranslates such texts or rarely experiences difficulty relating ideas or making inferences. Ability to comprehend many sociolinguistic and cultural references. However, may miss some nuances and subtleties. Increased ability to translate unusually complex structures and low-frequency idioms; however, accuracy is not complete.

In rendering translations, able to write the language in a few prose styles pertinent to professional/ educational needs. Not always able to tailor language to suit original material. Weaknesses may lie in poor control of low-frequency, complex structures, vocabulary or the ability to express subtleties and nuances.

**Level 4**

Able to translate fluently and accurately all styles and forms of the language pertinent to professional needs. Can translate more difficult prose and follow unpredictable turns of thought readily in any area directed to the general reader and all materials in his/her own special field, including official and professional documents and correspondence. Able to translate precise and extensive vocabulary, including nuances and subtleties, and recognize all professionally relevant vocabulary known to the educated nonprofessional native, although may have some difficulty with slang. Can translate reasonably legible handwriting without difficulty. Understands almost all sociolinguistic and cultural references.

In rendering translations, able to write the language precisely and accurately in a variety of prose styles pertinent to professional/ educational needs. Errors of grammar are rare, including those in low-frequency complex structures. Consistently able to tailor language to suit material and able to express subtleties and nuances.

**Level 4+**

Increased ability to translate extremely difficult or abstract prose. Increased ability to translate a variety of vocabulary, idioms, colloquialisms and slang. Strong sensitivity to sociolinguistic and cultural references. Increased ability to translate less than fully legible handwriting. Accuracy is close to that of an educated translator, but still not equivalent.

In rendering translations, able to write the language precisely and accurately, in a wide variety of prose styles pertinent to professional/educational needs.

**Level 5**

Can translate extremely difficult and abstract prose (i.e., legal, technical), as well as highly colloquial writings and the literary forms of the language. Translates a wide variety of vocabulary and idioms, colloquialisms, slang and pertinent cultural references. With varying degrees of difficulty, can translate all kinds of handwritten documents. Able to understand how natives think as they produce a text. Accuracy is equivalent to that of a well-educated translator.

In rendering translations, has writing proficiency equal to that of a well-educated native. Without nonnative errors of structure, spelling, style or vocabulary, can translate both formal and informal correspondence, official reports and documents and professional/educational articles, including writing for special purposes which might include legal, technical, educational, literary and colloquial writing.

# APPENDIX D: CHINESE TECHNICAL DICTIONARIES

*General Dictionaries*

**Far East Medium Chinese-English Dictionary,** Shih-chiu, L., Taipei: Far East Book Company (Cheng & Tsui Co.) 1999

**Handbook of Chinese Synonyms with Bilingual Explanations,** Beijing: China Today Press 1992 *Simplified characters.*

**Visual Dictionary,** Corbeil, J.C., Hong Kong: Readers' Digest As-sociation Far East Ltd. 1988

**English-Chinese Word-Ocean Dictionary**, 2 vols., Wang Tungyi, Beijing Defense Industry Press 1987

**Reverse Chinese-English Dictionary,** Beijing: Commercial Press 1985

**The Shogakukan Dictionary of New Chinese Words,** Tokyo: Shogakukan 1985

**Chinese Idioms and Their English Equivalents,** Chen Yongzhen and Spring Chen, Hong Kong: Commercial Press 1983 *A must for anyone translating general Chinese text.*

**A Chinese-English Dictionary,** Beijing Foreign Languages Institute, Chinese-English Dictionary Editorial Committee, Hong Kong: Com-mercial Press 1981 *A very good mid-sized dictionary. Entries are arranged alphabetically but there is also a character index.*

**A Dictionary of World Place Names,** Shanghai: Shanghai Cishu Chubanshe 1981

**A Classified and Illustrated Chinese-English Dictionary,** Hong Kong: Joint Publishing Company 1981

**Xinhua Cidian,** Beijing: Commercial Press 1980 *The most basic reference. Indispensable.*

**Chinese Cihai,** Shanghai: Shanghai Cishu Chubanshe 1979 *The staple reference of Chinese translators for years.*

**Xinhua Hanyu Cidian,** Dictionary Editorial Department of the Chinese Academy of Sciences' Language Research Institute, Hong Kong: Com-mercial Press 1977

**Chinese-English Dictionary of Contemporary Usage,** Wen-shun Chi, Berkeley: University of California Press 1977

**Handbook of Chinese-English Phrases,** Beijing: Waiwen Chubanshe 1970

**Tung-Fang Kuo-Yu Tz'u-Tien,** Taipei: Far East Book Company 1970

*Chinese: Aerospace/Aviation*

**English-Chinese Aviation Dictionary,** Hua Renjie, Beijing: Shangwu Yinshuguan 1982

**Chinese-English Rocketry Dictionary,** 7602nd Air Intelligence Group 1977

*Chinese: Agriculture*

**A Chinese-English Dictionary of China's Rural Economy,** Broadbent, K., Farnham Royal, Bucks, England: Commonwealth Agricultural Bureau 1978

*Chinese: Biology/Life Sciences*

**English-Chinese Dictionary of the Life Sciences,** Beijing: Zhongguo Kexuejishu Chubanshe 1992

*Chinese: Business and Related Fields*

**Midland Group English-Chinese Dictionary of Finance**, Adams, S.J., and Mathieson, T., I., AMCD (Publishers) Ltd.: Hong Kong University Press 1991

**Dictionary of International Trade and Finance,** Chung-hwa Cheng-hsin-swo Inc. Publishing Department Taipei, Taiwan: 1989

**New Chinese Dictionary of Economics and Trade,** Harbin Press, 1989

**Chinese-English Dictionary of Economic Terms**, China Commercial Press 1988

**An English-Chinese Dictionary of Finance, Economics and Ac-counting,** Chen Jinchi, Beijing Economics Institute, Beijing: Zhong-guo Caizheng Jingji Chubanshe 1987

**An English-Chinese Dictionary of Economics and Finance**, Hu Xisen, Yu Jialai and Qu Wanfang, Beijing: Shiyou Gongye Chubanshe 1986

**A Glossary of Economic and Commercial Terms (Chinese-English),** Xie Zhenqing, Beijing: Zhongguo Duiwai Jingji Maoyi Chubanshe 1986

**Nichi-Ei-Chu Boeki Yogo Jiten**, Shangwu Yinshuguan, Toho Shoten. Tokyo: Toho Shoten 1986 *Japanese-English-Chinese*

**Accounting Terminology in Use in the PRC & the USA,** Lou Er-Ying and Farrell, J.B., Hong Kong: Joint Publishing Co., and Shanghai: Shanghai Renmin Chubanshe 1985

**A Chinese-English Textile Dictionary,** Zhu Zhengdu, Lou Erduan et al., Beijing: Fangzhi Gongye Chubanshe 1985
**An English-Chinese Glossary of International Finance and Trade,** Beijing: Zhongguo Zhanwang Chubanshe 1984
**An English-Chinese Lexicon of International Economy,** Beijing: Zhongguo Shehui Kexue Chubanshe 1984
**English-Chinese Economics Glossary,** Chongqing: Zhongguo Shehui Kexue Chuabanshe 1983
**English-Chinese Accounting Dictionary**, Beijing: Shiyou Gongye Chubanshe 1982 *Good, reputable reference.*
**A Dictionary of Economic Management Terms,** Changchun: Jilin Renmin Chubanshe 1982
**Glossary of Foreign Exchange Terms** Caizheng Jingji Chubanshe 1980 *Chinese-English-French-Russian-German*
**English-Chinese, Chinese-English Dictionary of Business Terms,** Chu Hsiu-feng, Hong Kong: Chi Wen Publishing Co. 1973
**English-Chinese & Chinese-English Accounting Dictionary**, Ji Zehua, Hong Kong: Wan Li Book Co. 1964

*Chinese: Chemistry*
**English-Chinese Dictionary of Chemistry and Chemical Engineering,** 3rd ed., Beijing: Kexue Chubanshe 1994
**Chinese-English/English-Chinese Chemistry Dictionary on CD-ROM,** Beijing: Chemical Industry Press
**Chinese-English-Japanese Glossary of Chemical Terms,** Tokyo: Toho Shoten, Ltd 1977 *Far from complete, but there are very few other such sources available in this field. Entries are arranged by number of strokes in a character.*
*Chinese: Civil Engineering*
**English-Chinese Dictionary of Civil and Architectural Engineering Terms,** Hong Kong: Commercial Press 1979

*Chinese: Computers*
**English-Chinese Computer Software Dictionary,** Zhou Hanzong, Changsha: Hunan Kexue Jishu Chubanshe 1986
**A Comprehensive IBM Computer Dictionary**, Science Popularization Press 1985
**English-Chinese Computer Dictionary,** Beijing: Renmin Youdian Chubanshe 1984

*Chinese: Electrical Engineering/Electronics*
**English-Chinese Dictionary of Data Communications Technology,** Electrical Engineering Press 1990
**Chinese-English Dictionary of Electronics Technology,** Gan Dayon, Beijing: Dianzi Gongye Chubanshe 1987 *A valuable reference.*
**English-Chinese Dictionary of Electrical Engineering**, Beijing: Kexue Chubanshe 1987
**English-Chinese Dictionary of Television and Electronics,** Beijing: Kexue Chubanshe 1987
**English-Chinese Dictionary of Remote Sensing,** Li Wenlan, Beijing: Kexue Puju Chubanshe 1986
**English-Chinese Dictionary of Television and Video Recording,** Beijing: Renmin Youdian Chubanshe 1983

*Chinese: Environmental Sciences*
**Chinese-English Dictionary of Environmental Sciences,** Beijing: Zhongguo Huanjing Chubanshe 1993

*Chinese: Fiber Optics*
**English-Chinese Lightwave Communications and Optical Fiber Technical Dictionary**, Li Guangqian, Beijing: Renmin Youdian Chu-banshe 1985

*Chinese: Geology*
**Geology Dictionary,** Ministry of Geology and Mineral Resources, Beijing: Dizhi Chubanshe 1983
**English-Chinese Comprehensive Geology Dictionary,** Beijing: Kexue Chubanshe 1980

*Chinese: Highway Engineering*
**English-Chinese Dictionary of Highway Engineering,** Beijing:
Renmin Jiaotong Chubanshe 1978

*Chinese: Journalism*
**English-Chinese Glossary of Newspaper Terms**, Hong Kong: Commer-cial Press 1986

*Chinese: Laser/Infrared Technology*
**English-Chinese Dictionary of Lasers and Infrared Technique,** Zhou Rongsheng, Beijing: Kexue Chubanshe 1987

*Chinese: Medical*
**English-Chinese Medical Dictionary,** Commercial Press 1988

*Chinese: Military*
**English-Chinese Military and Technical Dictionary,** Jiang Kang, Lu Zuokang, Luoyang: Yuhang Chubanshe 1985
**Cihai, Military Supplement,** Shanghai: Shanghai Cishu Chubanshe 1980 *A must, as is the "Cihai" itself.*

*Chinese: Science and Technology*
**The Chinese-English Dictionary of Scientific and Technical Glossaries (Hanying keji dacidian)** (2 vol.), Beijing: Kexue Jishu Wenxian Chubanshe 1998 *A good comprehensive general technical dictionary.*
**Comprehensive Chinese-English Dictionary of Science and Tech-nology,** 2nd ed., Beijing: Science Press 1988
**Chinese-English Dictionary of Scientific and Technical Terms**, Harbin: Heilongjiang Renmin Chubanshe 1985 *One of the best, but unfortunately not available from the publisher.*
**Comprehensive Chinese-English Dictionary of Science and Tech-nology,** Beijing: Kexue Chubanshe 1983
**A Modern Scientific and Technical Dictionary,** Shanghai: Shanghai Scientific and Technical Publishing House 1980 *Highly recommended.*
**An English-Chinese Dictionary of Technology**, Qinghua University Spe-cialist Group, Beijing: Guofang Gongye Chubanshe 1978 *Recommended.*
**A Modern Science and Technology Dictionary,** Shanghai: Shanghai Kexue Jishu Chubanshe 1980

# APPENDIX E: SOURCES OF TRANSLATION WORK

> This book includes a CD (on the inside of the front cover) with lists of translations companies and international corporations who do a large volume of translation in all languages.

If you choose freelance translation, you should consider yourself a one-person translation company. Your main concern will be where to find work. The need for freelance translation is greater than anyone can estimate, and is clearly growing at a rapid rate. Worldwide, translation is a multibillion dollar industry. But finding translation work on your own is easier said than done. The main problem is that translation is hardly ever a steady, ongoing function of any particular work source, such as an embassy, a company, a government agency, or even a publisher. None of those needs translation every day of the year. Each of them may need a great deal of translation all at once (more than any one person can handle within the given time-frame), and then none for a long time. And, if any one of them needs translation on an ongoing basis, chances are a decision will be made to hire an in-house translator rather than farm out the work.

The fact remains, however, that a well-rounded freelancer can earn well over $50,000 a year, and, in the case of highly specialized technical translators in major languages like Spanish, German, Japanese or Russian, even $100,000 or more. The secret to all of this is establishing for yourself a good clientele. There are two ways of doing this. The first, and by far the hardest, is finding your own clients and working with them directly. You may want to contact embassies, law firms, publishers, government agencies and so on, and solicit work directly from them. If you are fortunate enough to find some good steady clients on your own, you will be doing quite well. But the problem often lies in the word "steady." What seems to be a steady client today may not be so steady tomorrow.

This brings us to the second, and by far the safer option, which is translation agencies. There are hundreds of them in the United States, and they handle huge amounts of translation business every year. In this chapter we will discuss translation agencies, as well as direct sources of translation available to the freelancer.

**Translation Agencies**

Translation agencies, also known as translation companies, or translation bureaus, are for the most part privately owned commercial establishments ranging in size from one or two employees to ten or more, but hardly ever larger than ten. Some are divisions of larger companies, such as Berlitz, which is primarily a language school and publisher, offering translation as a secondary function. Some specialize in one language only, such as Spanish, German, or Japanese. Most offer several languages, and quite a few bill themselves as offering "all languages." This last type is somewhat pretentious, since there are more languages in the world than any one person can identify. But what they really mean is that they will make the effort to find a translator in almost any language they may be called upon to translate.

As a general rule, translation agencies employ relatively few in-house translators, since the flow of work in any given language is usually uneven. Instead, they rely on the services of a network of hundreds of freelancers who can handle a great variety of subjects. Those freelancers are located all over the United States and even abroad. The ones who are most reliable and professional get the major share of the work, and some of them earn the above-quoted figures.

As a freelancer, you need to cultivate at least one such agency, preferably two or three. The problem in working with only one is that, with few exceptions, there may not be a steady flow of work coming out of any given agency in any given language, in subjects you are equipped to handle. Two or three will give you better coverage, and assure a better flow. On the other hand, you may find yourself in a situation where all three ask you to do something at the same time, and you may not be able to do it. You need to establish an understanding with your agencies that would make an allowance for such a scenario, so that you don't spoil your relationship with any one of them.

The worst thing you can do as a freelancer working with translation agencies is to overcommit yourself. Your most important personal asset is your reliability. Once you fail to meet deadlines (keep in mind—the agency stands to lose a client if deadlines are not met), your reliability becomes questionable, and if you do it once too often, you may soon find out that those phone calls from the agency offering you work assignments stop coming.

Where do you look for translation agencies? Below you will find a listing of hundreds of such agencies. You can find more in the Yellow Pages, or through the ATA (American Translators Association), which has local chapters around the country. My suggestion is to start with those close to home. In this day and age of international electronic communications, distance has little meaning. But then again, close to home still works, because you can meet the people there, befriend them, and in some instances even avail yourself of their dictionaries and other resources.

Keep in mind that a translation company has overhead, and also needs to make some profit to stay in business. They do the hard work of finding translation assignments, and therefore share with you the profit from the job. You can usually make more money by going directly to the client, and if you have enough of your own clients you don't need a translation company to send work your way. But most freelance translators do need those companies, which invariably provide a more steady flow of work than what a freelancer can get on his or her own.

The two things all translation companies appreciate and reward in a freelancer are honesty and loyalty. If you agree to a deadline, stick to it. Don't renege on it at the last minute. That's a sure prescription to spoil your association with your company. Equally important is not to go behind the company's back and try to solicit its own clients directly. Some companies will make you sign an agreement to this effect. Others will rely on the honor system. Don't abuse their trust. It usually doesn't pay off.

### Direct Sources of Work

Working with translation agencies usually does not stop you from finding your own clients, as long as there is no conflict of interest with the agency's clients. It would be impossible to list here all the potential sources of direct translation work, since they include practically the entire human race (everyone needs a document translated at some point). But there are some major sources which ought to be mentioned, and here are some of the more important ones.

### Law Firms

Law firms are a major source of translation work. Some of the larger firms hire full-time translators or staff members who are bilingual, especially if they do business on a regular basis with a foreign entity. Most firms use translators on an as-needed basis. Legal translation is a specialized field in which you need to acquire experience working with legal documents. There are several legal specialties, such as patent law, international law, immigration, and so on. Each specialty has its own style and terminology, which a translator needs to become acquainted with. As a freelancer, adding legal translation to your list of specialties is an excellent idea. You will find out that your volume of translation will increase considerably by doing so.

Quite often, a law firm needs both document translation and interpretation. Keep in mind that interpretation is a discipline separate from translation, and that there is a big difference between one-on-one consecutive interpreting and simultaneous conference interpreting. If asked by a law firm to do both text translation and interpreting, be sure to find out first exactly what the assignments consist of.

## Industry

Corporations doing business in other countries have to deal with documents originated in the languages of those countries or English documents that need to be translated into those languages. Here again we find the two approaches of either hiring translators or farming out work to freelancers and to translation services (or a combination of both). This field is perhaps the fastest growing source of translation in the closing years of the twentieth century. More and more major American companies are turning to international business as a way to offset the decline of business at home and to gain a share of the world market. Their need for translation is growing every day, and even those who have in-house translators are finding themselves using freelancers because of their volume of translation work.

If you are fortunate enough to form a relationship with a major company doing business overseas, you may find yourself in the enviable position of dealing with a major, steady source of translation. How does one get work with major corporations? If you have a special expertise in their field of work, say you are a telecommunications expert and you would like to translate for Sprint, find out who handles outside vendors or services, and give them a call or drop them a note. It also helps to know someone in the company, who can do some of the legwork for you and put you in touch with the right people. As a general rule, this is not easy to do. But persistence does pay off some of the time, and even if only a few respond, it is worth the effort.

## The U.S. Government

For several decades following World War Two, translation in the federal government enjoyed a boom. The onset of the Cold War resulted in wide-scale translation activities on the part of the U.S. Department of Defense (DoD), all the branches of the service (particularly the Army, Navy, and Air Force), and the Central Intelligence Agency (CIA). In addition, such multilingual organizations as the Voice of America (which started broadcasting in 1942 in 40 languages), sprang into being. These and other organizations employed a host of translators, and farmed out millions of words every year to be translated. Looking back, those were the feast years of government translation. During the nineties, however, a major shift has been taking place. Since 1992, there has been a sharp decline in government translations, and those translation agencies and freelancers who were dependent on government work for their bread and butter, are hurting. This is not to say that the U.S. Government is no longer a source of employment for translators. There are still many opportunities for translation in the government, offered by such bodies as the Language Services division of the U.S. Department of State (for in-house as well as freelance translators and interpreters), the Library of Congress, the U.S. Patent and Trademark Office, and so on (see list of U.S. Government Agencies, Appendix 4).

My translation company, Schreiber Translations, Inc. (STI), started out in life as a full-service translation company for the federal government. This was in the early eighties, when the boom was still on. We provided translation from and into over 50 languages and dialects, as well as interpreting, transcription, voice-over, graphics, and editing. Luckily for us, we realized early on that, as the world was changing, we were better off not being locked into government work, and we were able to develop a lucrative practice in the nongovernmental sectors. Today, government work makes up less than 50% of our total translation work.

What does all of this mean to linguists seeking translation work in the closing years of the twentieth century? There is no one simple answer. The government has been known to swing like a fast-moving pendulum. This author believes that before long the federal government will be launching new major translation projects, in such sectors as world trade and international relations. American interaction with other cultures and languages is far from diminishing. If anything, it is increasing day by day. One good example is the American space program, conducted by the National Aeronautics and Space Administration (NASA). Back in the sixties, there were two major space programs in the world—the Soviet and the American. Today, many countries in Western Europe and Asia have an active space program, and many of them are involved in cooperative efforts.

NASA is actively involved in this new international space scene, and the need for translation in this particular organization should not be underestimated. But all of this, of course, is speculative. The federal government is making a historical effort to reduce its enormous deficit, and since the lawmakers of our land are not necessarily attuned to the critical importance of translation, translation may well be a casualty of the budget wars. Translators would be well advised not to write off doing translation for the government, since it is, and will continue to be, the single biggest employer around. But they should put at least as much, if not more, effort into finding translation work outside the government, where indeed the field is all but limitless.

What are the pros and cons of translating for the government? For many linguists over the years, the government has offered job security. I know some fine translators who have worked for the government for many years and had interesting and fulfilling careers. On the other hand, career translators in the government are not paid exceptionally high salaries. Quite a few freelance on the side in an effort to supplement their income. As for freelancers who contract with the government, here we have mixed results. Some have found themselves a cozy niche and are kept busy on a fairly regular basis. Others go through the "feast and famine" syndrome. Some have been frustrated by spending a long time hunting for government assignments, with little result. To freelance effectively for the government, one should, in most instances, work in one of the top five languages the U.S. Government is interested in (Spanish, Russian, German, French and Japanese). Any other language, even Chinese or Italian, may not offer enough of a flow. One should also make many contacts.

On the downside, government agencies, with few exceptions, are notorious for not paying on time. A few years ago, the government passed a "prompt payment" act, which mandates 30-day net payment, with interest accruing thereafter. The problem is, more than a few agencies take at least another 30 days to process an invoice, claiming that it takes that long to get your invoice "into the system." Others take even longer, and simply neglect to add interest. If you try to get it, you may soon find out you waste more time going after it than it's worth. In some extreme cases—which are by no means rare—it can take six to twelve months to get paid. Your invoice simply gets lost in the system. Your remedy is to contact your congressperson, who will call that particular government office to make sure you get paid. The problem is, those folks in the finance office often resent being put on the spot in this manner, and while they will expedite your payment, you may not get work next time. It all sounds shocking, but having been there, it is my civic duty to let you know.

Another drawback of government freelancing is the incredible amount of paperwork you are asked to fill out in doing some of those jobs. I have done five and ten dollar jobs that required three detailed forms filled out, plus an invoice in six copies, mailed to three different offices (finance, procurement, and contract). It took me longer to do the paperwork than to translate, and clearly the whole thing was not worth my while. If you do a fair amount of freelancing for the government, you learn to overlook these excesses. Otherwise, you may have to decide whether it's all worth it.

A third major drawback to doing government work is the fact that quite often the translation standards of a particular agency may be quite low. As a result, you run the risk of developing poor translation habits, lack of attention to details, lack of sufficient editing and proofing, and so on. What that means in a practical sense is that when a more demanding job comes along, especially in the private sector, you may find out your performance is not satisfactory, and you may lose your client.

Having said all this, it behooves me to add that during the last seventeen years I have interacted with hundreds of government employees and dozens of agencies, and many of those have been a delight to work with, and overall I have been very fortunate to have this unique opportunity to take part in many historical events, including the peace treaty between Israel and Egypt, the Gulf War, the disarmament agreement with the former Soviet Union, the Bosnian peace agreement, and many more. Thus, working with the government as a linguist is by no means a dull experience, and if you learn how to take some of the problems in your stride, you can do quite well.

### State and Local Government

Government at all levels, from the municipal to the federal, needs translation. At the local level we find more and more city and county government translating their pamphlets, brochures and other documents into the languages of their immigrant populations, notably Asian languages and Spanish. In addition, local government has an ongoing need for interpreters, mostly for the court system, but also for social services, hospitals, and other local institutions. At this time of tight budgets, this may not be the most lucrative field, but it is definitely worth exploring, since it is local, and mostly uses local linguists.

### Major Organizations

Among the largest organizations that use a great deal of translation one should mention the United Nations, The World Bank, the World Health Organization, the Organization of American States, to cite only some of the better-known ones here in the U.S. Surely there are more in Europe, such as the World Court, the European Community, NATO, and many more. Most of these organizations use in-house linguists, and do not farm out translation work if they can help it. But quite often they have more documents to translate than they can handle in-house, and they look for outside help.

### Publishers

Book publishers use freelance translators in many different ways. This is not an easy field to break into, particularly for the beginner. Many publishers turn to academia for translators, and if you are in academia and can translate from or into another language in your field of expertise, there is a chance you can get the work. Others turn to established translators with name recognition. But it is certainly worth trying, to query publishers and find out if they need your services.

### Software Localization Companies

A fast-growing area of translation is software localization, or translation of software-related text into other languages and adapting the text to the target culture. Software localization companies specialize in computer subjects and in English-into-foreign language translation. They employ in-house translators, but they also use freelancers from time to time. Their work encompasses everything from computer manuals to localization of web-sites.

### Networking

An excellent source of work for freelance translators is personal contacts with other translators. The ATA's local chapters are one place where translators meet and get to know each other. The annual conference of the ATA holds a networking session, which is very valuable. One also meets translators through personal contacts in the translation field.

The latest way to meet translators is on the Internet. Entities such as the Foreign Language Forum on CompuServe bring together translators from all over the world. All you need to do is post a message on one of those programs, and before you know it you get a response from someone in your own town or half way around the world.

Keeping in touch with other translators is a prime means of finding out about work sources and assignments. There are clearly many advantages to networking in the translation field, and the more contacts one has the better.

The following is a list of translation companies who use freelance translators. The companies are not rated. It is up to you to find out which are best suited to your needs.

-A-

**ABC Worldwide Translations & Interpretations**, 8306 Wilshire Boulevard, Ste. 200, Beverly Hills, CA 90211
Phone: (310)260-7700 Fax: (310)260-7705
e-mail: info@wordexpress.com Website: www.wordexpress.net
Contact: Muriel Redoute Member: ATA

**ABS Translation & Interpreting Service**, 1685 Hampton Road, Abington, PA 19001 Phone: (215)886-2219 Fax: (215)886-7671
e-mail: ABStrans@aol.com
Contact: Aram Sarkisian Member: ATA

**A.C.E. InfoTech Group**, 1450 114th Ave SE, Ste. 1-230, Seattle, WA 98004
Phone: (425)453-4444 Fax: (425)453-0188
Website: www.aceinfotech.com
Contact: Maya Vengadasalam Member: ATA

**AE Inc. Translations**, 15995 N. Barkers Landing, Ste. 111, Houston, TX 77079 Phone: (281)870-0677 Fax: (281)556-9737
e-mail: translations@aetrans.com Website: www.aetrans.com
Contact: Stephen D. Ross, President Member: ATA

**ABLE Innovations, Inc.**, 1100 Lakeway Drive, Ste. 200, Bellingham, WA 98229 Phone: (360)714-1390
e-mail: sales@ableinnovations.com
Website: www.ableinnovations.com Member: ATA

**Academy of Languages Translation & Interpretation Services**, 216 First Ave. South, Ste. 330, Seattle, WA 98104
Phone: (206)521-8601
Fax: (206)521-8605 e-mail: translate@aolti.com Website: www.aolti.com
Contact: Chaouky Kaboul Member: ATA

**Accent on Language**, 160 East 56th St., 5th Fl., New York, NY 10022 Phone: (212)486-6790 Fax: (212)486-2439
e-mail: info@accentonlanguage.com Website: www.accentonlanguage. com
Contact: Brian E. McDermott Member: ATA

**ACCENT Translations, Inc.;** 442 Beaulieu Road, Neenah, WI 54956; Phone: (920) 751-8260
Fax: (920) 969_0320; E_mail: accent@ameritech.net; Contact: Kimberlee A. Heier, President Member: ATA

**Accento, The Language Company**, 5527 Dyer St., Dallas, TX 75206
Phone: (214)363-5353 Fax: (214)363-0067
e-mail: accento@accento.net Website: www.accento.net
Contact: James Mahler Member: ATA

**Access Transport & Translation Services, Inc.**, 528 S North Lake Boulevard, Ste. 1000, Altamonte Springs, FL 32701
Phone: (888)748-7575 Fax: (407)330-7959
e-mail: gengelman@accessontime.com Website: www.accessontime.com
Contact: Stacey L. Whidden Member: ATA

**Accura International Translations, Ltd.**, 915 S. High St., Denver, CO 80209 Phone: (303)280-1292 Fax: (303)280-1489
e-mail: accura@ix.netcom.com Website: www.accuratrans.com
Contact: David Anderson Member: ATA

**Accurapid Translation Services, Inc.**, 806 Main St., Poughkeepsie, NY 12603 Phone:(845)473-4550 Fax: (845)473-4554
Website: www.accurapid.com
Contact: Gabe Bokor
Founded 1978. Member: ATA. Translates German, Spanish, French, Hungarian and Japanese both from and into English, and Portuguese and Russian from English. Emphasis on Engineering, Patents, Law, Business and Finance trans-lation. Prospective translators should demonstrate competence and a professional attitude. Resumes are filed for future reference. The company pioneered the use of technological tools in the industry. The company counts freelance translators from Europe, Asia and the Americas in its professional pool. Maintains a pool of 600 translators.

**Accurate Spanish Translations by Spanish Business Services, Inc.**, P.O. Box 720519, Dallas, TX 75372
Phone:(214)821-2050 Fax: (214)821-7065 e-mail: sbscorp@swbell.net Website: www.spanishbusiness.com
Contact: Robert H. Brandao Member: ATA

**ACCUWORLD, LLC**, 200 West Madison St., Ste. 930, Chicago, IL 60606 Phone: (312)641_0441 Fax:(312)641_7370
E_mail: ts@inlinguachi.com
Contact: Human Resources Department
Founded 1968. Member: ATA. Translates all languages, both from and into English. Covers all areas, with specialties in foreign language voice_overs, health care, pharmaceuticals, insurance, and technical manual translation. Resumes are compiled in a database according to area of expertise. The company, headquartered in Hartford, Connecticut has over 300 worldwide locations. It provides language training, cultural training, translation/interpretation services, and foreign language typesetting and voicecovers. Maintains a pool of 800+ translators.

**Acentos, Marketing & Advertising & Translations**, 400 E. Lake St., Minneapolis, MN 55408 Phone: (612)824-6109 Fax: (612)825-1729
e-mail: fcurbelo1@csc.om
Contact: Franklin Curbelo Member: ATA

**AD-EX WORLDWIDE**, 1733 Woodside Rd., Ste. 115, Redwood City, CA 94061 Phone: (800)223-7753 Fax: (650)474-2531
e-mail: translations@ad-ex.net Website:www.ad-ex.net
Contact: Robert Addis
Founded 1957. Member: ATA. Translates in all major languages, in all industrial fields, especially in the power and aerospace industries. Prospective translators must have demonstrable years of experience and written evidence of competence, including resumes and work samples. Resumes are responded to with a request for samples which are then thoroughly examined. The company is always glad to hear from veteran professional translators. Their client base is worldwide. Maintains a pool of "hundreds" of translators.

**Adaptive Language Resources, Inc.**, 45 Mount Auburn St., Watertown, MA 02139 Phone: (617)924-0554 Fax:(617)924-0280
Website: www.adaptivelanguage.com
Contact: Adrian Spidle Member: ATA

**Advance Language Studios**, 500 N. Michigan Ave., Chicago, IL 60611 Phone:(312)782-8123 Fax:(312)782-8356
Contact: Patrick Schoorlemmer
Founded 1963. Member: ATA. Translates from English into Spanish, French, German, Italian, Portuguese, Dutch, Japanese, Korean, Mandarin, Russian, and Polish. Emphasis on Technical, Advertising, Financial, Legal, and Commercial translations. Prospective translators should be born and raised in country of target language. Resumes are entered in a database. Company services include Translation, Interpreting, Desktop Publishing, Video dubbing in in-house studio. Maintains a pool of 1000+ translators.

**Advanced Communication and Translation, Inc.**, 4332 Montgomery Avenue, Suite A, Bethesda, MD 20814 Tel: 301-654-2890 Fax: 301-654-2891; Web Page: http://www.act_translate.com
E-mail: act@act-translate.com
Contact: Monique-Paule Tubb Member: ATA

**Advanced Global Services, Inc.**, P.O. Box 965, Chesterton, IN 46304 Phone: (219)921-1733 Fax: (219)921-

0640; E-mail: ags-inc@ags-inc.com Web site: www.AGS_INC.COM
Contact: Sylvie Prudhomme  Member: ATA

**Advanced Language Translation Inc.**; 25 N. Washington St, Rochester, NY 14614; Toll Free: 800-218-9024 Tel: 585-697-0462 X18 Fax: 585-697-0467 E-mail: info@advancedlanguage.com Web Site: www.advancedlanguage.com
Contact: Scott Bass, President Member: ATA

**Affinity Language Services**, 101 S. Fairview Ave., Wind Gap, PA 18091
Phone: (610)863-3955 Fax: (610)863-8571
e-mail: info@affinity-languages.com Website: www.affinitylanguages.com
Contact: Michelle Zuccarini
Founded 1998. Member: ATA. Works in Spanish, German, French, Italian, and Dutch. Also in Japanese. Main areas: Technical, sci-tech, legal, medical, and business. Also provides interpretation, editing, proofreading, transcription, and copywriting. Uses translators worldwide.

**Agnew Tech-II**, 741 Lakefield Rd., Ste. C, Westlake Village, CA 91361 Phone: (805)494-3999 Fax: (805)494-1749 e-mail: agnewi @agnew.com Website: agnew.com Contact: Irene Agnew
Founded 1986. Member: ATA, NAWBO, WITI. Translates Spanish, Chinese, French, German, Japanese, Russian, Vietnamese, etc. from English. Also scripts and voiceover. Covers all technical areas. Prospective translators should have a B.A. degree or higher and 2-3 years experience. Resumes received via e-mail, reviewed, graded and scheduled for a translation test. The company is a full-service translation bureau, as well as providing desktop publishing, web page design, multimedia, and audiovisual services. Maintains a pool of 300-400 translators.

**AimTrans, Inc.**, 14752 Beach Blvd, Ste. 201, La Mirada, CA 90638 Phone: (714)522-8200 Fax: (714)522-7773 Website: www.aimtrans.com Contact: Irene Agnew member: ATA

**Airspeed Translations**, 4200 Westheimer Road, Ste. 201, Houston, TX 77027
Phone: (713)586-2577 e-mail: rknauth@att.net
Website: www.airspeedtranslations.com
Contact: Rick Knauth
**Alanguage Bank, Inc.**, 150 Lafayette St., 5th Floor, New York, NY 10013 Phone: (212)213-3336 Fax:(212)685-7263
e-mail: peiwens@alanguagebank.comWebsite: www.alanguagebank.com
Contact: Pei Wen Shih Member: ATA

**Albanian Translation Services,** 3738 Katie Place, Triangle, VA 22172
Home: (703)221-8837 Fax: (703)221-8836
E_mail: tirana@msn.com
Contact: Mirela M. Kuhn Member: ATA

**Albors and Associates, Inc.**, P.O. Box 5516 Winter Park, FL 32793 Phone: (800)785-8634Fax: (407)657-7004
e-mail: rene@albors.com Website: www.albors.com
Contact: René A. Albors, President
Founded 1996. Member: ATA, NAJIT, Hispanic Chamber of Commerce, Orlando Chamber of Commerce. Translates Spanish, French, Portuguese, Japan-ese, German, Chinese, Russian, Polish, Arabic and Italian, both from and into English. Emphasis on Legal, Medical and Business translations. Prospective translators should be experienced, expert with terminology, and prompt in their delivery of finished work. Accepts unsolicited resumes for translation and inter-pretation. Resumes are computer-filed, and a letter of thanks is sent to acknowledge receipt. Maintains a pool of 5300 translators.

**Alexandria Translations**, 8827 Fort Hunt Rd., Alexandria, VA 22308 Phone:(703)799-7606 Fax:(703)799-7607 e-mail: 102554.3407 @compu-serve.com Contact: Lidia Terziotti Member: ATA
Translates and edits documents in a variety of languages.

**Allegro Translations**, 4513 Vernon Blvd., Madison, WI 53705
Phone: (608)233-3208 Fax: (608)233-3511 e-mail: info@allegro.com
Website: www.allegro-translation.com
Contact: Yaël Bratzlavsky
Founded 1993. Member: ATA. Translates English into Spanish, German, French, Japanese, Chinese, Russian, Italian, Brazilian Portuguese, Hmong and Laotian. Technical manuals, user manuals, employee handbooks, and marketing. Has over 100 translators.

**Allen Translation Service**, Box 1529, Morristown, NJ 07962
Phone: (973)292-2737 Fax: (973)292-3954 Contact: Jeanette C. Fredericks Member: ATA

**Allslavic Translation Services;** 4930 NW 84th Ave., Ft. Lauderdale, FL 33351
Phone: (800)775-5504 Fax: (954)741-3898
e-mail: info@slavprom.com Web site: www.slavprom.com
Contact: Stanka Moskov Member: ATA

**ALLSPEAK Interpreting Services**, P. 0. Box 1606, Glendale, CA 91209
Phone: (818)246-1515 Fax: (818)246-4211 e-mail: allspeakint@aol.com Contact: Tatiana E. Vorobieff Member: ATA

**Allworld Language Consultants, Inc**., P.O. Box 2128, Rockville, MD 20847
Phone: (301)881-8884 Fax: (301)881-6877 Website: www.alcinc.com
Contact: Carlos Scandiffio Member: ATA

**Alpha Tech Communications,** 4440 Chastant St, Suite E, Metairie, LA, 70002; Phone: (504)454_6554 Fax: (504)454_6717; Web Page: www.ustranslations.com E_mail: alphaTC@aol.com; Contact: Giovanna Icaza Director of International Language Services Member: ATA
Founded in 1998. Alpha Tech Communications translates many languages including English into Spanish, French, German, Portuguese, Chinese and Arabic. Along with translating English into those languages they translate them back into their respective language. They also translate Italian_English, Japanese_English, Greek_English, Russian_English, Etc. Their main subjects of translation are medical handbooks and legal documents. They deal with a wide variety of documents, from journal articles to technical documents. They do accept resumes and they do use freelance. The resumes are reviewed, evaluated, classified and kept in their data files to contact freelancers when necessary. They require you to have a good command of the language pair(s) you work with. Experience, commitment and responsibility. Computer programs and internet tool skills. They have one in_house translator and about 20 freelancers. They also offer interpreting equipment rental/sales, video narration, transcription, proofreading/editing and ESL training..

**ALTA Language Services,**; 3355 Lennox Rd. NE, Ste. 510, Atlanta, GA 30326;
Phone: (404)240_1810 Fax: (404)239_9516; E_mail: robert@altalang.com
Contact: Robert Jones
Company founded 1982. Member: ATA, AAIT. Uses freelance translators and interpreters. Accepts unsolicited resumes. Resumes are filed by language. Requires outstanding translation skills. Main languages (both ways) are Spanish, German, French, Japanese, Portuguese, Dutch, Italian, Chinese, Korean, and Russian. Main subjects are legal, medical, and general. Does multilingual typesetting in addition to translation and interpretation. Engages around 300 translators.

**ALTCO Translations,** 1426 Ridgeview Rd., Columbus, OH 43221, USA
Phone: (614)486_2014 Fax: (614)559_6682
e_mail: trudypeters@sbcglobal.net
Contact: Trudy E. Peters, Owner.
Founded 1982. Member: ATA. Uses freelancers for translation and interpretation. Only experienced translators' applications accepted. Main languages: all European languages. Main subjects are patents, business, IT, manuals, brochures, advertising, medical/pharmaceutical.

**Always Ready Translation Services**, 11026 Ventura Blvd., Room 10, Studio City, CA 91604 Phone: (800)240-6601
Fax: (818)755-8959
e-mail: language@worldnet.att.net
Contact: Dan Prescott, President
Founded 1985. Accepts resumes. Translates Spanish, Asian languages, Russian, Armenian, and other European languages.

**Ambassador Translating, Inc.**, 442 Route 202-206 N., #PMB200, Bedminster, NJ 07921 Phone: (908)429-0200
Fax: (908)429-0333
e-mail: rosa@am-translating.com Website: www.am-translating.com
Contact: Rosa A. Stevenson Member: ATA

**America Translating Services**, P.O. Box 800272, Santa Clarita, CA 91380 Phone: (800)535-0555 Fax: (800)316-2230
e-mail: rstevenson@aol.com Website: am-translating.com
Contact: Rosa A. Steventon, Coordinator
Founded 1984. Member: ATA, CCIA. Translates all languages, both from and into English. Emphasis on Legal, Technical and Medical translation. Prospective translators should provide sample translations, reference list. Resumes are listed in a database. Specializes in voiceover work. Maintains a pool of over 1,000 translators.

**American Bureau of Professional Translators (ABPT),** 8989 Westheimer Rd., Ste. 112, Houston, TX 77063; Phone: (713)789_2500 Fax: (713)789_8920; E_mail: abpt@abpt.com Web site: www.abpt.com
Contact: Ms. Lu Waterhouse Member: ATA

**American Education Research Corp**., Box 996, West Covina, CA 91793
Phone: (626)339-4404 Fax: (626)339-9081
e-mail: aerc@cyberg8t.com Website: www.credencialsevaluation.com
Contact: John A. Sheety Member: ATA

**American Translation Partners, Inc.**, 200 Lincoln Street, Boston, MA 02111 Phone 617.350.9988; fax 617.350.6988
E_mail: info@americantranslationpartners.com
Web site: www.americantranslationpartners.com
Contact: Scott Crystal
Founded 1998. Member: ATA, NAJIT, NETA, MMIA, LPDAM, FIT, TTI, LISA, AIIC. Accepts resumes. Requires language proficiency and experience as well as computer proficiency. Translates Spanish, Portuguese, French, German, Italian, Japanese, Chinese, Korean, Vietnamese, Haitian Creole, Afrikaans, and all Indian dialects. Works in government, legal, medical, insurance, technical, financial, software subjects in more than 200 language pairs. Has 1500 translators in New England and 3500 worldwide.

**ANDALEX International, Inc**., 421 SW 6th Ave. Suite 1150, Portland, OR 97204 Phone: (503)24-.9756 Fax: (503)246-6002
e-mail: info@telelanguage.com www.telelanguage.com
Contact: Andrei Lupenko Member: ATA

i**Antiquariat Literary Services, Inc.**, 12042 Trumbull Way, Reston, VA 20190 Phone:(703)707-8531 Fax:(703)707-8532
e-mail: alstranslation.com Website: www.alstranslation.net
Contact: Rebecca Marie Hindrichs Member: ATA

**APS International Ltd;** 7800 Glenroy Rd., Minneapolis, MN 55439; Phone: (952)831-7776 Fax: (952)-831-8150
E-mail: trans@civilactiongroup.com
Contact: Ann Mickow Member: ATA

**Arab American Translators**, 5827 Columbia Pike, #415, Falls Church, VA 22041
Phone: (703)820-5612 Fax: (703)820-1318
e-mail: info@translatearabic.com Website: www.translatearabic.com
Contact: Radwan Hakim Member: ATA

**ArchiText Inc.,** 23 Main St., Andover, MA 01810
Phone: (978)409-6112 Fax: (978)409-6096
e-mail: hansf@architext-usa.com Web site: www.architext-usa.com
Contact: Hans Fenstermacher Member: ATA

**Argo Translation, Inc.,** 3747 S. Howell Ave., Milwaukee WI 53207 Phone: (414)615-6000 Fax: (414)615-6005 e-mail: sales@argotrans.com Website: www.argotrans.com
Contact: Jacqueline LaCarelli
Founded 1995. Member: ATA. Uses freelance translators and interpreters. Accepts unsolicited resumes. Works in all languages and subjects, viz., medical, technical, legal, commercial. Always on the lookout for professional translators. Has 575 translators.

**Around The World, Inc.**, 12281 Butterfield Drive NW, Pickerington, OH 43147
Phone: (614)575-2424 Fax: (614)575-2423
e-mail:atw@nls.com Website: www.atwtranslation.com
Contact: Gary West Member: ATA
Founded 1998. Member: ATA, BBB. Translates all languages, mainly technical, advertising, business and legal. Has satellite offices in Kansas City, Columbus, Brussels (Belgium), and Paris (France). Translates and typesets for private and business sectors. Utilizes over 5000 translators.

**ASET International Services Corporation**, 2009 North 14th St., Ste. 214, Arlington, VA 22201 Phone:(703) 516-9266 Fax:(703)516-9269
e-mail: Khendzel@asetquality.com Website: asetquality.com
Contact: Kevin S. Hendzel, Director of Language Services
Founded 1987. Member: ATA. Translates in over 100 languages, both from and into English. Emphasis on Equipment Manuals, Pharmaceuticals and Medical Equipment, Software Localization, Nuclear, Chemical, Industrial and Structural Engineering, Law and Legislation, Regulations and Codes, Education and Consumer Goods translation. Prospective translators are required to have 10 years professional translating experience and formal technical training in a specialty area. Resumes are archived in database and assignments given when appropriate match arises. Resumes *must be faxed or submitted by e-mail.* The company also works with engineering drawings and specifications and possesses full AutoCad and full-color printing capabilities. They provide interpreting services and are an authorized Master Distributor for the Philips interpreting equipment series. Welcomes voice-over talent. Maintains a pool of 1000 translators.

**Asian Link Corp.**, 1108 W Valley Blvd., Ste. 4, Alhambra, CA 91803
Phone: (626)300-9191 Fax: (626)300-8955
e-mail:sophia@asialink.com
Contact: Sophia N. Yang Member: ATA

**Asian Translation Service;** 7393 S. Locust St., Midvale, UT 84047 Phone: (801)565-8281 Fax: (801)365-6560
E-mail:ats@asiantranslation.com Web site: www.asiantranslation.com
Contact: Steve Stevens
Founded 1992. Member: ATA. Translates English into Hmong, Vietnamese, Cambodian, Thai, Korean, Japanese, Chinese, Tagalog, Malay, and Indonesian, mainly health_related, business, personal documents, and product catalogues. Provides full range of translation and interpretation. Uses about 30 translators.

**Asian Translations, Inc.**, 3702 E. Lake St., Ste. 102, Minneapolis, MN 55406
Phone: (612)712-5432 Fax: (612)721-5778
e-mail: atrans@asiantranslations.com
Website: www.asiantranslations.com
Contact: Sokunthea (Sue) Hendry Member: ATA

**ASIST Translation Services**, 4663 Executive Drive, Ste. 11, Columbus, OH 43220 Phone: (614)451-6744 Fax: (614)451-1349
e-mail: asist@asisttranslations.com
Contact: Elena Tsinman, President

Founded 1983. Member: ATA. Uses freelance translators and interpreters. Accepts unsolicited resumes. All resumes are entered in a database. If qualified, translator is contacted immediately. Applicant must be experienced, native speaker, and have a university degree. Main languages are English into French, Spanish, Chinese, Japanese, Russian, Arabic, German, Somali, Portuguese and Italian. Additional languages are Dutch, Swedish and Danish. Does 2-3 million words a year. Does also typesetting, Website translation, software translation, localization, audio-visual productions, and desktop publishing. Maintains pool of 2000 translators.

**Atlantic International, Translators, Inc.**, 4956 Vermack Rd., Atlanta, GA 30338
Phone: (770)350-9050 Fax: (770)350-9051
e-mail: atlanticit@aol.com Website: www.atlanticitinc.com
Contact: Rogelio Cipriano Member: ATA

**Atlas Translation Services**, 336 North Central Ave., Ste. 6, Glendale, CA 91203 Phone: (818)242-2400 Fax: (818)242-2475
e-mail: atlas @atlaspvs.com
Contact: Sorina Kalili
Founded 1993. Uses freelancers for translation. Accepts unsolicited resumes. Main languages (both ways) are Farsi, German, Spanish, French, Arabic, Chin-ese, and Japanese. Main subjects are legal, business, and scripts. Also does legal interpretation.

**Audio To Go, Inc.**, 42 West 89th St., New York, NY 10024
Phone: (212)721-1183 Fax: (212)721-1273
e-mail: info@a2g.com Website: www.a2g.com
Contact: Gayle Goldfarb
Founded 1991. Member: NYCT. Accepts resumes. Requires certification, experience, native speakers in target language. Translates all languages. Translates audio and video programs with narrators in their native language.

**Avant Page**, 1138 Villaverde Lane, Davis, CA 95616
Phone: (530)750-2040 Fax: (530)750-2024
E-mail: luis@avantpage.com Web site: www.avantpage.com
Contact: Luis Miguel, President
Founded 1996. Member: ATA. Accepts resumes. Requires 3 years exp., certification/accreditation where available. Translates English into Spanish, Japanese, Chinese (simplified and traditional), Korean, French, German, Vietnamese, Arabic, Hebrew, Italian, and Portuguese. Also Farsi, Thai, Tagalog, and MORE!. Main areas are business, hi tech, biotechnology, government documents, and advertisements. Does multilingual desktop publishing. Does over one million words per year. Utilizes over 200 translators.

**Avantext**, 2991 Shattuck Avenue, Ste. 200, Berkeley, CA 94705
Phone: (510) 644-3490 Fax: (510) 644-3492
E-mail: info@avantext-usa.com Web site: www.avantext-usa.com

## -B-

**BBC Multilingual Translations**, 1231 Somerset Drive, McLean, VA 22101 Phone: (703)448-0893 Fax: (703)448-8077
e-mail: mansourf@aol.com

**Babel Tower, Inc.**, P.O. Box 491023, Ft. Lauderdale, FL 33349
Phone: (954)731-9180 Fax: (954)731-1366
e-mail: babeltower@aol.com Website: www.babeltowerinc.com
Contact: Sandra Fernandez
Founded 1996. Member: ATA. Translates all languages.

**Barinas Translation Consultants, Inc.**, 1100 NW Loop 410, Ste. 700, San Antonio, TX 78213 Phone: (210)545-0019 Fax: (210)545-4731 160424 E-mail: info@barinas.com Website: www.barinas.com
Contact: Sonia Barinas, President
Company founded 1980. Member: MPI, AAHA, TSHE, SATC, San Antonio Chamber of Commerce, GSHMA, ISMP, THMA. Uses freelance translators and interpreters. Accepts unsolicited resumes. Resumes are checked for quality and experience, then filed by language and areas of expertise. Please submit sample with resume, and indicate degree in translation and/or interpretation. Degree in law, medicine etc. is a plus. Main language pairs are Spanish/English, French/ English, French/Spanish, Portuguese/English,

German/English, Chinese/English, Japanese/English. Main subjects are legal, medical, technical, telecom. Specializes in simultaneous interpretation for meetings and conventions. Does about 350 projects a year. Uses hundreds of freelancers.

**Berkeley Scientific Translation Service, Inc**, P.O.Box 150, Berkeley CA, 94701; Phone: (510)548_4665 Fax: (510)548_4666; E_mail: marlo@berksci.com Web site: www.berksci.com
Contact: Dr. Marlo R. Martin
Founded 1974. Member: ATA. Translates Japanese, Korean, Chinese, and other major European and Asian languages, both from and into English. Emphasis on Mechanical, Automotive, Chemical and Chemical Engineering, Computers and Software, Electronics, Biotechnology, Pharmaceuticals, Physics and Patent translations. Prospective translators should be able to produce autho_ritative translations into their native language within a specialized area. Resumes are screened for educational background and subject expertise as related to translation experience. The company was founded by a physicist and engineer and seeks translators with similar qualifications. Maintains a pool of 70-100 translators.

**Betmar Languages**, 6260 Highway 65 NE, Ste. 308, Minneapolis, MN 55432 Phone: (612)572-9711 Fax: (612)571-3467
e-mail: best@betmar.com Contact: Elizabeth A. Loo Member: ATA

**BioMedical Translators**, 3477 Kenneth Drive, Palo Alto, CA 94303 Phone:(650)494-1317 Fax:(650)494-1394
e-mail: biomed@biomedical.com Contact: Monique Vazire
Founded 1992. Member: ATA, NCTA. Main languages translated are French, German, Italian, Spanish, Dutch, Swedish, Portuguese, Danish, Japanese, and Chinese. Emphasis is on Medical and Biological translation, including equipment, studies and software. Prospective translators should possess at least one year experience, have knowledge of the medical field, and have access to medical dictionaries. Their equipment should include a PC and modem or e-mail; software should include Word and WordPerfect. Resumes are reviewed by the recruiting department and responded to with a test translation, which is then evaluated. The company specializes exclusively in the medical field and its peripherals. Their services also include desktop publishing. Maintains a pool of 500+ translators.

**Bloomberg L.P.**, 100 Business Park Drive, P.O. Box 888, Princeton, NJ 08542 Phone:(609)279-4955 Contact: Elsa Shilling

**Bowne Translation Services**, 345 Hudson Street, New York, NY 10014
Tel. (212) 229-7370 Fax. (212) 229-7395
Email: lisa.dimeglio@bowne.com

**BRADSON Corporation**, 1735 Jefferson Davis Highway, Ste. 705, Arlington, VA 22202 Phone: (703)413-3050 Fax: (703)413-3056
Contact: John S. Horner

**BRIDGE-LINGUATEC LANGUAGE SERVICES**, 915 South Colorado Blvd., Denver, CO 80246 Phone: (303)777-7783 Fax:(303)777-7246
e-mail: translators@bridgeschool.com
Website: www.bridge-linguatec.com Contact: Michelle Duvall
Founded 1981. Translates mainly Spanish, French, German, Arabic, Dutch, Russian and Portuguese. Emphasis on legal and medical. Prospective translators should, by preference, be native speakers. Resumes are filed by language and translators contacted by need.. The company also provides ESL training for executives, foreign language instruction, and interpretation services. Maintains a pool of 150-200 translators.

**Brigham and Women's Hospital**, 75 Francis St., Boston, MA 02115
Phone: (617)732-6640 Fax: (617)975-0813 e-mail: igarcia@partners.org
Contact: Ileana Jimenez Garcia Member: ATA

**Bromberg & Associates**, 28475 Ranchwood Drive, Southfield, MI 48076
Phone: (248)827-7164 Fax: (248)827-3621
E-mail: jinny@linguacity.com Web site: www.linguacity.com
Contact: Jinny Bromberg Member: ALC

**Bruce International, Inc.**, 10550 SW Allen Blvd., Ste. 123, Beaverton, OR 97005
Phone: (503)643-8448 Fax: (503)643-7174
E-mail: info@bruceinternational.com

Web site: www.bruceinternational.com
Contact: Oscar Andrino   Member: ATA

**Burg Translation Bureau, Inc.,** 29 South LaSalle, Ste. 936, Chicago, IL 60603 Phone: (312)263-3379 Fax:(312)263-4325
E-mail: burg@interaccess.com  Web site: www.burgtranslations.com
Contact: Lodovico Passalacqua, President
Founded 1936. Member: ATA. Emphasis on technical translation. Translators carefully "screened" _ Strong Project Management - QC procedure en-forced.Translation and Typesetting.

## -C-

**CC Scientific, Ltd.,** 73920 Mountain View Ave, Palm Desert, CA 92260
Phone: (760)341-7544   Fax: (760)341-7514 e-mail: CCSLtd@aol.com
Contact: Dr. Jaime R. Carlo-Casellas   Member: ATA

**C.P. Language Institute**, 225 West 57th St., Ste. 404, New York, NY  10019 Phone: (212)246-2054  Fax: (212)247-2258
e-mail: info@cpli.com   Website: www.cpli.com
Contact: Yuki Saito
Founded 1980. Member: ATA. Translates Chinese, Japanese, Korean, Spanish, Arabic, Russian, French, German, Hebrew, Hindi, Urdu, Vietnamese, Italian, Portuguese, Thai, Khmer, Tagalog and Indonesian, both from and into English. Emphasis on Advertising, Technical, Patent, Financial, Medical, Legal, Personal Document and Textbook translation. Prospective translators should show pro-ficiency in English and the target language and should be experienced. Resumes are responded to with a call-in or an e-mailed test translation in order to assess the candidate's ability. The company has two departments - programs and services. Programs is a language school providing small group and private language instruction. Services comprise translation, typesetting, formatting, interpretation, voiceovers and subtitling. Maintains a pool of 300 translators.

**Carolina Polyglot, Inc.**, PO Box 36334, Charlotte, NC 28236
Phone:(704)366-5781 Fax:(704)364-2998
e-mail: wdepaula@carolinapolyglot.com
Website: www.carolinapolyglot.com Contact: Dr. William DePaula
Company founded 1971. Member: ATA, CATI. Accepts unsolicited resumes. Resumes are filed by language pair. E-mail and fax filed electronically. Require-ments for applicants include academic degree, previous experience, professional affiliation/accreditation, references. Main languages (both ways) are French, Spanish, Italian, Portuguese, Romanian, German, Dutch, Arabic, Chinese, Vietnamese, and Japanese. Also translates Turkish, Farsi, Africaans, Hindi, Danish, Norwegian, Swedish, and Finnish. Main subjects are immigration, education, law, business, medicine, insurance, theology, ecology, literature, and computers. Uses over 30 translators.

**Caterpillar, Inc.**, Dealer Capability Dept., Corp Translation, 501 SW Jefferson Ave., Peoria, IL 61630
Phone: (309)494-5216   e-mail: opherk_jorg@CAT.com   Member: ATA
Contact: Dr. Jorg Opherk   Member: ATA

**CDNOW, Inc.**, 1005 Virginia Drive, Fort Washington, PA 19034
Phone: (215)619-9696 Fax: (215)619-9559
e-mail: emcpartland@cdnow.com   Website: www.cdnow.com
Contact: Erica A. McPartland   Member: ATA

**Certified Interpreters & Translators (CIT),** PO Box 390006, San Diego, CA 92149  Phone: (619)475-8586  Fax: (619)472-2157
Company founded 1983. Uses freelance translators and interpreters. Accepts unsolicited resumes. Resumes are filed by language and geographical area. Interpreters have to be certified. Main language pair is English-Spanish, followed by English into German and Tagalog, Russian, Arabic, and Japanese into English. Also Portuguese, Polish, and Vietnamese into English. Main subjects are legal, medical, technical, literary, commercial, as well as manuals. Does conference interpreting. Also does translator and interpreter training.

**Certified Languages International,** 4700 SW Macadam Ave., #200, Portland, OR 97201  Phone: (503)525-9601

Fax: (503)525-9607
E-mail: Kristin@certifedlanguages.com
Web site: www.certifiedlanguages.com
Contact: Kristin Quinlan Member: ATA, ALC

**Certified Translation Services**, One Harbison Way, Ste. 105, Columbia, SC 29212 Phone: (800)730-9970 Fax: (803)781-5052
e-mail and website: certifiedtranslationservices.com
Contact: Ed Crosby Member: ATA

**CETRA, Inc;** 4312 Oak Avenue, Melrose Park, PA 19027; Phone: (215)635-7090 Fax: (215)635-9239; Web Page: www.cetra.com E-mail: info@cetra.com;
Contact: Dr. Jiri Stejskal, President; Member: ATA
Founded in 1994. The main languages that they translate are English into French, German, Spanish, Japanese and Chinese. They also translate Central/East European languages. The subjects that they translate are business, legal and surveys. CETRA does use freelance and they do accept resumes. The resumes are reviewed and filed together with information provided by the vendor via online form. You may fill out a form at http://www.cetra.com/trans_appl.html.

**Cherry Creek Language Centre, Inc.,** 1071 Jersey St., Denver, CO 80220
Phone: (303)756-2520 Fax: (303)782-5686
e-mail: ignacio@translationlinks.com Web site: www.translationlinks.com
Contact: Ignacio Jimenez (DBA.Translationlinks tradename.)

**Choice Translating & Interpreting**, 8701 Mallard Creek Rd., Charlotte, NC 28262 Phone: (704)717-0043 Fax: (704)717-0046
e-mail: hr@choicetranslating.com Website: www.choicetranslating.com
Contact: Sophie David-Gunn Member: ATA
**CinciLingua, Inc.**, 322 East Fourth St., Cincinnati, OH 45202 Phone: (513)721-8782 Fax:(513)721-8819
email: translat@cincilingua.com Website: www.cincilingua.com
Contact: Michael Sum
Founded 1972. Member: ATA, ASME. Translates in Spanish, French, German, Chinese, Japanese, etc., both from and into English. Prospective translators should have college degree, professional experience in a technical specialty, and references. Should have a computer. Resumes are reviewed by the Project Manager and entered in a database. Qualified candidates may be asked to translate a short sample for additional information.

**CITI Translation Center, Inc.,** 1025 Kane Concourse, Ste. 208, Bay Harbor Islands, FL 33154 Phone: (305)868-1746 Fax: (305)868-1748
e-mail: info@cititran.com Website: www.cititran.com
Contact: Fernando Velez-Pardo
Founded 1987. Member: ATA, FLATA. Translates German, Russian, Japanese, Chinese, French, Italian and Spanish, both from and into English. Emphasis on Technical, Communication Manuals, Medical, Business and Personal Documents translation. Prospective translators should be experienced, preferably with accre-ditation and/or certification. Resumes are reviewed and the applicant contacted if there is a specific need for that language or specialty area. The company supports markets in the Americas, Europe and the Pacific Rim. Maintains a pool of 60 translators.

**CME Corporation**, 2945 Three Leaves Drive, Mount Pleasant, MI 48858 Phone: (517)773-0377 Fax: (517)773-1105
Contact: Fumiko Lobert Member: ATA

**Columbia Language Services**, 11818 SE Mill Plain Blvd., #307,
Vancouver, WA 98684 Phone: (360)896-3881 Fax: (360)896-4074
e-mail: mail@columbia-language.com
Website: www.columbia-language.com
Contact: Sveltana Linchuk Member: ATA

**CommGap International Language Services**

PO Box 71248, Salt Lake City, Utah 84171
Phone: (801) 944-4049 Fax: (801) 944-4046
e-mail: info@commgap.com Web site: www.commgap.com
Contact: Lelani P. Craig Member: ATA

**Community Interpreter Services**, Catholic Charities/Greater Boston, 75 Kneeland St., 8th Floor, Boston, MA, 02111
Phone: (617)350-4811 Fax: (617)629-5768
e-mail: inna_persitsgimelberg@ccab.com Web Page: www.cccis.org
Contact: Inna P. Gimelberg, Program Manager
Founded in 1986. Member: ATA, MMIA, NETA. Accepts resumes. Translates Haitian Creole, Spanish, Cape Verdean Creole, Vietnamese, Russian, Portuguese, Cantonese-Chinese, Vietnamese, Polish, Farsi, Bosnian and Albanian. Also Somali, Swahili, Italian, French, Arabic, Khmer and Laotian. They translate a total of 50 languages. Emphasis on Personal Document translation. Prospective translators and interpreters should live in Massachusetts or a bordering state, and possess at least a Bachelor's degree, past translating experience, and fluency in at least two languages. Qualified resumes are responded to with an interview appointment. They are a nonprofit service operated by Catholic Charities. Maintains a pool of 200 translators and interpreters.

**ComNet International,** 31255 Cedar Valley, Ste. 212, Westlake Village, CA 91362 Phone:(818)991-1277 Fax:(818)991-1699
Website: comnetint.com Contact: Dr. Elias Agel
Founded 1989. Member: ATA. Translates all languages, in all subjects. Pro-spective translators should have extensive experience and should provide references. Resumes are reviewed and entered into a database. The company also provides desktop publishing, art production and printing services. It also does voice-overs and dubbing. Specialties include Middle East consulting services, electronic update filing and interagency network cooperation. Maintains a pool of 600 translators.

**Comprehensive Language Center**, 4200 Wilson Blvd., Ste. 950, Arlington VA 22203 Phone: (703)247-0700 Fax: (703)247-4295
e-mail: kjdresen@comlang.com Website: www.comlang.com
Contact: Kelly Jones Dresen
Company founded 1980 as CACI. Member: ATA. uses freelance translators and interpreters. Accepted unsolicited resumes, but not unsolicited phone calls. Qualified applicants are sent a database form which is processed and are called upon when needed in their area of expertise. Requirements include college degree, 2 years professional experience as linguist, or appropriate certification/ specialized degree. Over 100 languages. Main areas are technical, legal, promotional, business. Company also does training, transcription, software and web page localization, and video narration.

**Continental Communications Agency,** 5105 E. Los Angeles Ave. #145
Simi Valley, CA 93063 Phone:(805)527-4446 Fax:(805)527-4460 e-mail:
cca1@adelphia.net or cca_inc@ix.netcom.com
Contact: Peter Charbonneau Member: ATA

**Continental Interpreting Services, Inc**., 3111 N. Tustin Ave., Ste. 235,
Orange, CA 92865 Phone:(800)201-7121 Fax:(714)283-9045
e_mail: veronica@wespeakyourlanguage.com
Web site: www.wespeakyourlanguage.com
Contact: Veronica Amador Member: ATA

**Copper Translation Service,** 18 Joseph Lane, Gansevoort, NY 12831
Phone: (518)691-0155 Fax: (518)691-0157
e-mail: angelos@coppertranslation.com
Web site: www.coppertranslation.com
Contact: Angelos G. Tzelepis
Company founded 1971. Member: ATA. Uses freelance translators and interpreters. Accepts unsolicited resumes. Applicant must be native speaker of target language. Main areas are technical legal, medical, and business. Over 700 translators in pool.

**Corporate Translations**, 1300 Aviation Blvd., Redondo Beach, CA 90278
Phone: (860)450-0405 Fax: (860)450-0409

e-mail:ctoomey@corptrans.inc.com Website: www.orptrans.inc.com
Contact: Carolyn Toomey
Founded 1995. Member: ATA

**Cosmopolitan Business Communication**, 8025 Marshall Circle, Arvada, CO 80003 Phone: (303)422-6702 Contact: Maya León Meis

**Cosmopolitan Translation Bureau**, 53 West Jackson Blvd., Ste. 1260, Chicago, IL 60604 Phone: (312) 726-2610 Fax: (312)427-8591
Contact: Emanuel H. Steen Member: ATA

**Coto Interpreting, Translating & Graphics**, 447 Burchett St., 2nd Floor, Glendale, CA 91203 Phone: (818)551-4545 Fax: (818)551-1123
Contact: Melanie Coto-Trevor Member: ATA

**Course Crafters,** 44 Merrimac St., Newburyport, MA 01950
Phone: (978)465-2040 Fax: (978)465-5027
E-mail: LBRagan@coursecrafters.com Web site: www.coursecrafters.com
Contact: Lise B. Ragan Member: ATA

**Creo International**, 520 Marquette Ave., Ste. 700, Minneapolis, MN 55402
Phone: (612)342-9800 Fax: (612)342-9745
e-mail:cthudson@creo-works.com Website: www.creo-works.com
Contact: Christa Tiefenbacher Member: ATA

**Counterpoint Language Consultants, Inc.**, P.O. Box 6184: Bridgewater, NJ 08807 Phone: (908)231-0991 Fax: (908)231-266
E-mail: ctpt@ctpt.net Web Page: www.ctpt.net
Contact: Erik Greb
Founded 1979. Member: ATA. Company uses freelance translators and interpreters. Accepts unsolicited resumes. Main languages (both ways) are French, German, Spanish, Chinese, Japanese, Portuguese, Italian, Russian, Greek and Hindi. Also Thai, Gujarati and Slovak. Main Areas are pharmaceuticals, telecom and legal. Provides worldwide language training.

**Cross Cultural Communications Systems, Inc:** 10 Converse Place, P.O. Box 860, Winchester, MA 01890 Phone: 781-729-3736 ext.110
Fax: 781-729-1217 E-mail: vphillips@cccsorg.com
Contact: Vonessa Phillips; Member: ATA

**Crossword Translation & Interpreting,** 16350 Park Ten Place, Ste. 201,
Houston, TX 77084 Phone: (281) 578-1300 Fax: (281) 578-1334
e-mail:language@crosswordtranslation.com
Contact: Office Staff
Founded 1997. Member: ATA. Accepts resumes. Translates and interprets most languages in all fields. Uses many translators and interpreters.

**Cybertec USA, Inc.,** 153 W. Westfield Ave., Roselle Park, NJ 07204-1816
Phone: (908)245-3305 Fax: (908)245-5434
E-mail: mail@cybertecusa.com Web site: www.cybertecusa.com
Contact: Joseph Nunes
Technical Translation Bureau founded in 1990. Member: ATA, NYCT. Uses in-house and freelance professional translators. Accepts unsolicited resumes. Resumes are filed by language and specialty. Translators are required to be experienced, professional translators, preferably with language or other diploma and accreditation/certification. Translates mainly Portuguese (Euro, African and Brazilian) and Western European languages. Specialized in technical and commercial subjects, including many industries, petroleum, biotech. Does over 4 million words per year. Over 100 translators in company's pool. Offices in the USA and Portugal.

**CyraCom International Inc.**, 7330 N Oracle Rd., Tucson, AZ 85704
Phone: (520)745-9447 Fax: (520)745-9022 Website: www.cyracom.com
Contact: Paul Burns
Company founded 1997. Member: ATA. Provides telephonic inter-pretation services on demand 24 hours a day, 7 days a week in about 150 languages. Has a secure system that provides rapid access to interpreters.

## -D-

**DFP Translating Service**, 42 Frederick Place, Bergenfield, NJ 07621
Phone: (201)343-2258 Fax: (201)343-4155
e-mail: info@ translationservices.net
Website: www.translationservices.net Contact: Doris Pacheco

**DTS Language Services, Inc.**, 308 W. Rosemary St., Ste. 210, Chapel Hill, NC 27516 Phone: (800)524-0722 Fax: (919)942-0686
e-mail: sales@dtstrans.com Website: www.dtstrans.com
Contact: Lucia Apollo Shaw
Founded 1972. Member: ATA, DIA, STC. Accepts resumes only electronically. Requires 5 years min. professional technical translation experience with related degree. Translates mainly Portuguese, French, Spanish, German, Italian, Czech, Vietnamese, Japanese, and Korean. Also Dutch, Finnish, Norwegian, Swedish. Mainly technical, medical, marketing, patents.

**Detroit Translation Bureau**, 30800 Telegraph Rd., Ste.1930, Bingham Farms, MI 48025 Phone: (248)593-6710 Fax: (248)593-6720
e-mail: info@dtbonline.com Website: www.dtbonline.com
Founded 1946. Member: ATA, LISA, SAW. Accepts resumes. Translates mainly Spanish (Mexico, Spain), Canadian French, German, Japanese, Italian, Norwegian, Dutch, Finnish and Korean. Mainly automotive – technical, training and marketing. Uses hundreds of translators.

**Digital Publishing, Inc.**, 1805 Hicks Rd., Rolling Meadows, IL 60008
Phone: (847)776-0200 Fax: (847)776-0249
e-mail: translation@digitalpub.com Website: www.digital pub.com
Contact: Debbie Shulman

**Digitek International, Inc./SAKHR**, 7631 Leesburg Pike, Ste. B, Fall Church, VA 22043 Phone: (703)883-0134 Fax: (703)883-0137
Contact: Youb Benyoucef
**Diplomatic Language Services**, 1901 N. 19th St., Ste. 600, Arlington, VA 22209 Phone:(703)243-4856 Fax:(703)358-9189
e-mail: resume@dls-inc.com Website: www.dls-inc.com
Founded 1985. Member: ATA, NCATA, NAJIT. Accepts resumes. Requires 5 years professional experience. Translates all languages. Provides all translation and interpretation services as well as language training.

**DocuTrans, Inc.,** 4712 S. 2675 W, Roy, UT 84067
Phone: (801)916-3924 Fax: (801)776-4027
e-mail: translate@docutrans.com Web site: www.docutrans.com
Contact: Gabariele H. Johnson Member: ATA

**Dragon Crest Associates, Inc.**, 11026 Ventura Blvd., Ste. 10, Studio City, CA 91604 Phone: (800)240-6601 Fax: (818)755-8959
e-mail: language@worldnet.att.com
Contact: Dan Prescott Member: ATA

## -E-

**800-Translate**, 865 United Nations Plaza, New York, NY 10017
Phone: (800)872-6752 Fax: (888)872-6752
Website: www.800-translate.com Contact: Ken Clark

**echo international**, Three Gateway Center, Floor 14 W, Pittsburgh, PA 15222 Phone: (412) 261-1101 Fax: (412) 261-1159
e-mail: dutka@echotrans.com Contact: Leslie A. Dutka

**Echo Translation**, P.O. Box 15301, Minneapolis, MN 55415
Phone: (612) 822-3473 Fax: (612)339-2122 e-mail: echobea@aol.com
Contact: Bea Cabrera

**Eiber Translations** 65-11 174th St., Fresh Meadows, NY 11365
Phone: (718) 463-2900 Fax: (718) 359-4073 e-mail: ibertrans@aol.com
Contact: Edna H. Eiber

**El Andar Translations**, P.O. Box 7745, Santa Cruz, CA 95061
Phone: (831) 457_8353 Fax: (831) 457_8354
e-mail: translations@elandar.com Web site: www.elandar.com
Contact: Marga Vaquer

**eLocale, Inc.,** 815 Park Blvd., Ste. 255, Boise, ID 83712
Phone: (208)336-5530 Fax: (208)336-6445info@

elocale.com Web site: www.elocale.com
Contact: Cary Clark

**Eriksen Translations Inc.,** 32 Court St., 20th Fl., Brooklyn, NY 11201
Phone: (718) 802-9010 Fax: (718) 802-0041
e_mail: info@erikseninc.com Web site: www.erikseninc.com
Contact: Leah Ruggiero
Founded 1986. Member: ATA, NYCT, STC. Translates into and from all major languages. Emphasis on Legal, Financial, Advertising, Education, Pharmaceutical and Health Care. Translators are encouraged to register on Web site. The company also provides typesetting services and Web site globalization. Maintains a pool of 3000 translators.

**eTranslations,** 1930 Village Center Circle #3-930, Las Vegas, Nevada 89134
Phone: 1-888-262-3468 (USA only) / (303)388-4488 Fax: (303)388-2255
E-mail: info@etranslations.com Web site: www.etranslations.com
Contact: Desiree Blum

**Eurasia International**, 16530 Ventura Blvd., Ste. 206, Encino, CA 91436 Phone: (818)907-9718 Fax; (818)907-9763
e-mail: VMordukhay@worldnet.att.net Website: www.eurasia-usa.com
Contact: Violetta Mordukhay
Founded 1993. Member: ATA. Accepts resumes. Translates mainly Spanish, German, Hebrew, Russian, French, Arabic, Farsi and Indonesian. Also Romanina, Slovak, Malay, Japanese, Polish, Czech and Chinese. Mostly immigration, legal, and book publishing. Pool of over 200 translators.

**Eureka-Foreign College Evaluators & Translators,** 6601 W. Irving Park Rd., Ste. 204, Chicago, IL 60634
Phone:(773)545-1700 Fax:(773)545-1716
e-mail: eureka@interaccess.com Website: www.polishtranslations.com
Contact: Maria Drewicz, Executive Director

Founded 1992. Member: ATA, The Translators and Interpreters Guild. Translates Polish, both from and into English, and German and Spanish into English. Emphasis on University Admission Documents, Immigration & Naturalization, Business, Technical, Medical and Legal translation. Prospective translators should have IBM-compatible PC, Word Perfect 5.1 DOS or Windows, minimum Bachelor's Degree. Resumes are reviewed, and qualified persons contacted. The company specializes in credential evaluation and Polish-American consulting services for business cooperation, cultural and marketing advisement, and is currently looking for Polish translators and interpreters. Maintains a pool of 10 translators.

**EuroNet Language Services**, 295 Madison Ave., 45th Fl., New York, NY 10017 Phone:(212)271-0401 Fax:(212)271-0404
e-mail: euronet@mindspring.com
Contact: Anouk, HRM
Founded 1989. Member: NYCT, ATA. Uses freelance translators and interpreters. Accepts unsolicited resumes. Translates Spanish, French, Portuguese, Italian, Dutch, German, Swedish, and other European languages, both from and into English. Translates all subjects. Prospective translators must be native speakers with bilingual capacity in English and possess a university degree. Resumes are reviewed and added to a database. Maintains a pool of 300 translators.

**Eurotext Translations Rosetta Stone,** 34 Franklin St., Ste. 200A, Nashua, NH 03063 Phone: (603)883-9388 Fax: (603)595-8673
e-mail: translate@rosettastoneinc.net
Web site: www.etrosettastoneinc.com
Contact: John Furey, CVO
Founded 1972. Member: GALA, STC, NHITA. Accepts resumes. Translates all major languages including French, Italian, German, Spanish, Russian, Chinese, Japanese, Arabic, Portuguese and Greek. Mostly industrial, medical, legal, scientific, marketing, computers, software and localization. Also provides the following services: interpretering, voice_overs, localization, language instruction and cross-cultural training. Aquired by Eurotext Translations, Dublin, Ireland in October 2002.

**Excel Translations, Inc.**, 660 Market St., Ste. 206, San Francisco, CA 94104 Phone: (415)434-4224 Fax: (415)434-4221
e-mail: info@xltrans. com Web site: www.xltrans.com
Contact: Hervé Rodriguez
Founded 1995. Offices in California, Pennsylvania and Spain. Member: ATA, NCTA, STC, HTML Guild. ISO 9001:2000 certified. Translates into and from all major European and Asian languages. Emphasis on Software Localization and Life Sciences. Prospective translators should have three years' translation experience and a specialty field. They should be native speakers and have access to the Internet. Most translations done using TM tools. Applicants will need to take a test. Resumes are screened and entered into a database if test is successful. Applicants are notified by postcard. The company works with both freelancers and in_house translators and provides full DTP services. Maintains a pool of 1,000 translators.

**Executive Linguist Agency, Inc**., 500 S. Sepulveda Blvd., Ste. 300, Manhattan Beach, CA 90266 Phone: (310)376-1409 Fax (310)376-9285 e-mail: mail@executivelinguist.com Website: www.executivelinguist.com Contact: Ronald R. Randolph

**Expert Translators,** 10621 N. Kendall Drive, Ste. 111, Miami, FL 33176. Phone: (305)279-8353 Fax: (305)273-4407
e-mail: experttranslators.com Website: www.experttranslators.com
Contact: Emily Correal

## -F-

**FLS, Inc.,** 3609 A-5 Memorial Parkway SW, Huntsville AL 35801
Phone: (205)881-1120 Fax: (205)880-1112
e-mail: mail@flstranslation.com Website: www.flstranslation.com
Contact: Judith H. Smith
Company founded 1979. Member: ATA. Uses freelance translators and interpreters. Unsolicited resumes accepted. Translates over 60 languages, mainly Japanese, Spanish, French, Chinese, Korean, German and East European languages. Mostly technical and legal. Over 200 translators.

**Federal News Service**, 620 National Press Building NW, Washington, DC 20045 Phone: (202)347-1400 Fax: (202)626-2630
e-mail: info@fednews.com Website: www.fednews.com
Contact: Marina Makanova
Founded 1987. Accepts resumes. Requires college degree. Translates mainly Spanish, French, Russian, Chinese, and Arabic. Uses 63 translators. The company is a news wire that provides government transcripts, online newsclipping, news monitoring services, and translations in almost any language.

**First Translation Services**, 3072 Brighton, 1st St., Brooklyn, NY 11235
Phone: (718)372-7723 Fax: (718)265-6653
Contact: Jack Kleyman Member: ATA

**Foreign Exchange Translations, Inc.**, One Richmond Square, Providence, RI 02906 Phone: (401)454-0787 Fax: (401)454-0789
e-mail: adnresh@fxtrans.com Website: www.fxtrans.com
Contact: Andres Heuberger Member: ATA

**Foreign Ink, Ltd.**, 5735 Washburn Ave. S, Minneapolis MN 55410 Phone: 612)920-4884 Fax: (612)924-9075
e-mail: greg@fornink.com Web site: fornink.com
Contact: Gregory Stricherz Member: ATA

## -G-

**GES Translation Services,** 836 Manhattan Ave., Brooklyn, NY 11222
Phone: (718)389-8453 Fax: (718)389-4442 e-mail:ges@flashcom.net
Contact: Richard Rzeznik

**Garcia-Shilling International,** 1402 Corinth, L.B. 139, Dallas, TX 75215
Phone: (214)428-4428 Fax: (214)428-4458
e-mail: acento@swbell.net Contact: Luis A. Garcia, Sr.

**Gene Mayer Associates**, 9 Depot St., 2nd Fl., Milford, CT 06460
Phone: (203)882-5990 Fax: (203)882-5995
e-mail: info@design4language.com
Founded 1985. Member: ATA, AIGA, Design Management Institute, National Investor Relations Institute, CT Art Directors Club. Provides graphic design, translation and production of complex printed material used by global corporations. Emphasis on business (employee information, annual reports, marketing brochures, corporate policy manuals). The firms handles translation, design, book layout and production in 30 languages. Prefers to work with agencies or with translators with a qualified track record with large corporate clients.

**Geneva Worldwide Inc;** 62 West 22nd Street, New York, NY 10010 Phone: (212)255-8400 Fax: (212)255-8409;
E-mail: genevaworldwide@aol.com
Web Page: www.genevaworldwide.com
Contact: Craig Buckstein, VP Operations.
Member: GSA, ATA, NAJIT, RID, NYCT, OGS. Geneva Worldwide was founded in 1903. They translate Spanish, Creole, Chinese (T+S), Arabic, Polish, Korean, Bengali, Urdu, Russian, Albanian. In addition they also translate 180 more languages. Their main subjects are business, medical, legal, general, technical, and financial. They specialize in various types of translation. They do accept freelance along with resumes. The resumes are filed by language and coded by experience and SME. Requirements for applicants are professional resumes. Geneva Worldwide provides face to face interpretation and document translation in over 180 different languages. They provide multilingual services to many Federal, State, City and Private agencies. They have several hundred translators in their pool.

**The Geo Group**, 6 Odana Court, Ste. 205, Madison, WI 53719
Phone: (608)230-1000 Fax: (608)230-1010

e-mail: translation@thegeogroup.com Website: www.thegeogroup.com
Contact: Translation Manager
Founded 1991. Accepts resumes. Requires min. 3 years translation/inter-preting experience. Main languages are French, German, Hmong, Italian, Portuguese, Spanish, Japanese, Chinese and Dutch. Also other European languages. Main subjects are medical, automotive, marketing, computers, dairy equipment, legal and audio/video. Uses a pool of over 500 translators.

**Geotext Translations,** 259 W. 30th St. 17th Floor, New York, NY 10001
Phone: (202)631-7432 Fax: (202)631-7407
e-mail: translations@geotext.com Web site: www.geotext.com
Contact: Randon Burns

**German Language Services**, 2658 48th Ave., SW, Seattle, WA 98116
Phone: (206)938-3600 Fax: (206)938-8308
e-mail: GermanLanguage@GermanLanguageServices.com
Web site: www.GermanLanguageServices.com
Contact: Maia Costa
Founded 1979. Member: ATA, NOTIS, GACC. Accepts resumes only in electronic form. Requires formal training in translation or interpretation and 5 years experience. Only translates German.

**Global Advanced Translation Services, Inc**., 501 S. Fairfax Ave., #212, Los Angeles, CA 90036
Phone: (323)937-1525 Fax: (323)937-6568 e-mail: mteper@aol.com
Contact: Marina Teper Member: ATA
Founded 1979. Member: ATA, NOTIS, GACC. Accepts resumes in electronic form. Requires training in translation or interpretation and 5 years experience. Only translates German.

**The Global Institute of Languages and Culture, Inc.**, 7301 NW 4th st., Ste. 110, Plantation, FL 33317 Phone: (954)327-1662 Fax: (955)327-8116 e-mail: globalin@gate.net Website: www.globalinstitute.com
Contact: Antonieta Mercado
Member: ATA. Translates Spanish, Portuguese, Italian, French, German, etc., both from and into English. Emphasis on General, Computer, Medical and Legal translation. Prospective translators should have a college degree, experience, and should be native speakers of the target language. Resumes are responded to based on the applicant's qualifications and the company's needs. Maintains a pool of 20 translators.

**Global Languages & Cultures, Inc.**, 680 N. Lake Shore Drive, Ste. 919, Chicago, IL 60611 Phone: (312)981-4444
Fax: (312)981-4445
e-mail: yozturk@e-translation.com Website: www.e-translation.com
Contact: Sedef Olcer

**Global Language Solutions/The Russian Word, Inc.**, 19800 MacArthur Blvd., Ste. 520, Irvine, CA 92612
e-mail: info@globallanguages.com Website: www.globallanguages.com
Contact: Inna Kassatkina

**Global Translation Systems Inc.**, 910 Airport Rd., Chapel Hill, NC 27514 Phone:(919)967-2010 Fax:(919)929-1333
e-mail: mike@globaltranslation.com Website: www.globaltranslation.com
Contact: Michael Collins Member: ATA

**Global Visions LLC,** 900 Commonwealth Place, Suite # 218., Virginia Beach, VA 23464 Phone: (757)495-3719
Fax: (757)495-6398
e-mail: globalvisions48@msn.com
Contact: Kristi B. Emerson Member: ATA

**The Global Word**, Inc., 63 Grand Ave., River Edge, NJ 07661
Phone: (201)343-0015 Fax: (201)343-4155
e-mail: info@globalword.com Website: www.globalword.com

Contact: Michael Fundaro  Member: ATA

**Global Works.Com**, 129 W. 27th St., New York, NY 10001
Phone; (212)414-1300  Fax: (212)414-8700
e-mail: emantello@globalworks.com Website: www.globalworks.com
Contact: Elisabeth Mantello  Member: ATA

**Go Global Translations, Inc**., 19515 Rosedale Ave., Excelsior, MN 55331  Phone: (952)474-6413 Fax: (952)474-3756
e-mail:TeresaGoGlobal@cs.com Website: www.goglobalranslations.com
Contact: Teresa A. Crespo  Member: ATA

**The Golf Channel, Inc.**, 7580 Commerce Center Drive, Orlando, FL 32819  Phone: (407)248-3344 Fax: (407)248-1344
e-mail: jkrisand@tgcinc.com
Contact: James R. Krisanda  Member: ATA

## -H-

**H&K Translations, LLC**, 701 Brickell Ave., Suite 3000, Miami, FL 33131  Phone: (305)789-7521 Fax: (305)789-7799
Contact: Maury M. Scharrer  Member: ATA

**Health Outcomes Group**, 3600 West Bayshore Road, Suite 106, Palo Alto, California 94303  Tel: (650) 858-8033
Fax: (650) 858-8034
e-mail: david_himmelberger@healthoutcomesgroup.com
www.healthoutcomesgroup.com

**Hernandez & Garcia, LLC**, 7360 N. Lincoln Ave., Ste. 100, Lincolnwood, IL 60712  Phone: (847)676-4445 Fax: (847)676-1420
e-mail: mhernandez@hernandezgarcia.com
Contact: Maritza Hernandez  Member: ATA

**Hightech Passport Limited**, 1590 Oakland Rd., Ste. B202, San Jose, CA 95131 Phone: (408)453-6303 Fax: (408)453-9434
e-mail: magdalena@htpassport.com Website: www.htpassport.com
Contact: Magdalena Enea, VP of Market Development
Founded 1992. Member: ATA, NCTA. Translates French, German, Spanish, Italian, Portuguese, Swedish, Dutch, Russian, Japanese, Chinese, and all Scandinavian from English. Emphasis on Computer Software, Documentation (both printed and online), Marketing Materials, Tapes, and Computer Training Literature translations. Complete range of internationalization and localization services, mainly to IT and medical industry. The company also provides software localization and testing, videotape localization, and desktop printing services. Maintains a pool of 150 translators.

**Honda R&D North America, Inc.**, 21001 State Route 739, Raymond,
OH 43067  Phone: (513)645-6164  Fax: (513)645-6341
e-mail: knason@oh.hra.com  Contact: Kay T. Nason

## -I-

**IDEM Translation**, 550 S. California Ave., Ste. 310, Palo Alto, CA 94306
Phone: (650)329-0170  Fax: (650)329-0266
e-mail: idem@compuserve.com
Contact: Mariam Nayiny  Member: ATA

**ISI**, 3501 Market St., Philadelphia, PA 19104
Phone: (215)386-0100 Fax: (215)243-2208
e-mail: ellen.boyar@isinet.com Website: www.isinet.com
Contact: Ellen A. Boyar

**ISI (Interpreting Services International Inc.)**, 6180 Laurel Canyon Blvd., #245, N. Hollywood, CA 91606 Phone: (818)753-9181 Fax: (818)753-9617 e-mail: info@isitrans.com
Contact: Cathi Rimalower

**INAWORD**, 811 W. 7th St., Ste. 204, Los Angeles, CA 90017
Phone: (213)688-6200 Fax: (800)805-7994
e-mail: info@inaword.net Website: www.inaword.net
Contact: Stella Fridman Member: ATA

**Information Builders, Inc.**, Two Penn Plaza, New York, NY 10121
Phone: (212)736-4433 Fax: (212)967-6404 Website: www.ibi.com
Contact: Georgina Channer Member: ATA
**Inline Translation Services, Inc.**, 100 W. Broadway, Suite 520, Glendale, CA 91210 Tel: (818)547-4995 Fax: (818)547-4013 www.inlinela.com

**Inlingua Language & Intercultural Services**, 15500 Wayzata Blvd., Suite 819, Wayzata, MN 55391 Phone: (952)929-9155 Fax: (952)929-0020
e-mail: info@inlingua-mn.com
Web site: www.inlingua.com/minneapolis.htm
Contact: Carolyn Leavenworth Meyers Member: ATA

**Inlingua Translation Service,** 95 Summit Ave., Summit, NJ 07901
Phone: (908)522-0622 Fax: (908)522-1433 e-mail: summit@inlingua.com
Contact: Erica Alicea
Founded 1968. Uses freelance translators and interpreters. Accepts unsolicited resumes. Resumes are kept on file for future jobs. Applicants must have computer, fax, and modem. Ten top languages are Spanish, French,Italian, Portuguese, Russian, German, Chinese, Japanese, Danish, and Polish. Also translates Korean and Romanian. Main areas are lincenses, birth certificates, and transcripts. Has pool of some 30 translators.Operates as language school with translation services.

**Inlingua, Inc.,** 171 East Ridgewood Ave., Ridgewood, NJ 07450 Phone: (201)444-9500 Fax: (201)444-0116
E-mail: ridgewood@inlingua.com Web site: www.inlingua.com, 2nd website: www.inlinguanorthnj.com
Contact: Sandra Stern, Translation Services Coordinator
Founded 1977. Member: ATA. Accepts resumes from translators and interpreters.. Requires ATA accreditation. Main languages are Spanish, French, Portuguese, German, Italian, Chinese, Japanese, Russian, and Arabic. Also Hindi, Hungarian, Polish, Romanian and Dutch Czech, Serbo-Croation, Haitain-Creole, French Canadian. Mainly legal, pharmaceutical, financial. Additional subjects that we translate: websites, medical, cosmetics,electronics subjects, tape transcriptions. Uses some 150 translators.

**Intermark Language Services Coporation,** 2555 Cumberland Pkwy, Ste. 295, Atlanta, GA 30339 Phone: (770)444-3055 Fax: (770)444-3002
e-mail: info@intermark-languages.com
Website: www.intermark-languages.com
Contact: Tom West
Founded 1995. Member: ATA. Accepts resumes. Interested in translators with with a law or business degree. Translates mainly French, Spanish, German, Portuguese and Swedish. Emphasis is on Law and Business translation. Prospective translators *must* provide a sample translation in every combination they wish to translate; ATA accreditation is preferred.

**InterNation, Inc.,** 299 Broadway, Ste. 1400, New York, NY 10007
Phone:(212)619-5545 Fax: (212) 619-5887
e-mail: info@internationinc. com Web site: www.internationinc.com

Founded 1990. Member: ATA, NYCT. Uses freelance translators and interpreters. Accepts unsolicited resumes. Prospective translators are invited to register themselves in the online database at www.internationinc.com. All applicable database forms must be filled out completely. Translates from and into all major languages, but predominantly works with Spanish, Portuguese, Italian, French, German, Japanese, Chinese, Russian, Korean, Arabic, Polish, Dutch and the Scandinavian languages. InterNation specializes in foreign language voiceovers and subtitling for corporate sales, image, training, safety, advertising videos and informercials as well as documentaries. Maintains a state-of-the-art digital recording studio in-house and has an online voice talent database with audio samples of 400 native language voice actors in over 40 languages. Employs narrators and character actors mainly in the New York City area. Also translates commercial, financial, legal, technical, scientific, medical, pharmaceutical, PR material and advertising copy. Maintains a pool of some 5,000 translators.

**International Bureau of Translations, Inc,** 10291 North Meridian St.,
Ste. 350, Indianapolis, IN 46290 Phone: (317)581-0060 Fax: (317)
581-1160 e-mail: ibtinc@ibtworld.com Web site: www.ibtworld.com
Contact: Demetria Gecewicz
Founded 1976. Member: OTIAQ, Indianapolis Chamber of Commerce, IUPUI, Indiana University. Translated 56 languages last year. Emphasis on Medical, Technical, Legal, Business and Personal Document translation. Prospective translators should be native speakers with access to a computer, modem, or fax. They should send a rate chart with their resume. Resumes are filed and the translator contacted as the need arises. In addition to translation and desktop publishing, the company does foreign videos, court interpretation, cultural presentations, and conducts language classes. They research the cultural acceptability of company names, product names and slogans, and are the official translators for the International Violin Competition. Maintains a pool of 150 translators.

**International Communication by Design, Inc.,** 1726 North First St., Milwaukee, WI 53212 Phone:(414)265-2171
Fax:(212)265-2101
e-mail: info@icdtranslation.com Website: www.icdtranslation.com
Contact: Jennifer Marquardt, Office Manager
Founded 1991. Member: ATA, Wisconsin World Trade Center, STC. Translates mainly Italian, Spanish, French, German, Portuguese, Dutch, Arabic, Greek, Japanese and Chinese. Also Korean, Russian and Swedish. Emphasis on Technical Manuals, medical and Legal translation. Also website localization. Prospective translators should be native speakers and ATA accredited, with a specific area of expertise and must be able to send projects in via CompuServe. Resumes are filed and used as a resource for new translators, interpreters and typesetters. It is a translation service company with a wide range of clients, from large corporations to smaller cottage industries. The company is actively community involved. Maintains a pool of over 60 translators.

**International Contact, Inc.,** 351 15th St., Oakland, CA 94612
Phone:(510)836-1180 Fax:(510)835-1314
e-mail: info@intlcontact.com Web site: www.intlcontact.com
Contact: Carla Itzkowich Member: ATA

**International Effectiveness Centers**, 360 Pine St., 3rd Floor, San Francisco, CA 94104 Phone:(415)788-4149
Fax:(415)788-4829
e-mail: iec@ie-center.com Website: www.ie-center.com
Contact: Taryk Rouchdy
Founded 1972. Member: ATA, NCTA. Translates Spanish, Chinese, Russian, and Portuguese, both from and into English, French and Vietnamese from English, and Japanese into English. Emphasis on Legal, Technical and Children's Book translation. Uses freelance translators and interpreters. Accept unsolicited resumes. Prospective translators must have at least 3 years experience and be tested unless they hold current ATA accreditation. Resumes are screened for qualifications and appropriate equipment and, if qualified, entered into a data base The company also does desktop publishing in all languages, as well as voiceovers, dubbing, promotional work, crosscultural and language training, and international business consulting. Maintains a pool of 7000 translators in its data base, 170 of whom are used regularly.

**International Institute of Wisconsin,** 1110 N. Old World 3rd St.,
Milwaukee, WI 83203 Phone: (414)225-6220 Fax: (414)225-6235
E-mail: iiw@exepc.com Web site: www.iiwisconsin.org
Contact: Alexander P. Durtka, Jr.

**International Language Center**, 1416 S. Big Bend Blvd., St. Louis, MO 63117 Phone: (314)647-8888 Fax: (314)647-8889

e-mail: ilc@ilcworldwide.com Website: www.ilcworldwide.com
Contact: Dede S. Brunetti

**International Language Services, Inc.,** 5810 Baker Rd., Ste. 250, Minnetonka, MN 55345 Phone: (612)672-9600 Fax: (612)672-9400
e-mail: info@ilstranslations.com Web site: www.ilstranslations.com
Contact: John Funk
Founded 1982. Translates Spanish, French, German, Italian, Portuguese, Japanese, Swedish, Dutch, Danish, Chinese and most other languages from English. Emphasis on Medical, Technical, Business and Legal translation.Prospective translators should have ATA accreditation, references, a minimum 3_5 years experience, and be native speakers of the target language. Resumes are read and filed by language. Their primary focus is on biomedical instrumentation. Maintains a pool of over 300 translators.

**International Language Source, Inc.,** P.O. Box 338, Holland, OH 43528
Phone:(419)865-4374 Fax:(419)865-7725
e-mail: ilsource@adelphia.net Web site: www.ilsource.com
Contact: Ryan Stevens, Account Manager
Founded 1981. Member: TAITA, ATA. Uses freelance translators and interpreters. Accepts unsolicited resumes. Prospective translators should have a specialty area and the appropriate resources for projects in that area. Resumes are kept for 6 months in an active database. Contact may involve the paid translation of a short sample. Translates mainly French, Spanish, German, Italian and Chinese. Also Japanese, Portuguese and Hebrew. Emphasis on Glass Manufacturing and Retail, Automotive OEM and Aftermarket, Furniture, Legal, Industrial and Healthcare translation. In addition to translation services, the company provides video and interactive CD-ROM translation and voiceovers. The company is willing to consider internships and cooperative projects with other translation companies.

**International Translating & Typesetting Company**, 2730 Stemmons Freeway, Ste. 302, Dallas, TX 75207-2248
Phone:(214)630-0840
Fax: (214)630-6482 e-mail: 102462.161@compuserve.com
Contact: Javier Galdeano, Translation Manager
Founded 1969. Member: Greater Dallas Chamber of Commerce. Translates Spanish, Chinese, French, German, Arabic, Russian, Japanese, Portuguese, Korean, Vietnamese, Bulgarian, Cambodian, Serbo-Croatian, Czech, Danish, Dutch, Farsi, Finnish, Greek, Gujarati, Hebrew, Hindi, Indonesian, Kurdish, Latin, Norwegian, Polish, Punjabi, Romanian, Hungarian, Swedish, Tagalog, Thai, Turkish, Ukrainian, and Urdu, both from and into English. Emphasis on Petroleum, Electronics, Legal, Business, Advertising, Food Export, Chemical, and Civil Engineering translations. Prospective translators must accept work *only* from translation companies, and *never directly from end users*. They must have either IBM or Macintosh computers, a modem and a fax. Resumes are filed until a need arises. In addition to translation, the company also provides high-resolution typesetting in most languages. Maintains a pool of 200 translators.

**International Translating Bureau**, 16125 West 12 Mile Rd., Southfield, MI 48076-2912 Phone:(248)559-1677
Fax:(248)559-1679
e-mail: itbinc @itbtranslations.com
Contact: Mariano Pallarés, President
Founded 1977. Translates all language pairs. Emphasis on Automotive, Engineering, Machine Tool, Legal, Medical, and Public Relations translation. Prospective translators should be native speakers of the target language, have at least 5 years residence in the source-language country, and have academic training or on-job experience in a specialized field. Candidates must have computer, fax and current software, particularly WordPerfect and Word for Windows for PC or Mac. Re-sumes are scanned for qualifications in which the company is interested and filed for future use. The company offers accurate, native-like translations. Maintains a pool of 250 translators.

**International Translation Service**, P.O. Box 188331, Sacramento, CA 95818 Phone: (530)753-7482 Fax: (530)753-7482
E-mail: its@yolo.com Web site: www.geocities.com/its worldwide Contact: Garry Pratt
Founded 1970. Uses freelance translators and interpreters. Accepts unsolicited résumés. Prospective translators must be experienced in both their languages and specialty fields, and should possess a variety of means of communications, including phone, fax and e-mail; they should have computers with the appropriate language fonts. Résumés are filed by language. Translates mainly Scandinavian, German, Spanish, and French, and also Estonian, Irish, Italian, Russian, Finnish, Portuguese, Polish, Dutch and more. Translates mainly legal, scientific, commercial, and medical. Maintains a pool of some 80 translators.

**International Translation Solutions (ITS)**, 990 Lumber Exchange Building, 10 South 5th Street, Minneapolis, MN

55402
Phone: (612) 339-4660 General e-mail: translate@intransol.com
Web site: http://www.intransol.com
Contact: Jason Wood, President and CEO
Founded 1989. Member: ATA, STC, NADTP, GBCC. ITS translates all major languages to and from English. Emphasis on technical, medical, legal, B to B, advertising and marketing materials. Prospective translators must have professional experience, be subject pecialized and be proficient with TRADOS or other CAT tools. Submit resumes to hr@intransol.com. ITS also provides multilingual typesetting and desktop publishing, graphic design, and audio and video production services. Maintains a pool of over 3,000 translators

**Interpretations, Inc.,** 8665 W. 96th St., Ste. 201, Overland Park, KS 66212 Phone: (913)338-2434 Fax: (913)338-2636
e-mail: interp@accessus.net Web site: www.exactwords.com
Contact: Gloria J. Donohue
Founded 1991. Member: ATA, MICATA, International Trade Club, International Relations Council, Women's Resources Network. Translates mainly Spanish, French, German, Portuguese, Russian, Dutch, Swedish and Italian. Also Danish, Finnish and Korean. Emphasis on Instructional and Technical, Legal, Advertising, Video Script and Educational Materials translation. Prospective translators must be native speakers and have five years' experience; ATA accreditation is a must. They should be up_to_date on hardware and software. Resumes are reviewed and filed; a select number are asked to provide samples of their work and/or translate short paragraphs. The company also provides interpreters for meetings, conferences and telephone conferencing. Maintains a pool of about 100 translators.

**Interpreters' Index.com**, P.O. Box 880872, San Diego, CA 92168
Phone: (619)850-8279 Fax: (619)334-9473
e-mail: info@interpretersindex.com
Website: www.interpretersindex.com
Contact: Juana Esther Blanco Member: ATA

**InterSol, Inc.,**Three Point Drive, Ste. 301, Brea, CA 92821
Phone: (714)671-9180 Fax: (714)671-9188
email: solutions@intersolinc.com Website: intersolinc.com
Contact: Susana Turbitt
Founded 1996. Member: ATA. Accepts resumes. Translates mainly French, Italian, German, Spanish, Portuguese, Japanese, Chinese, Danish, Swedish and Finnish. Mostly medical, electronics, computers, automotive, general business, travel and sports. Also software localization. Uses some 30 translators.

**Interspeak Translations, Inc.,** 114 East 32nd St., New York, NY 10016 Phone: (212)679-4772 Fax: (212)679-5084
Contact: Silvia Zehn Member: ATA

**IRU Language & Translation Services;** 2909 Hillcroft Ave, Suite 538, Houston, TX, 77077; Phone: (713)266-0020
Fax: (713)266-1716; Web Page: www.iru_services.com e-mail: IRU2000@aol.com
Contact: Elke Krause;
Member: AATG, ATA, HITA, WBEA, GACC, Houston-Leipzig Sister City Association; Founded In 1989. The main languages that IRU translates are English, German, Spanish, French, Italian, Portuguese, Russian, Chinese, Korean and Indonesian. In addition they translate all other languages. The main subjects that they translate are legal, commercial, medical, technical and individual. IRU does use freelance and they do accept resumes. Once they have received a resume it is checked if all the information needed is enclosed and then it is added to a freelance database. They require translators to hold a translation degree or equivalent, interpreters to be court certified and teacher have to hold a degree for foreign language education. IRU Language & Translation Service is a well-established company, serving not only the greater Houston area, but also Baytown, Clear Lake, Orange and Freeport, Texas. Some more of their services include foreign language and ESL classes, private language tutoring with an emphasis on German, cross-cultural seminars and tour-guiding/chaperon services for visitors. They offer prompt, accurate and confidential services at competitive prices. They are also listed in the membership directory of the German American Chamber of Commerce. Their average work load per year is 1,500 translations per year. They have about 40 translators in their pool.

**Italian Language Connection, Inc.**, 5225 Pooks Hill Rd. Ste. 504-S, Bethesda, MD 20814 Phone: (301)897-3728
Fax: (301)897-0872
E-mail: ItalTranslations@cs.com
Contact: Mark L. Pisoni

Founded 1991. Member: ATA. Accepts resumes. Only translates Italian. Main subjects are economics and finance, legal, business, marketing and medical. Uses 15 translators.

**Iverson Language Associates, Inc.,** P.O. Box 511759, Milwaukee, WI 53203 Phone:(414)271-1144 ext.21 Fax:(414)271-0144
e-mail: steve@iversonlang.com Web site: www.iversonlang.com
Contact: Steven P. Iverson, President
Founded 1986. Member: ATA, STC, ASTD. Translates French, Spanish, Japanese, Italian, Arabic, Dutch, and Korean from English, and Portuguese, German,Polish, Chinese and all other languages, both from and into English.Emphasis on Technical Manuals (large machines), Medical Operators' Manuals, Spec Sheets, Financial, Software, Advertising Packaging, and Legal translations. Prospective translators should have computer, fax, current software, e-mail. Must be native speakers in the target language, with a technical background and formal training in a specific field of concentration. Three years experience in the industry and good writing skills are preferred. Resumes are reviewed internally for the required criteria. Interested translators should complete the translator listing format http://www.iversonlang.com/contact/translator.asp. The company provides translation, interpretation, typesetting and video narration services in most major languages, as well as technical writing and illustration. Typesetting capabilities include Chinese and Japanese. Maintains a pool of 600 translators. Iverson Language Associates is a long-standing member of the American Translators Association, and a Founding Member of the Association of Language Companies.

**-J-**

**JLS Language Corporation**, 135 Willow Rd., Menlo Park, CA 94025 Phone: (415)321-9832 Fax: (415)329-9864
e-mail: info@jls.com Website: jls.com
Contact: Ms. Rikko Field, President
Founded 1977. Member: ATA. Translates Japanese, Chinese, German, French and Spanish, both from and into English, with other languages on request. Emphasis on High Tech translation. Prospective translators should have ATA accreditation, education and industry experience. Resumes are screened and filed, and the promising applicants tested. In addition to High Tech, the company also does Agribusiness, Biomedical and Patent translations, and provides Chinese and Japanese desktop publishing. Maintains a pool of "hundreds" of translators.

**JTG, Inc.**, 105 N. Washington St., Ste. 300, Alexandria, VA 22314
Phone: (703)548-7570 Fax: (703)548-8223
e-mail: hr@jtg-inc.com Website: www.jtg-inc.com
Contact: Muriel Jérôme-O'Keeffe Member: ATA

**Japan-America Management, Ltd.**, 2020 Hogback Rd., Ste. 17, Ann Arbor, MI 48105 Phone: (734)973-6101 Fax: (734)973-1847
e-mail: jamltdmi@ameritech.net
Contact: Landon Bartley Member: ATA

**Japan Communication Consultants**, 236 E. 47th St., 28th Fl., New York, NY 10017 Phone: (212)759-2033 Fax: (212)759-2149
e-mail: jcc@japancc.com Website: www.japancc.com
Contact: Mariko N. O'Hare Member: ATA

**Japan Pacific Publications, Inc.**, 419 Occidental Ave. S. #509, Seattle, WA 98104 Phone: (206)622-7443 Fax: (206)621-1786
e-mail: andrewt@japanpacific.com Website: www.japanpacific.com
Contact: Andrew Taylor, President
Founded 1983. Member: ATA. Uses freelance translators and interpreters. Accepts unsolicited resumes. Resumes are entered into database and evaluated for skills and experience. Main language is Japanese. Also translates Chinese and Korean. Main areas are agriculture, business, bio-med, tourism, marketing, software and wood products. Maintains pool of 35 translators. Translation, DTP, pre-press, image setting.

**John Benjamins Publishing Company,** P.O. Box 27519, Philadelphia PA 19118 Phone: (215)836-1200 Fax: (215)836-

1204
email: paul@ benjamins.com Contact: Paul Peranteau Member: ATA

**Josef Silny & Associates, Inc.**, 7101 SW 102 Ave. Miami, FL 33173
Phone: (305) 273-1616 Fax: (305) 273-1984
e-mail: translation@jsilny.com Web site: www.jsilny.com
Contact: Marisa di Giovanni Member: ATA

**JPMorgan Chase**, 575 Washington Blvd., Jersey City, NJ 07310
Phone: (201)595-8000 e-mail: maria.ricci@jpmchase.com
Contact: Maria Ricci Member: ATA

## -K-

**The Kaiser Permanente Medical Group**, 2241 Geary Blvd., Rm. 146, San Francisco, CA 94115 Phone: (415)202-2888 Fax: (415)202-3829
e-mail: gayle.tang@kp.org
Contact: Gayle Tang Member: ATA

**Kern Corporation**, 230 Park Ave., Ste. 925, New York, NY 10169 Phone: (212)953-2070
Contact: Eric Schloss

**Korean Consulting & Translation Service;** P.O. Box 154773, Irving, TX 75015 Phone: (972)255-4808 Fax: (214)853-5374
e-mail: sbammel@koreanconsulting.com
Web Page: www.koreanconsulting.com
Contact: Steven S. Bammel, President
Member: ATA, founded in 1999. The main language pair that this company translates is Korean & English. They do any type of subject and translate any type of Korean. They do use freelance and they do accept resumes. The resumes are filed once they are received. The requirements for applicants are that they are native English-speaking and translate Korean into English. They specialize in Korean and are always looking for translators that speak English natively for Korean to English translation. They do not need translators for English to Korean. They have many translators in their pool.

**Kotru Direct**, 1001 Avenue of the Americas, #1214, New York, NY 10018 Phone: (212)840-2300 Fax: (212)840-0004
e-mail: kdiny@aol.com
Contact: Ravi Kotru Member: ATA

**Kramer Translation**, 893 Massasso St., Merced, CA 95340
Phone: (209)385-0425 Fax: (209)385-3747
e-mail: keith@thailinguist.com Website: www.thailinguist.com
Contact: Keith & Marisa Ensminger Member: ATA

## -L-

**LRA Interpreters, Inc.**, 5150 Wilshire Blvd., #506, Los Angeles, CA 90036 Phone: (323)933-1006 Fax: (323)933-1153
e-mail: Ira@Lrausa.com Website: www. Lrausa.com
Contact: Abel Plockier Member: ATA
**LangTech International**, 5625 SW 170th Ave., Aloha, OR 97007
Phone: (503)646-2478 (to fax, call first)
e-mail: LangTech@oregonvos.net Website: www.oregonvos.com
Contact: Douglas Foran, Owner
Founded 1994. Member: Latin American Trade Council of Oregon. Does not accept resumes. Translates French (European and Canadian), Spanish, Italian and Portuguese (Brazilian and Lusitanian), both from and into English. Emphasis on Scientific/Technical, Mechanical, Electronics, Automotive, Agricultural, Legal, Health Care/Medical and Employee Relations translation.

Also interpretation and audio/visual narration.

**Langua Translations, Inc.**, 30150 Telegraph Rd., Ste. 300, Bingham Farms, MI 48025 Phone: (248)645-6663 Fax: (248)645-5376
e-mail: rneely@languatutor.com Web site: www.languatutor.com
Contact: R.P. Neely

**The Language Bank**, 875 O'Farrell St., Ste. 105, San Francisco, CA 94109 Phone: (415)885-0827 Fax: (415)885-1304
Contact: Yen Nguyen-le, Manager
Founded 1987. Uses freelance translators and interpreters. Accepts unsolicited resumes. Resumes are screened for qualifications. Main languages are Spanish, Chinese, Vietnamese, Russian, Tagalog, Thai, Laotian, Cambodian, and French. Emphasis on social services. Pool of more than 100 translators.

**The Language Bank, Inc.**, 1323 Lancaster Drive, Orlando, FL 32806
Phone: (407)894-3300 Fax: (407)894-7825
e-mail: info@languagae-bank.com Website: www.language-bank.com
Contact:Dennis Ray Merritt

**The Language Center**, 144 Tices Ln., E. Brunswick, NJ 08816
Phone: (732)613-4554 Fax: (732)238-7659
e-mail: tlc@thelanguagectr.com Website: www.thelanguagectr.com
Contact: Mary Majkowski
Founded 1967. Member:ATA, TCD. Accepts resumes. Translates all languages. Main areas are health care, pharmaceutical, medical equipment and technical manuals.

**The Language Center Inc.**, 7 Gilliam Ln., Riverside, CT 06878-0520 Phone: (203)698-1907 Fax:(203)698-2043
e-mail: thelanguagecenterinc@worldnet.att.net
Contact: Siri Ostensen, President
Founded 1978. Translates (both ways) Spanish, French, German, Portuguese, all Scandinavian languages, Italian, Japanese, Chinese, and Russian. Emphasis on Technical, Commercial and Legal translation. Prospective translators should provide sample translations. Resumes are entered into a data base. Maintains a pool of 30 translators.

**Language Company Translations, L.C.**, P.O. Box 721507, Norman, OK 73070 Phone: (405)321-5380 Fax: (405)366-7242
e-mail: 71564.2044 @compuserve.com
Contact: Nancy T. Hancock, Director
Founded 1982. Member: ATA. Translates all languages in all technical disciplines. Potential translators should have experience and total fluency. They should be able to produce translations on disk if needed. Resumes are acknowledged and filed. Freelancers are contacted when appropriate work comes in. The company can take materials through final printing, working with commercial printers and supervising production. They also accept resumes from freelance interpreters. Maintains a pool of 40 translators.

**Language Direct**, 9801 Westheimber, Ste. 302, Houston, TX 77042
Phone: (713)917-6870 Fax: (713)917-6806
e-mail: jylan@langdirect.com Website: www.langdirect.com
Contact: Jylan Saleh-Maloy Member: ATA

**Language Dynamics**, 931 Howe Ave. #107, Sacramento, CA 95825
Phone: (916)920-4062 Fax: (916)920-3594 e-mail: juanvallej@aol.com Contact: Rhody Vallejo
Founded 1979. Translates Spanish, French, Italian, Russian and Chinese and Hmong. All subject areas are translated. Prospective translators should be of high quality. Resumes are read and kept on file for contact on an as-needed basis.

**The Language Exchange, Inc.**, P.O. Box 750, Burlington, WA 98233
Phone: (360)755-9910 Fax: (360)755-9919
e-mail: Langex@langex.com Website: www.langex.com
Contact: Jaye Stover Member: ATA

**The Language Group**, 2421 Bowland Pkwy, Ste. 104-B, Virginia Beach, VA 23454 Phone: (757)431-9004 Fax: (75)431-0447
e-mail: info@thelanguagegroup.com
Website: www.thelanguagegroup.com
Contact: Evelin Schuyler
Founded 1999. Member: ATA, TCD, NAJIT, ASTM, NCMA, ABWA, NCATA. Accepts resumes via e-mail. Translates mainly Chinese, Croatian, Czech, French, German, Italian, Japanese, Norwegian, Polish and Spanish. Mostly technical, engineering, finance and marketing. Uses some 150 translators.

**Language Innovations, LLC**, 1725 I St. NW, Ste. 300, Washington, DC 20006 Phone: (202) 349-4180 Fax: (202) 349-4182
e-mail: Translate@languageinnovations.com
Web site: www.Languageinnovations.com
Contact: Brian S. Friedman Member: ATA

**Language Intelligence, Ltd.**, 16 North Goodman Street, Rochester, NY 14607 Tel. (585) 244-5578 Website: www.languageintelligence.com

**Language Learning Enterprises (LLE),** 1627 K Street NW, Suite 610,
Washington, DC 20006 Phone: Phone: 888.464.8553 x224 Fax: (202)785-5584 e-mail: hlacy@lle-inc.com Web site: www.lle-inc.com
Contact: Heidi G. Lacy
Founded 1979. Resumes are carefully screened; prospective translators and interpreters are then interviewed over phone, references checked, and then tried out on a small project first. Requires minimum 2 years experience. Translates all languages "from Arabic to Zulu," both from and into English. Emphasis in all technical areas, with a specialty in medical interpretation. The company is the creator of LLE-Link, a 24-hour-a-day, 365 days-a-year telephone interpretation service using conference calling. Maintains a pool of 12 full-time people with 1000 linguists on call. With its rapidly growing client base LLE(tm) has opportunities for highly qualified linguists in each of its business units: instruction, face-to-face interpretation, translation, and telephonic interpretation. If you are interested in working with LLE on a freelance basis, please go to our website at www.lle-inc.com for information on positions and languages we are currently recruiting for. Resumes may be submitted under the Jobs tab/Contract Positions.

**Language Line Services**, 1 Lower Ragdale Drive, Bldg. 2, Monterey, CA 93940 Phone: (831)648-5819 Fax: (800)752-0073
e-mail: danyune@languageline.com Website: www.languageline.com
Contact: Daynune Geertsen

**Language Link Corporation**, 3100 Broadway, Ste. 110, Kansas City, MO 64111 Phone: (816)753-3122 Fax: (816)753-3262
e-mail: translation@languagelinkcorp.com
Website: www.languagelinkcorp.com
Contact: Carrie Hewitt
Founded 1989. Member: ATA, ACTFL, MICATA, ASTM. Uses freelance translators and interpreters. Accpts unsolicited resumes. Main languages are Spanish, Russian, Chinese, Vietnamese, Arabic, Croatian, Japanese, Somali, Korean and Farsi.

**Language Matters,** 1445 Pearl St., Ste. 215, Boulder, CO 80302
Phone: (303)442-3471 Fax: (303)442-5805
e-mail: info@languagematters.com Web site: www.languagematters.com
Contact: Rosangela Fiori
Founded 1992. Member: ATA. TCA. Translates medical, technical, legal documents, patents, marketing material, in all languages. Has a pool of over 800 translators.

**The Language Network, Inc.**, 5151 Belt Line Rd., Ste. 452, Dallas, TX, 75240 Phone: (972)960-9980 Fax: (972)960-9904
e-mail: Language@flash.net
Contact: Christine J. Finck Member: ATA

**LanguageOne,** 2305 Calvert St. NW, Washington DC 20008
Phone: (202)328-0099 Fax: (202)328-1610

e-mail: translations@languageone.com Web site: www.languageone.com
Contact: Lorraine B. Smith Member: ATA

**Language Plus,**4110 Rio Bravo, Ste. 202, El Paso TX 79902
Phone: (915)544-8600 Fax: (915) 544-8640
e-mail: langplus@aol.com Website: www.languageplus.com
Contact: Connie Gyenis Member: ATA

**The Language Service, Inc.**, 806 Main St., Poughkeepsie, NY 12603 Phone: (845)473-4303 Fax:(845)473-4467
e-mail: info@tlsmedtrans.com Website: www.tlsmedtrans.com
Contact: Jeanne De Tar

Founded 1950. Member: ATA, FIT. Uses freelance translators and interpreters. Accepts unsolicited resumes. Qualified linguists are filed for future reference. Main languages (both ways) are German, French, Spanish, Italian, and Portuguese, and Japanese into English. Also Dutch and Swedish into English. Main areas are medical, pharmaceutical, chemical and environmental. Does about one million words a year. Works with various translators, but mainly with a steady group of about ten. Owner is co-founder and former president of the ATA.

**Language Services Associates, Inc.,** 607 North Easton, C, PO Box 205,
Willow Grove, PA 19090 Phone: (215)657-6571 Fax: (215)659-7210
e-mail: lschriver@lsaweb.com Web site: www.lsaweb.com
Contact: Laura T. Schriver

Founded 1991. Member: ATA, DVTA, NAJIT, CHICATA, NOTA. Uses freelance translators and interpreters. Accepts unsolicited resumes. Resumes are acknowledged, kept, and used when needed. Applicants should have ATA accreditation. Main languages (both ways) are Spanish, German, French, Chinese, Japanese, Korean, Vietnamese, Russian, Hindi, Italian, and Tamil. Also Cambodian, Arabic, Farsi, Hebrew, Dutch and more. Emphasis on Legal and Medical translation. Maintains a pool of 745 translators. We have 4,000 subcontractors.

**Language Services Consultants, Inc.**, P.O. Box 412, Ardmore, PA 19003 Phone: (610)617-8962 Fax: (610)617-9108
e-mail: ruth.karpeles@verizon.net
Contact: Ruth S. Karpeles

Founded 1992. Member: ATA, DVTA. Accepts resumes. Translates mainly Spanish, Vietnamese, Cambodian, Russian, Chinese, Korean, French, Portuguese, Greek, Dutch and Albanian. Mostly medical, education and social services. Uses some 150 translators.

**Language Source;** P.O. Box 13114, Wauwatosa, WI 53213
Phone: (414)607-8766 Fax: (414)607-8767
e-mail: langsource@aol.com
Contact: Elizabeth Brudele-Baran

**Language Training Centre, Inc.:** 5750 Castle Creek Parkway, Suite 387, Indianapolis, IN, 46250: Phone: (317)578-4577 Fax: (317)578-1673; Web Page: www.languagetrainingcenter.com
e-mail: mgeorge@languagetrainingcenter.com
Contact: David Hunt

Member: ATA, TESOL, IFLTA, INTESOL. Founded in 1993. The Language Training Center translates English to Spanish, Spanish to English, English to German, German to English, French to English, English to French, Chinese to English, English to Chinese, Japanese to English and English to Japanese. The main subjects that they translate are handbooks and legal contracts. They specialize in corporate documents. They do use freelance and they also accept resumes. One they receive them, they file them by language and special area. They require that you have experience. They are a full-service language center that teaches, translates and acclimates clients in the languages of the world. A leader in the translation field for over 20 years. They have 40 translators in their pool.

**The Languageworks, Inc.,**1123 Broadway, Ste. 201, New York, NY 10010 Phone: (212)447-6060 Fax: (212)447-6257
e-mail: talwood@languageworks.com Website: www.anguageworks.com
Contact: Thomas Alwood Member: ATA

**Latin American Translators Network, Inc.**,1970 Cliff Valley Way NE, Ste. 208, Atlanta, GA 30329
Phone: (404)634-2635 Fax: (404)634-9683
e-mail: latn@latninc.com Web site: www.latninc.com

Contact: Alicia V. Mitchell Chacón Member: ATA

**Lazar & Associates**, 2444 Wilshire Blvd., Ste. 411, Santa Monica, CA 90403 Phone: (310)453-3302 Fax: (310)453-6002
e-mail: languages@lazar.com Website: www.lazar.com
Contact: Elaine Lazar
Founded 1995. Member: ATA. Accepts resumes occasionally.Main languages are Spanish, French, Chinese, Japanese and German. Mostly medical, pharmaceutical, IT, business, legal and technical equipment manuals. Has a pool of over 3000 translators.

**Le Chateau Enterprises Group, Inc.**, 10051 McGregor Blvd, Ste. 105
Ft. Myers, FL 33919 Phone: (941)574-5600 Fax: (941)574-3273
e-mail: info@letspeak.com Website: www.letspeak.com
Contact: Allendy Doxy Member: ATA

**Legal Interpreting Services, Inc.**, 21-50 44th Drive, Long Island City, NY 11101 Phone: (718)786-7890 Fax: (718)786-8034
e-mail: accutran@aol.com Website: www.accuratetranslation.com
Contact: Alexandra Gerenburg Member: ATA

**Leggett & Platt, Inc.**, PO Box 757, Carthage, MO 64836
Phone: (417)358-8131 Fax: (417)359-5767
Website: www.leggett.com
Contact: Tomasita Hernandez Member: ATA

**Lemoine International, Inc.**, 339 E. 600 N., American Fork, UT 84003
Phone: (801)763-5644 Fax: (801)763-5660 e-mail: brigittem @lemoine-international.com Website: www.lemoine-international.com
Contact: Brigitte L. Morales Member: ATA

**Letspeak, Inc.**, Phone: (239) 274-5700 Fax: (239) 274-9709
e-mail: info@letspeak.com Web site: www.letspeak.com
Contact: Allendy Doxy Member: ATA

**Liaison Language Center**, 3500 Oak Lawn Ave., Ste. 110 LB 32, Dallas, TX 75219 Phone: (214)528-2731 Fax: (214)522-7167
e-mail: liaison@liaisonlanguage.com Website: www.liaisonlanguage.com
Contact: Gerda Stendell
Founded 1978. Member: ATA. Uses freelance translators and interpreters.. Translated mainly Spanish, Portuguese, German, French, Italian, Korean, Japanese, Chinese (Madarin and Cantonese) and Vietnamese. Mostly legal, oil, insurance. Has a pool of around 100 active translators and interpreters.

**Liaison Multilingual Services**, 3261 Cherryridge Rd., Englewood, CO 80110 Phone: (303)762-0997 Fax: (303)762-0999
e-mail: liaison@ecentral.com Website:eMultilingual.com
Contact: Suzanne Robinson Member: ATA

**Lingo Systems**, 15115 SW Sequoia Pkwy, #200, Portland, OR 97224
Phone: (503)419-4856 Fax: (503)419-4876
e-mail: info@lingosys.com Website: www.lingosys.com
Contact: Maja Bailey
Founded 1992. Member: ATA. LISA, SAO. Accepts resumes. Requires 5 years experience and knowledge of CAT tools. Translates mainly French, German, Italian, Spanish, Japanese, Chinese, Korean, Dutch, Scandinavian languages and Eastern European. Also Asian. Mostly IT, computer hardware and software, websites, marketing and training materials. Maintains some 500 translators.

**Lingua Communications Translation Services**, 9321 Lavergne, Ste. 101, Skokie, IL 60077 Phone:(847)673-1607 Fax:(847)673-1669
Contact: Alex Babich, General Partner
Founded 1989. Member: ATA. Translates Russian and German, both from and into English, and Polish, Ukrainian, Latvian, French and Japanese into English. Emphasis on all subject translations. Prospective translators should possess experience, speed and quality at market-level pricing. Resumes are filed against need; translators are then contacted. **Lingua** maintains a pool of 250 translators.

**Lingua Language Center**, 1730 Main St., Ste. 226, Weston, FL 33326
Phone: (954)349-8088 Fax: (954)349-1799
e-mail: info@linguaschool.com Website:linguaschool.com
Contact: Andreina Ojeda Member: ATA

**Lingualink Incorporated,** 5777 W. Century Blvd., Ste. 1000, Los Angeles, CA 90045 Phone: (310)642-2920 Fax: (310)642-2945
e-mail: lingualinkinfo@ccscom.com Website:
www.ccscom.com/ lingualink
Contact: Keir Milan Member: ATA

**Linguistic Consulting Enterprises, Inc.**, 251 W. Marlboro Rd., Oro Valley, AZ 85737 Phone: (520)297-6420 Fax: (520)297-2629
e-mail: LCEAZ1@aol.com
Contact: Maria Elisa Rivera

**Linguistic Systems, Inc.**, P.O. Box 390031, 130 Bishop Allen Drive, Cambridge, MA 02139 Phone:(617)864-3900 Fax:(617)864-5186
e-mail: info@linguist.com Website: www.linguist.com
Contact: Martin Roberts, President
Founded 1967. Member: ATA. Uses freelance translators and interpreters. Applicants should have relevant education and experience. Translates mainly Spanish, French, German, Italian, Portuguese, Chinese, Japanese, Korean, Greek and Swedish. Mostly legal, medical and commercial. The company provides translation, interpretation, voiceover, and machine translation editing services. Maintains a pool of about 4000 translators.

**Lionbridge**, 301 Mission St., Ste. 350, San Francisco, CA 94105
Phone: (415)546-6885 Fax: (415)495-4926
Website: www.lionbridge.com
Contact: Allison Smith Member: ATA

**Littleton & Associates, Inc.**, 6006 W. 159th St., Bldg. C, Ste. 2 East, Oak Forest, IL 60452 Phone: (708)429-3336 Fax: (708)429-3414
e-mail: lcs62258@aol.com
Contact: James M. Littleton Member: ATA

**Lucent Technologies Global Translation**, 2400 Reynolda Rd., Winston-Salem, NC 27106 Phone: (336)727-6218 Fax: (336)727-3221
e-mail: mrhodes@lucent.com Website: www.lucent.com/translations
Contact: Marta C. Rhodes Member: ATA

**LUZ**, 202 Potero Ave., San Francisco, CA 941103
Phone: (415)241-0520 Fax: (415)241-0504 Website: www.luz.com
Contact: Sanford Wright Member: ATA

**-M-**

**M² Limited**, 9210 Wightman Rd., Montgomery Village, MD 20886
Phone: (301)977-4281 Fax: (301)926-5046
e-mail: info@m2ltd.com Website: www.m2ltd.com
Contact: Audrey Moyer
Founded 1979. Member: ATA, STC, World Trade Center. Accepts unsolicted resumes. Applicants should be native speakers of the target language, with 2-5 years minimum experience. Translates mainly Spanish, French, Italian, German, Porutguese, Chinese, Japanese, Korean, Dutch and Russian. Emphasis on Computer Software, technical documentation, web pages and localization. The company does not provide interpreting services. The company has become a specialist in the localization of computer-based equipment and software, and is heavily involved in software development, training, and adaptation of English-language materials for use in other cultures and languages. In addition to translators, the company is interested in proofreaders and editors in all languages. Maintains a pool of 2,000 translators.

**M/C International**, 7207 Chagrin Rd., Unit #4, Chagrin Falls, OH 44023 Phone:(440)247-2277 Fax:(440)247-0453
e-mail: mcinternational @stratos.net
Contact: Mrs. E. Marchbank
Founded 1969. Translates Spanish, French, German, Italian, Portuguese, Russian, Accepts resumes. Translates mainly French, German, Dutch, Italian, Portuguese, Spanish, Arabic, Chinese and Japanese. Emphasis on technical, legal and commercial translation. The company is a full-service translation bureau. It also provides 4-color printing services, desktop publishing and typesetting, both to clients and to other translators. In addition, they operate their own travel agency. Maintains a pool of 50 translators.

**MGE Lingual Services**, 136 36th St. Drive SE, Ste. A-4, Cedar Rapids, IA 52403 Phone: (319)366-1038 Fax: (319)366-1047
e-mail: mike@mge-lingual.com Website: www.mge-lingual.com
Contact: Michael G. Elliff Member: ATA

**MTS Multinational Translating Service,** 928 Connetquot Ave., Central Islip, NY 11722 Phone: (631)581-8956 Toll Free: (800)864-5069, 70 & 71 Fax: (631)224-9435 e-mail: info@mtsinc.us Web site: www.mtsinc.us
Contact: Lisa Alesci Member: ATA

**Madison Linguistic Services**, 301 Keezell Hall, MSC 1802, Harrisonburg, VA 22807 Phone: (540)568-3512 Fax: (540)568-6904
e-mail: rethorcx@jmu.edu Web site: jmu.edu/forlang/trans
Contact: Christophe Rethore Member: ATA

**MAGNUS International Trade Services Corp.**, 1313 North Grand Ave., #280, Walnut, CA 91789 Phone: (909) 595-8488 Fax: (909)598-5852 Website: www.manuscorp.com
Contact: Nora K. Schwartz
Member: ATA, PCLA, HPRMA, LA-FTA, NOTA. Translates Spanish, Chinese, Vietnamese, Tagalog, Korean, Portuguese, French, German and Russian from English, as well as Hindi, Farsi, Armenian, Hmong, Lao and Arabic. Emphasis on Healthcare, Medical, Pharmaceutical, Engineering, Legal, Technical, and General Business translation. Prospective translators should have certification (if possible), appropriate education and field experience. Resumes are responded to with a standard contract, and contractors called as needed.

**Marion J. Rosley Secretarial, Transcription & Translation Services**, 41 Topland Rd., Hartsdale, NY 10530 Phone: (914)682-9718 Fax: (914) 761-1384 e-mail: mrosley@rosley.com Website: rosley.com
Contact: Marion J. Rosley, President
Founded 1977. Member: NYCT, World Trade Council of Westchester, Westchester County Assn., Westconn. Translates all languages. Emphasis on Legal, Medical, Technical, and Business Correspondence translation. The company provides interpreting services in all languages. Prospective translators should have excellent skills and reasonable prices. Resumes are filed for future use. Maintains a pool of "hundreds" of translators. The company provides secretarial, transcription and translation services, including cassette transcription of conferences.

**MasterWord Services, Inc.**, 303 Stafford, Ste. 204, Houston, TX 77079 Phone:(713)589-0810 Fax:(713)589-1104
e-mail: masterword@ masterword.com Website: www.masterword.com

Contact: Mila Green

Founded 1993. Member: ATA, Azeri Translators Association. Translates Russian, Spanish, Azeri, Brazilian Portuguese and Chinese, both from and into English. Emphasis on Oil and Gas, Drilling, Legal and Medical translations. Prospective translators should have significant translation experience, especially in the oil/gas or legal areas, and show quality performance on the company's certification exam. All resumes are acknowledged, and after prescreening, ap-proximately 10% are sent an in-house certification exam, primarily in Russian or Spanish. They are then phoned for an in-person interview. The company also has offices in Baku, Azerbaijan, and is involved in ongoing projects in Europe, South America and Asia.They also have affiliates in Washington, DC, New York, London and Moscow. Maintains a pool of 35-50 translators.

**Masua Funai Eifert & Mitchell, Ltd.**, 1701 Golf Rd., Ste. 800, Rolling Meadows, IL 60008
Contact: Yasuyo Wakuta Member: ATA

**McNeil Multilingual**, 6564 Loisdale Court, Ste. 800, Springfield, VA 22150 Phone: (703)921-1600 Fax: (703)921-1610
e-mail: rnelson@mcneilmultic.com Website: www.mcneilmultic.com
Contact: George E. Washington, Jr. Member: ATA

**ME Sharp, Inc., Publisher**, 80 Business Park Drive, Armonk, NY 10504 Phone: (914)273-1800 Fax: (914)273-2106
e-mail: journals@mesharpe.com Website: www.mesharpe.com
Contact: C. P. Chetti Member: ATA

**Mena's International Corp.**, 2548 Nicollet Ave., S., Minneapolis, MN 55404 Phone: (612)872-8392 Fax: (612)872-7861
e-mail: menastrave@aol.com
Contact: Maximo Mena Member: ATA

**Mercury Marine**, W6250 West Pioneer Rd., Fond du Lac, WI 54936 Phone: (414)929-5299 Fax: (414)231-8916
e-mail: Gary_Fenrich@mercmarine.com
Contact: Gary Fenrich Member: ATA

**Metropolitan Interpreters and Translators Worldwide, Inc.**, 110 E. 42nd St., Ste. 802, New York, NY 10017
Phone: (212)986-5050 Fax: (212)983-5998 e-mail: metlang@aol.com Website: metlang.com
Contact: Joe Citrano

Founded 1990. Member: ATA, NYCT, NAJIT, IAFL. Uses freelance translators and interpreters. Accept unsolicited resumes. Resumes are entered in a database. Translates all languages. Emphasis on legal and law enforcement. About 500 in translator pool.

**Merrill Translations;** 225 Verick St., New York, NY 10014
Phone: (212)367-5970 Fax: (212)367-5969
e-mail: translations@merrillcorp.com Web Page: www.merrillcorp.com resumes: resumestrans@merrillcorp.com
Contact: Thomas Alwood

Member: ATA, ITI; Founded in 1998. Translates mainly English to Spanish, French, German, Italian, Portuguese, Japanese, Chinese, Korean, Swedish and Russian. They work in 64 different languages. Subjects translated are legal, financial, advertising, medical and technical. They primarily focus on document translation. They also do some interpreting. Merrill Translations does use freeland and they do accept resumes. The resumes are all reviewed and qualified candidates are contacted to continue the registration process. They are mainly interested in applicants with college education and experience in legal and financial work. Merrill Translations is the foreign language services division of Merrill Corporation, a diversified document services company. They have offices in over 50 locations in the US and Europe. Merrill Translations production offices, located in New York and London, offer a full range of foreign language services, focused on the financial, life sciences, advertising, advertising and legal industries as well as general corporate clients. In addition to translation, localization, interpreting and foreign language typesetting services they also coordinate services with Merrill Corporation's other document management solutions, including printing and distribution anywhere in the world. They have more than 2,000 translators in their pool.

**Monti Interpreting & Translation Services, Inc.**, 101 S. Wymore Rd., Ste. 315, Altamonte Springs, FL 32714 Phone: (888)686-6007 Fax: (407)830-1860
e-mail: montitrans@yahoo.com Website: www.montitrans.com
Contact: Caroline Montalvo

Founded 1997. Member: ATA. Accepts resumes. Translates mainly Spanish, Creole, Vietnamese, French, Chinese, Arabic, Bosnian, Croatian, Cambodian, Portuguese and Turkish. Mostly medical, legal and corporate literature. Maintains a pool of 50 translators and 500 interpreters.

**Morales Dimmick Translation Service, Inc.**, 1409 W S Slope, Emmett, ID 83617 Phone: (208)365-2622
e-mail: projects@mdtranslation.com Website: www.mdtranslation.com
Contact: Chris
Founded 1989. Member: ATA, IMA. Accepts resumes. Main languages are Spanish, Bosnian, Laotian, Vietnamese and Arabic. Mostly business, medical, legal and insurance. Maintains a pool of 65 translators.

**Morgan Guaranty Trust Company**, 60 Wall St., 34th Fl., New York, NY 10260 Phone: (212)552-5474 Fax: (212)552-8128
e-mail: lisa.gallo@chase.com
Contact: Lisa Gallo Member: ATA

**The Multi-Lingual Group**, 8 Faneuil Hall Marketplace, 3rd Fl., Boston, MA 02109 Phone: (617)973-5077 Fax: (617)787-3124
e-mail: multilg @aol.com
Contact: Felice Bezri
Founded 1994. Member: NAJIT. Translates Spanish, French, Italian and Portuguese, both from and into English, German, Swedish, Arabic and Cantonese into English, and Japanese and Mandarin from English. Emphasis on Medical Studies, Computer, Legal and Military translation. Prospective translators should be ATA members with extensive experience in written translation and specialization in one or more fields. Resumes are reviewed on a regular basis with a particular eye to the experience of the candidate. The company also provides simultaneous interpreting in over 50 languages and offers cross-cultural consulting. Maintains a pool of approximately 320 translators.

**MultiLing International, Inc.**, 55 N. University Ave., Ste. 225, Provo, UT 84601 Phone:(801)377-2000 Fax:(801)377-7085
e-mail: translation@ultiling.com Website: www.multiling.com
Contact: Michael V. Sneddon
Founded 1988. Member: ATA, STC, Utah Information Technology Assn., Software Publishers Assn. Translates Spanish, French, Dutch, German, Italian, Japanese, Chinese, Swedish, Danish, Russian and all other languages, both from and into English. Emphasis on High-Tech Product Localization and the translation of related documents. Prospective translators must be native speakers of the target language with an undergraduate and, preferably, a master's degree, with an area of special expertise. They should have a good software and desktop publishing background and several years of experience and accreditation. The company works in all areas of translation, including working with translation software and aiding in its further development. Maintains a pool of1400 translators.

**Multilingual Communications Corporation**, P.O. Box 7164 Pittsburgh, PA 15213 Phone:(412)621 7450 Fax:(412)621 0522
e-mail: mktg @mccworld.com Website: www.mccworld.com
Contact: Cathy Rosenthal
Founded 1977. Member: ATA. Translates Spanish, French, German, Chinese, Japanese, Russian, Italian, Korean, Portuguese, Arabic and Korean, both from and into English. Emphasis on Technical, Legal and Medical Software translation. Prospective translators should possess native proficiency and background in a specialized field. Resumes are evaluated on receipt, then contacted and tested. Their services include software localization. Maintains a pool of 500 translators.

**Multilingual Solutions**, 22 W. Jefferson St., Ste. 402, Rockville, MD 20850 Phone: (301)424-7444 Fax: (301)424-7331
e-mail: laurie@msolutions.com Website: www.mlsolutions.com
Contact: laurie Campos Sandler Member: ATA

**Multilingual Translations, Inc.**, 1510 Front St., Ste. 200, San Diego, CA 92101 Phone: (619)295-2682 Fax: (619)295-2984
e-mail: mcardenas@multitrans.com Website: www.multitrans.com
Contact: Michael Ramírez Cardénas, J.D. Member: ATA
**Multilingual Word**, 2631 Salem Ave. S, Minneapolis, MN 55416
Phone: (952)929-4203 Fax: (952)922-4344 e-mail: mlivon@aol.com
Contact: Michelle Livon Member: ATA

## -N-

**NCS Enterprises, Inc.,** 1222 Hope Hollow Rd., Carnegie, PA 15106 Phone: (412)278-4590 Fax: (412)278-4595
e-mail: cnagy@ncs-pubs.com Web site: www.ncs-pubs.com
Contact: Charlene Nagy
Founded 1992. Member: ATA. Uses freelance translators and interpreters. Accepts unsolicited resumes. All resume are reviewed and entered into database.

**NiS International Services**, 1913 Dundin Drive, Old Hickory, TN 37138 Phone:(615)758-6459 Fax:(615)758-6459
e-mail: Nisintl@aol.com Website: www.nisintl.com
Contact: Bill Hollaway
Founded 1987. Member: ATA. Translates Japanese, Korean, Chinese, Spanish, German, French, Italian, and Russian, both from and into English. Emphasis on Automotive, Electrical Engineering, Mechanical Engineering, Patent, Contract and Agreement, and other technical document translation. Prospective translators should send a sample of previous work. A specialized technical background is a plus. Resumes are saved in a database, and the translator contacted when a job is available. The company provides translation, interpretation, and teaching services. Maintains a pool of 600-700 translators.

**N.O.W. Translations**, 23054 Covello St., West Hills, CA 91307
Phone: (818)716-9112 Fax: (818)888-6962
e-mail: thomasc@nowtranslations.com
Website: www.nowtranslations.com
Contact: Thomas Clement Member: ATA

**Narragansett Translations & Interpreting, Inc.**, 32 East Ave., Pawtucket, RI 02860 Phone: (401)722-1222 e-mail: morra_red@ids.net
Contact: Mike D. Chea Member: ATA

**Nelles Translations,** 104 South Michigan Ave., Room 1004, Chicago, IL 60603 Phone: (312)236-2788 Fax: (312)236-0717
Contact: Lawrence R. Kramer, Product Manager
Founded 1956. Member: ATA, Chicagoland Chamber of Commerce, Chicago Convention & Tourism Bureau. Translates Spanish, French, German, Italian, Portuguese, Polish, Russian, Japanese, Chinese, Korean and numerous other languages, both from and into English. Emphasis on Patent, Print Advertising, Legal, Brochures and Manuals, and Personal Document translation. Prospective translators should be experienced with references. They may be tested at the discretion of the company. Resumes are acknowledged and promising applicants are contacted. The company provides interpreting and voiceover services in addition to translation.

**NetworkOmni Multilingual Communications**, 1329 E. Thousand Oaks Blvd., 2nd Fl., Thousand Oaks, CA 91362
Phone: (805)379-1090
Fax: (805)379-2467 e-mail: omni@networkomni.com
Website: www.networkomni.com Contact: Irena Stone
Founded 1978. Member: ATA. Translates French, Italian, German, Spanish, Chinese, Korean and Japanese, both from and into English. Handles a variety of subjects. Excellence is the primary requirement for prospective translators. Resumes are followed up with a call and a registration skills packet. The company has five separate divisions: Interpretations, Translations, Teleinterpretations, Transcriptions and Videointerpretations and all are supported by Omni's Quality Control staff. Maintains a pool of 800 translators.

**New England Translations**, 59 Temple Place, Ste. 204, Boston, MA 02111 Phone: (617)426-4868 Fax: (617)695-9349
e-mail: netranslations@langcenters.com
Website: newenglandtranslations.com
Contact: Ken Krall, Director
Founded 1986. Member: ATA. Uses freelance translators and interpreters. Accepts unsolicited resumes. Resumes are entered into databse by language and specialty. Requires experience. Translates Spanish, Portuguese, French, German, Italian, Chinese, Vietnamese, Korean and Japanese from English, and Spanish into English. Emphasis on Finance, Legal, Marketing, Industrial and Medical translation, with specialties in Financial and Medical. Prospective translators should have PC or Mac, fax, modem. A small sample translation should be sent with the resume. Resumes are entered into a database by language pair and technical specialty after qualifications are reviewed. The company is dedicated to the translation of all major languages. It also provides instruction in

Spanish only. Maintains a pool of 800 translators.

**Newtype, Inc.**, 1259 Route 46 E, Bldg. 1, 2nd Fl., Parsippany, NJ 07054
Phone: (973)263-5000 Fax: (973)263-5522
e-mail: tbias@newtypeinc.com Website: www.newtypeinc.com
Contact: Thomas Bias Member: ATA

**Northwest Translations**, 2636 E. Greentree Ct., Eagle, ID 83616
Phone: (208)938-5005 Fax: (509)351-7529
e-mail: sales@nwtranslations.com Website: www.nwtranslations.com
Contact: Jeff Scott Allen Member: ATA

**NovaTrans Enterprises, Inc.**, P.O. Box 3903, Boca Raton, FL 33427
Phone: (561)368-0865 Fax: (954)255-5161
e-mail: mail@novatrans.net
Contact: Janet T. Aliaga Member: ATA

## -O-

**Okada & Sellin Translations, LLC** 1950 Addison St., Ste. 101, Berkeley CA 94704 Phone: (510)843-5600 Fax: (510)843-5603
e-mail: okada@ostrans.com Website: www.ostrans.com
Contact: Robert G. Sellin
Founded 1996. Member: ATA, STC. Uses freelance translators and interpreters. Accepts unsolicited resumes. Resumes are reviewed and graded. Work sample are welcome. Requires e-mail. Translates all major Asian and European languages. Focuses on patents and other technical, scientific, pharma/biotech, and legal subjects.

**Omega Translation Service**, 331-A North Brand Blvd., Glendale, CA 91203 Phone: (818)545-3626 Fax: (818)545-0364
e-mail: omega2@earthlink.net
Contact: Jill Massehian
Founded 1985. Translates Spanish, French, German, Japanese, Italian and Chinese, both from and into English. Emphasis on Scientific, Businese and Computer translation. Prospective translators should have good references. Resumes are filed by specialty and language. The company needs qualified translators and interpreters with various specialty fields. Maintains a pool of 1000 translators.

**OmniLingua, Inc.**, 306 6th Ave. SE, Cedar Rapids, IA 52401 Phone: (319)365 8565 Fax:(319)365 7893 e mail: omnilingua @omnilingua .com Website: www.omnilingua.com
Contact: Elizabeth Miller
Founded 1980. Member: ATA, MACHETE, NCATA. Accepts resumes. Translates mainly French, Italian, German, Spanish, Portuguese, Chinese, japanese, Korean, Greek and Russian. Mostly automotive, heavy equipment, medical products, IT, consumer durables and marketing. Prospective translators should complete a written application form and a short translation test. Experience and educational requirements vary; great emphasis is placed on test results. The company also provides desktop publishing services. Maintains a pool of 300 translators, editors, proofreaders, narrators, and word-counters, all freelance.

**OneWorld Language Solutions**, 2909 Cole Ave., Ste. 300, Dallas, TX 75204 Phone: (214)871-2909 Fax: (214)871-2907
e-mail: flctans@connect.net Website: www.oneworldlanguage.com
Contact: Gabriele Hayes, Director
Founded 1990. Member: ATA, META. Uses freelance translators and interpreters. Accepts unsolicited resumes. Requires experience, prefers ATA members. Resumes are entered in database and applicants are contacted when the need arises. Translates (both ways) mainly Spanish, French, German, Italian, and Russian. Also Japanese, Dutch, and Chinese. Provides interpretation and language training. Maintains a pool of over 400 translators.

**Openworld**, 2673 NE University Village, Ste. 1, Seattle, WA 98105
Phone: (206)523-1100 Fax: (206)522-3345
e-mail: orders@openworldtranslations.com

Website: www.penworldtranslations.com
Contact: Helen Tereshina Member: ATA

**Origin - The Language Agency**, P.O. Box 1648, Makawao, HI 96768
Phone: (808)573-1453 Fax: (808)573-6446
e-mail: info@origin.to Website: www.origin.to
Contact: Chelsea Hill
Founded 1998. Member: ATA, Aquarius, Proz.com. Accepts resumes via website. Translates mainly Chinese, Korean, Indian Languages, Spanish, French, Russian, German, Japanese, Ukrainian and Romanian. Mostly medical, computer-related, business, marketing, telecommunications, tourism, pharmaceuticals and automotive. Has a pool of 600 translators.

**OSTrans, LLC** 1950 Addison St., Ste. 101, Berkeley CA 94704
Phone: (800)803-9896 Fax: (510)843-5603
e-mail: okada@ostrans.com Web site: www.ostrans.com
Contact: Robert G. Sellin
Founded 1996. Member: ATA, STC. Uses freelance translators and interpreters. Accepts unsolicited resumes. Resumes are reviewed and graded. Work sample are welcome. Requires e-mail. Translates all major Asian and European languages. Focuses on patents and other technical, scientific, pharma/biotech, and legal subjects.

**O'Sullivan Menu Corporation**, 110 Triangle Blvd., Carlstadt, NJ 07072
Phone: (201)507-1449 Fax: (201)507-4920
Contact: Adriana Marton Member: ATA

## -P-

**PSC, Inc.**, 12330 Pinecrest Rd., Reston, VA 20191
Phone:(703)716-5000 Fax:(703)716-5005
e-mail: translat@pscusa.com
Contact: Fred Lothrop
Founded 1988. Member: ATA. Translates Spanish (all dialects) to and from English, and Arabic, Chinese (all dialects), Farsi, Haitian Creole, Russian, Serbo/Croatian, Japanese, and Central and West African languages into English. Emphasis on technical (computer, communications, radar), legal, and business translation. Specialty in transcription and translation for law enforcement agencies. Translators must have a specialized area and security clearance before being matched with an appropriate job. Unsolicited resumes for freelance work are processed through internal channels of selection. PSC, Inc. is a privately-owned firm with a major business area, also providing foreign language services for the private and public sectors. Maintains a pool of 1500 linguists.

**Pacific Dreams, Inc.,** 525 Glen Creek Rd., #230 NW, Salem, OR 97304
Phone: (503)588-7368 Fax: (503)588-7549
e-mail: pacific.dreams@viser.net Web site: www.pacificdreams.org
Contact: Ken Sakai Member: ATA

**Pacific Interpreters, Inc.**, 520 SW Yamhill, #320, Portland, OR 97204
Phone: (800)311-1232 Fax: (800)881-2565
e-mail: recruitment@pacificinterpreters.com
Website: www.pacificinterpreters.com
Contact: Joana Laitinen
Founded 1992. Member: ATA, SOMI, NOTIS, NAJIT, ASTM. Accepts resumes. Translates mainly Spanish, Vietnamese, Chinese, Cambodian, Hmong, Laotian, Arabic and Farsi. Mostly health care. Maintains pool of about 100 translators.

**Pacific Ring Services, Inc.**, 1143 Christina Mill Drive, Newark, DE 19711
Phone: (302)269-1518 Fax: (302)269-1618
e-mail: pacific@dca.net Web site: www.pacificring.com
Contact: Motoko Yuasa, Registered US Patent Agent
Member: ATA. Pacific Ring House, Inc is a patent house.

**Pangea Lingua**, 3620 N. Washington Blvd., Indianapolis, IN 46250

Phone: (317)920-1600 Fax: (317)920-1601
e-mail: staff@pangealingua.com Website: www.pangealingua.com
Contact: Alessandra Matas
Founded 1994. Member: ATA. Accepts resumes. Translates mainly Spanish, Japanese, German, Chinese, French, Dutch, Portuguese and Russian. Mostly medical, pharmaceutical, promotional, legal and automotive. Maintains pool of over 1000 translators.

**Paragon Language Services,** 5657 Wilshire Blvd., Ste. 310, Los Angeles, CA 90036 Phone: (323)966-4655 Fax: (323)651-1867
e-mail: info@paragonls.com
Web site: www.paragonls.com
Contact: Hanne R. Mintz Member: ATA, ALC

**Peritus Precision Translations, Inc.**, 727 Industrial Rd., #710, San Carlos, CA 94070 Phone: (650)631-6667 Fax: (650)631-6664
e-mail: info@peritustranslations.com Website: www.peritustranslations.com
Contact: Dagmar Dolatshko Member: ATA

**Phoenix Translations**, 2110 A White Horse Trail, Austin, TX 78757
Phone (512) 343-8389 Toll-free (877)452-1348 Fax (512) 343-6721
email: phoenixtranslations@ev1.net www.phoenixtranslations.com
Contact: Jennifer Ruggio

**Precision Translating Services**, 150 W. Flagler St., Penthouse II, Miami, FL 33130 Phone: (305)373-7874 Fax: (305)381-7874
e-mail: vince@pretran.com Website: www.pretran.com
Contact: Vicente J. de la Vega Member: ATA

**Premier Translation Services, Ltd.**, 62 Stonicker Drive, Lawrenceville, NJ 08648 Phone: (609) 538-9333 Fax:(609)530-0079
e-mail: rzarelli@premiertranslationsusa.com
Web site: www.premiertranslationsusa.com
Contact: Renée Zarelli, Esq., President
Founded 1994. Member: ATA. Accepts resumes. The language pairs we translate are French into English, Italian into English, and Spanish into English. Only translate legal and business documents.. Prospective translators should be ATA members, accredited if applicable. Three+ years full time experience, college education or higher. Equipment should include WP or Word and modem. Resumes are reviewed on a monthly basis. The company specializes in using lawyers and individuals with a strong legal background, in both U.S. and other legal systems, for translation and editing. Freelance translators do not have to be members of ATA, or accredited by ATA, for consideration. Three or more years' full-time translating experience is desirable. Maintains a pool of 50 translators.

**Princeton Technical Translation Center**, 333 Bolton Rd., East Windsor, NJ 08520 Phone: (609)443-6770 Fax: (609)443-6778
Contact: Charles Teubner, Director
Founded 1982. Member: ATA, STC. Translates French, German, Spanish, Italian, Portuguese, Chinese, Japanese, Russian and Scandinavian languages, both from and into English. Prospective translators should have advanced technical degrees and be proficient in Word/WordPerfect and related software.

**Professional Translating Services Inc.**, 44 West Flagler St., Ste. 540, Miami, FL 33130 Phone: (305)371-7887 Fax: (305)381-9824
e-mail: translate@protranslating.com Website: www.protranslating.com
Contact: Luis A. de la Vega
Founded 1973. Member: ATA. Accepts resumes. Translates mainly Spanish, Portuguese, French, Italian, German, Japanese, Russian, Chinese, Arabic and Hebrew. Translations are in legal, technical, financial and advertising. Has a pool of over 350 translators.

**ProZ.com**, 1448 Madison St., Apt. 410, Oakland, CA 94612
Phone: (510)682-3231 e-mail: henry@proz.com Website: www.proz.com Contact: Henry J. Dotterer Member: ATA

**-Q-**

**Quality Interpreting**, 367 University Ave., Ste. 4, Saint Paul, MN 55103 Phone: (651)244-0066 Fax: (651)312-0270
Contact: Paul Yang Member: ATA

**Quantum, Inc.**, 240 S. 9th St., Philadelphia, PA 19107
Phone: (215)627-2251 Fax: (215)627-5570
e-mail: www.quantumtrans@msn.com
Contact: Quan Pham Member: ATA

**Quintana Multi-Lingual Services, Inc.**, 3050 W. Cermak Rd., Chicago, IL 60623 Phone: (773)277-0000 Fax: (773)277-1804
e-mail: quintana@compuserve.com
Contact: Gloria K. Quintana

**-R-**

**RIC International, Inc.**, 955 Massachusetts Ave., PMB 342, Cambridge, MA 02139 Phone: (617)666-4555 Fax: (617)666-8896
e-mail: r-i-c.com Website: www.r-i-c.com Member: ATA

**R.R. Donnelley Financial Translation Services**, 75 Park Place, New York, NY 10007 Phone: (212)341-7416 Fax: (212)341-7532
e-mail: FBUTRansServ@rrd.com
Contact: Aouck F. Le Fur
Member: ATA

**Ralph McElroy Translation Company**, PO Box 4828, Austin, TX 78765 Phone: (512)472-6753 Fax: (512)472-4591
e-mail: tc@mcelroytranslation.com
Website: www.mcelroytranslation.com
Contact: Patricia Bown
Founded 1968. Member: ATA, STC. Accepts resumes. Translates mainly German, Japanese, French, Spanish, Italian, Portuguese, Russian, Chinese, Dutch and Korean. Mostly engineering, technical, medical, legal, pharmaceutical, chemical, patents, localization and high tech. Several hundred active translators.

**Rancho Park Publishing**, 2203 Balsam Ave., Los Angeles, CA 90064
Phone:(310)470-7488 Fax:(310)470-7930
e-mail: sales@ranchopark.com Website: www.ranchopark.com
Contact: Stan Cheren
Founded 1988. Translates Spanish, French, German, Portuguese and German. Mostly sales and marketing, books and brochures. Prospective translators should have 10+ years experience and full computer /online capabilities. Resumes are filed for future projects. The company also has desktop publishing capabilities. Maintains a pool of over 700 translators.

**Rapport International**, 3 Stonegate Lane, #3 Middleboro, MA 02346 Phone: (508)946-3443 Fax: (508)946-3533
e-mail: rapport@rapportintl.com Website: www.rapportintl.com
Contact: Lisa Gavigan Member: ATA

**Rennert Bilingual Translations**, 216 East 45th St., 17th Fl. New York, NY 10025 Phone:(212)867-8700 Fax:(212)867-7666
e-mail: translations@rennert.com Website: www.rennert.com
Contact: Mikael Poulsen, Director
Founded 1973. Member: ATA, New York Circle of Translators. Translates all languages. Emphasis on all aspects of Patent Law, Marketing, Public Relations, Business and Finance, Videos and Educational Material translation, and website localization. Prospective translators should possess training and experience in the specific fields. Resumes are reviewed for education and experience, and a Rennert application is sent to the translator for completion. Maintains a pool of 3000 translators.

**Rescribe**, P.O. Box 503981, San Diego, CA 92150
Phone: (858)487-5292 Fax: (858)487-5292
e-mail: erin@rescribe.com Website: www.rescribe.com
Contact: Erin Berzins
Founded 2001. Member: ATA. Accepts resumes. Translates mainly Spanish, French, Chinese, Vietnamese, Japanese, Italian, German, Korean and Russian. Mostly legal, insurance, medical, finance and insurance. Has a pool of several thousand translators.

**Richard Schneider Enterprises, Inc.**, 27875 Berwick Drive, Suite A, Carmel, California 93923
Telephone: (800)500-5808 x25 Fax: (831)622-0524
e-mail: sandra@idioms.com Website: www.idioms.com
Contact: Richard A. Schneider Member: ATA

**Rosetta**, 2261 Market St. #318, San Francisco, CA 94114
Phone: (415) 550-9151 Fax: (415)550-9162 e-mail: oshea@sirius.com
Contact: Christina O'Shea, Director
Founded 1995. Member: ATA. Translates Japanese, Chinese, French, German and Korean, both from and into English, and Italian, Spanish, Thai, Swedish, Norwegian, Polish, Danish, Dutch, Portuguese and Russian into English. Emphasis on Computer (hardware and software), Semiconductors, Chemical, Medical, Pharmaceutical, Automotive, Patent, Business, and Marketing translation. Prospective translators should have at least five years experience as translators, plus five years experience in a technical field or in business, and a degree in their area of specialization. Resumes are entered into a data base and sent a test if they fulfill company requirements. The company hires translators with technical specialties as opposed to "generalists" and has every document reviewed for accuracy by a technical editor. Maintains an "active" pool of 50 translators.

**Rosetta Stone Associates, Inc.**, 34 Franklin St., Ste. 200A, Nashua, NH 03063 Phone: (603)883-9388 Fax: (603)595-8673
e-mail: translate@rosettastoneinc.net Website: www.rosettastoneinc.net
Contact: Jana Coughlin
Founded 1972. Member: ATA, STC. Accepts resumes. Translates mainly French, Italian, German, Spanish, Russian, Chinese, Japanese, Arabic, Portuguese and Greek. Mostly industrial, medical, legal, scientific, marketing, computers, software and localization. Uses pool of over 2000 translators.

**Russian and Slavic Language Services**, 271 Madison Ave., 3rd Fl., New York, NY 10016 Phone: (212)481-4980
Fax: (212)683-4801
e-mail: karina@russiantranslation.com
Website: www.russiantranslation.com
Contact: Karina Gukasyan Member: ATA

**RussTech**, 1338 Vickers Rd., Tallahassee, FL 32303
Phone: (850)562-9811 Fax: (850)562-9815
e-mail: Contact: Cynthia Seaborn Member: ATA

## -S-

**S.B.F. TRANSLATIONS INC.**, 5601 Collins Ave #1021, Miami Beach, Florida 33140 Phone: (305) 866-6079
Fax: (305) 866-6162
e-mail: SBFTRANS@AOL.COM
Contact: Silvia B. Fernandez
Founded 1994. Member: ATA. Accepts resumes. Translates Spanish, Portuguese and Creole. Mostly legal, medical, immigration and Christian books. Has three translators.

**SH3, Inc.**, 5338 East 115th St., Kansas City, MO 64137
Phone: (816)767-1117 Fax:(816)767-1727
e-mail: chubbard@sh3.com Website: www.sh3.com
Contact: Cathy Hubbard, General Manager
Founded 1980. Member: ATA, STC. Translates mainly French, German, Spanish, Italian, Dutch, Portuguese, Swedish, Chinese and Japanese. Emphasis on Agricultural and Industrial Equipment, and Consumer Equipment translation. Prospective translators should

have Windows-based computer, modem and fax; they should have experience in the agriculture, industrial and mechanical areas. Translator's Workbench is a definite plus. Resumes are reviewed by subject specialty, experience, and language, and flagged for a future contact. Does around 20 million words a year. The company deals in high volume, highly technical manuals. Maintains an active pool of 70 translators.

**Sajan, Inc;** 215 N 2nd St, River Falls, WI 54022 Phone: (715)426-9505 Fax: (715)426-0105 e-mail: info@sajan.com Web Page: www.sajan.com; Contact: Angel Zimmerman, Director of Operations
Member: ATA; Founded in 1997. They translate English in to European Spanish, Latin American, European Portuguese, European French, Canadian French, German, Italian, Norwegian and Swedish. They also Translate English into all Western European Languages, all Eastern European Languages and all Asian Languages. Main subjects are medical, medical devices, engineering, technical, dentistry, and general. They specialize in translation services and editing/proofing. Accepts freelance resumes. They require 5 or more years translating experience and translating in particular fields. Also ATA accreditation or equivalent in target language country. Their annual work_load is about 2,500,00 words per year. They have 300-400 translators in their pool.

**SARJAM Communications, Ltd.**, 4370 NE Hulsey St., Ste. 122, Portland, OR 97213 Phone:(503)287-9277 Fax:(503)287-9277 e-mail: 70314. 1226@compuserve.com
Contact: Seth A. Reames
Founded 1987.Member: ATA. Translates Japanese, Korean, Chinese, Spanish, German, French, Italian and Russian, both from and into English. Translates all subjects. Prospective translators should have 5+ years experience, a computer (MAC or PC), fax and modem. Resumes are examined and filed by language. The company also offers desktop publishing and graphic design. Their in-house computers are Macintosh. Maintains a pool of 40-50 translators.

**Schreiber Translations, Inc.**, 51 Monroe St., Ste. 101, Rockville, MD 20850 Phone:(301)424-7737 Fax:(301)424-2336
e-mail: translation@schreibernet.com Website: www.schreibernet.com Contact: Walter Stankewick, Director, Translation Services
Founded 1984. Member: ATA. Uses freelance translators and interpreters. Accepts unsolicited resumes only on website. Translates (both ways) mainly Japanese, Russian, German, French, Spanish, Chinese, Italian, Arabic, Korean, Vietnamese, Hebrew, Polish, and Dutch, and close to 90 additional languages and dialects. Emphasis on patents, aerospace, law, medicine, communications, computers, engineering, public relations, military and maritime subjects, chemical subjects, and business and finance. Maintains a pool of over 1300 translators - 350 active, and 200 of those very active. In addition to translation and interpretation, the company produces multilingual brochures and advertisements, prints manuals and business literature in a variety of multinational fonts, and does voiceovers for video and films. Maintains a pool of over 1300 translators—350 active, and 200 of those very active.

**SinoMetrics International, Inc.,** 3503 188th St. SW, Lynnwood, WA 98115 Phone: (425)776-5648 Fax: (425)776-6648
email: info@sinomet.com Website: www.sinomet.com
Member: ATA

**Speak Easy Languages**, 757 South Main St., Plymouth, MI 48170 Phone:(734)459-5556 Fax:(734)459-1460
e-mail: selanguages@earthlink. net
Contact: Cristina Clark
Founded 1980. Member: ATA. Translates all major language pairs. Emphasis on Automotive business, Brochure, Advertising and Legal translation. Prospective translators should be ATA accredited and possess fax and modem capabilities. Resumes are filed and the applicant called upon as the circumstance arises. The company also provides talent for voiceover work. Maintains a pool of 100.

**State Farm Insurance**, One State Farm Plaza, SC-2, Bloomington, IL 61710 Phone: (309)766-3760
Contact: Joan Epperson Member: ATA

**Superior Translations**, 1924 Minnesota Ave., Duluth, MN 55802
Phone: (218) 727-2572 Fax: (218)727-2572
e-mail: towardinc@aol.com Web site: www.isuperiortranslations.com
Contact: Elisa A. Troiani
Founded 1993. Member: ATA. Uses freelance translators and interpreters. Accept unsolicited resumes. Resumes for translation and interpretation should be mailed. Applicants are carefully screened and required to submit samples, references, and tests.

Requirements are honesty, accuracy, editing/proofing skills, reasonable rates, punctuality, and an eye for detail. Translates mainly Spanish, French, German, Japanese, Chinese, Russian, Portuguese, Italian, Polish and Hmong. Emphasis on all subject areas. Has 250_300 translators in its pool.

**Suzuki, Myers & Associates, Ltd.**, P.O. Box 852, Novi, MI 48376 Phone:(248)344-0909 Fax:(248)344-0092
e-mail: language@suzukimyers.com Website: www.suzukimyers.com
Contact: Kumiko Oh
Founded 1984. Member: ATA, MITN, Japan-America Society. Translates Japanese and Korean only, both from and into English. Emphasis on Manufacturing-related translation (Autos, Engineering, Quality Design, Robotics, Plastics, Assembly, Electronics, Paint, Contracts, Product Liability).Prospective translators should be competent and diligent. Resumes are responded to with a phone call. The company provides translation, interpretation, and consultation services in North American-Japanese relations. They also provide DTP services. Maintains a pool of about 40 translators.

**-T-**

**Techno-Graphics and Translations, Inc.**, 1451 East 168th St., South Holland, IL 60473 Phone: (708)331-3333 Fax: (708)331-0003
e-mail: techno@wetrans4u.com Website: www.wetrans4u.com
Contact: Pinay Gaffney
Founded 1972. Member: ATA. Uses freelance translators and interpreters. Accepts unsolicited resumes. Resumes are entered in database. Requires native ability and technical background. Translates (both ways) mainly European, Asian, and Middle Eastern languages. Main areas are telecommunications, agriculture, industry, automotive, and medical. Worldwide pool of 200 translators.

**TechTrans International, Inc.**, 2200 Space Park Drive, Ste. 410, Houston, TX 77058 Phone: (281)335-8000 Fax: (281)333-3503
e-mail: techtrans@tti-corp.com Website: www.tti-corp.com
Contact: Beth Williams Member: ATA

**Techworld language Services, Inc.**, 1250 W. 14 Mile Rd., Ste. 102, Clawson, MI 48017 Phone: (248)288-5900 Fax: (248)288-7900
e-mail: info@techworldinc.com Website: www.techworldinc.com
Contact: Fred Meinberg Member: ATA

**Telelingua International;** 46 Sayre Drive, Princeton, NJ 08540
Phone: (609)951-9511 Fax: (609)951-0550
e-mail: lmellet@telelingua.com Web Site: www.telelingua.com
Contact: hbaraona@telelingua.com
Member: LISA, GALA; Telelingua International was founded in 1985. Jean-Didier Boucau is the CEO of the company. They translate English to FIGS, Japanese, Korean, Chinese, Dutch, French and Spanish. The main subjects that they translate are ERP software, medical/pharma, banking and manufacturing. They do not use freelance translators. They do accept resumes. The resumes are human resources processed. You must be certified. Telelingua is headquartered in Brussels, Belgium and has sales and manufacturing operations in Paris, France and Princeton, NJ. It also has strategic alliances in Latin America and Asia, thus providing it's customers with a global solution to its GILT requirements. Telelingua is also recognized for its leadership in developing cutting edge translation technologies. T-Remote Memory, its best-selling application, is a web-services based Translation Memory technology allowing multiple remote translators to work on the same job at the same time using the same TMs. They have approx. 1,500 translators in their pool.
**TermSeek Inc./Lingotek;** 1257 W. 75 N., Centerville, Utah 84014
Phone: (801)294-7700 Fax: (801)294-7711
e-mail: hr@termseekinc.com Web Page: www.termseekinc.com
Contact: Charles
Member: ATA; TermSeek Inc./Lingotek was founded in January of 2001. They translate English to Spanish, Chinese, Japanese, German, French, Italian, Bosnian, Russian, Arabic and Punjabi. They also did work in over 50 language pairs.The main subjects are medical, legal, engineering, manuals, manufacturing, marketing and genomics. They use freelancers. They also accept resumes. Applicants need to list native language and their rates. They typically employ 4 independent translators on every job. They also develop software to assist their translators in doing the work at a higher level of quality and speed. They currently have about 3,000 translators in their pool.

**TerraSpan, Inc.**, 12647 Alcosta Blvd., Ste. 150, San Ramon, CA 94583
Phone: (925)866-3030 Fax: (925)866-3036
e-mail: galiloupour@terraspan.com Website: www.erraspan.com
Contact: Gloria Aliloupour Member: ATA

**TEXTnology CORPoration**, 20 Trafalgar Square, Ste. 456, Nashua, NH 03063 Phone:(603)883-8398 Fax:(603)883-8998
e-mail: nadeau@textcorp.com Website: www.textcorp.com
Contact: Ronald Nadeau Member: ATA

**Thomson Scientific**, 3501 Market Street, Philadelphia, PA 19104
e_mail: ellen.boyar@thomson.com Web site: www.thomsonisi.com
Contact: Ellen A. Boyar

**3 Way Talk**, 2255 Skyfarm Drive, Hillsborough, CA 94010
Website: www.3waytalk.com
Contact: Dr. B. Goldstein Member: ATA

**3DWord, Inc.**, 4325 Athens High Way, Ste. 4-13, Loganville, GA 30052
Phone: (770)613-0879 Fax: (770)849-9627
e-mail: julieMacgregr@3word.com Website: www.3word.com
Contact: Julie MacGregor Member: ATA

**TLS - Translation Service**, 69 Broad St., Red Bank, NJ 07701
Phone: (732)530-4542 Fax: (732)849-6755
e-mail: trans90@aol.com
Contact: Ingeborg Perndorfer
Founded 1982. Member: ATA. Uses freelancers and accepts unsolicited resumes. Resumes are checked and filed until needed. Applicants must show experience. Translates all languages and all subjects. Maintains a pool of 30-50 translators.

**Total Benefit Communications, Inc.**, 5775-B Glenridge Drive, Ste. 120, Atlanta, GA 30328 Phone: (404)256-5042 Fax: (404)256-5101
Contact: Anne McKillips Member: ATA

**Total System Services, Inc.**, 1600 First Ave., TSYS Corporate Campus, 1st Fl., #1318, Columbus, GA 31901 Phone: (706)649-5450 Fax: (706)649-8148 Contactl: Evan Latham.

**Toward,** 1924 Minnesota Ave**.,** Duluth, MN 55802
Phone: (218)727-2572 Fax: (218)727-2572
e-mail: towardinc@aol.com Web site: www.superiortranslations.com
Contact: Dr. Elisa A. Troiani Member: ATA

**TRADOS Corporation**, 113 S. Columbus St., Ste. 400, Alexandria, VA 22314 Phone: (703)683-6900 Fax: (703)683-9457
e-mail: edith@trados.com Website: www.trados.com
Contact: Edith Westfall Member: ATA

**Traducciones LinguaCorp**, Poba International, #1-20072, P.O. Box 02-5255, Miami, FL 33102 Phone: 58(2)7625745 Fax: 58(2)7625745
e-mail: linguacorp@compuserve.com
Contact: Francisco J. Pance Member: ATA

**Trans Global Translation & Immigration Services**, 175 Fontainbleau Blvd., Ste. 2G 8, Miami, FL 33172

Phone: (305)552-9793 Fax: (305)223-4080
e-mail: trnsglobal@aol.com Member: ATA

**TransACT Inc.**, 8423 Mukilteo Speedway, Ste. 100, Mukilteo, WA 98275 Phone:(206)348-5000 Fax:(206)348-3095
e-mail: support @transact.com Website: www.transact.com
Contact: Ms. Tomi Renshaw
Founded 1994. Member: ATA, NOTIS, Washington Software Assn., ASCD. Translates Spanish, Russian, Cambodian, Korean, Chinese, Lao, Thai, Arabic, Japanese and Vietnamese from English. Emphasis on Education, Medical and Utilities translation. Prospective translators must have computer skills and PageMaker experience. Resumes are reviewed and applicants contacted if needed. The company specializes in translation and typesetting for school districts in the US. Their software division creates custom CD-ROMs for Mac/Win in all languages. Maintains a pool of 20 translators.

**Trans-Caribe Communications, Inc.**, 9109 Queen Elizabeth Court, Orlando, FL 32818 Phone: (407)260- Fax: (407)260-6349
e-mail: transcc@aol.com Website: www.iotrak.com/trans-caribe.html
Contact: Sherry E. Allen-Diaz Member: ATA

**Transemantics, Inc.**, 4301 Connecticut Ave. NW, Ste. 146, Washington, DC 20008 Phone: (202)686-5600 Fax: (202)686-5603
Contact: M-L Wax Cooperman Member: ATA

**Transimpex Translations,** 8301 East 166th St., Belton, MO 64012 Phone: (816)561-3777 Fax:(816)561-5515
e-mail: transmpx@sound.net Web site: www.transimpex.com
Contact: Ingrid Pelger, Doris Ganser or Brian White
Founded 1974. Member: ATA, Board member International. Trade Club of Greater Kansas City. Uses freelance translators and interpreters. Accepts unsolicited resumes. Resumes are put in database until needed. Requires degree in linguistics or translation. Main languages translated are German, French, Spanish, Portuguese, Italian, Japanese, Russian, and Arabic. Translates all subjects, with long experience in localization. Has overall pool of some 5000 translators, with about 150 active ones.

**Transfirex Translation Services, Inc.**, 12509 Village Sq. Terr., #201, Rockville, MD 20852 Phone: (301)984-9753 Fax: (630)604-8323
e-mail: info@transfirex.com Website: www.transfirex.com
Contact: Margaret Johnson
Founded 2001. Member: ATA. Accepts resumes. Main languages are Turkish, German, Spanish, Italian, French and Portuguese. Mostly scientific, engineering, social sciences, and safety, emergency and rescue. Has a pool of 12 translators.

**TRANSGLOBAL Language Services**, 534 Princeton Cove, Memphis, TN 38117 Phone: (901)680-0927
Contact: Robyn Hassell

**Translate4me Inc.;** 9720 Wilshire Boulevard, Suite 205, Beverly Hills, CA 90212; Phone: (310)274-9771 Fax: (310)274-9431
e-mail: translation@translate4me.com Web Page: www.translate4me.com Contact: Olessia Laird
Member: ATA, ITI, BBB. The main languages that they translate are English to French, German, Spanish and Italian. They also translate into 80 languages. They translate into all subjects. Translate4me Inc does use freelance and they do accept resumes. You may send your resume to olessia@translate4me.com. Suitable applicants are sent an application form, terms of business nad are reference checked. They require that applicants have graduated and have at least 5 years translation experience. They should also have professional translator's qualifications. They have about 3,000 translators in their pool.

**Translation Aces, Inc.**, 29 Broadway, Ste. 2301, New York, NY 10006 Phone: (212)269-4660 Fax: (212)269-4662
Contact: Serge Nedeltscheff
Founded 1952. Member: NY Circle, NY Chamber of Commerce. Translates Spanish, French, German, Japanese Italian, Portuguese, Russian and Greek, both from and into English, as well as *all* other language pairs. Emphasis on Legal, Patent, Medical Financial, Scientific, Advertising, Engineering, and almost all other areas of translation. Prospective translators should have "experience, experience, experience." Resumes are responded to with the company's application form. The company has 45 years experience

in providing the legal, financial, advertising, medical and governmental communities with translation, interpreting, voiceover and consulting services. Maintains a pool of about 400 translators.

**Translation Company of America, Inc.**, 10 West 37th St., New York, NY 10018 Phone:(212)563-7054 Fax:(212)695-2385
e-mail: trude@tcany.com Website: www.languagematters.com
Contact: Trudi Mathys Member: ATA

**Translation Company of New York,** 8 South Maple Ave., Marlton, NY 08053 Phone: (856)983-4733 Fax: (856)983-4595
e-mail: tcny2000@cs.com Web site: www.tcny.net
Contact: Jennifer C. Thompson

Founded 1983. Member: ATA. Uses freelance translators and accepts unsolicited resumes. Translates mainly French, German,Spanish, Italian, Japanese, Portuguese, Dutch, Russian, Chinese and Swedish. Main areas are pharmaceutical, chemical, medical, engineering, and electronics. Does about 7_8 million words a year. Has active pool of 200 translators.

**Translation Services, Inc.**, 5860 Forward Ave., Office #1, Pittsburgh, PA 15217 Phone: (412)242-8240 Fax: (412)242-1241
e-mail: ATA-info@translations.us.com
Website: www.translations.us.com
Contact: Lisa M. Heinrich Member: ATA

**Translation Services International**, 1100 South Mint Street, Suite 107, Charlotte, NC 28203 Ph: (704)347-5882 Fax: (704)347-5899
e-mail: info@tsitranslation.com Web: www.tsitranslation.com
Contact: Victor M. Guzman, President/CEO

**Translations & Language Consulting**, 8105 Hearthstone Place, Antelope, CA 95843 Phone: (916)729-4222 Fax: (916)729-4232
e-mail: emorrow@trans-language.com
Website: www.trans-language.com
Contact: Elena Morrow Member: ATA

**Translations Unlimited,** 1455 Forest Hill SE, Grand Rapids, MI 49546 Phone:(616)942-5742 Fax: (616)526-8583
e-mail: lmathews@calvin.edu Contact: Leslie Mathews, Director
Founded 1980. Member: ATA. Accepts resumes. Main languages are French, Spanish, German, Japanese, Portuguese, Italian, and Vietnamese. Main areas are patents, sales literature, video scripts, and voice-overs, employee handbooks, sales literature, legal documents, and technical specifications. Translator pool of 25-30.

**translations.com**, 3 Park Ave., 37th Fl., New York, NY 10016
Phone: (212)689-1616 Fax: (212)685-9797
e-mail: LRC@translations.com Website: www.translations.com
Contact: Pamela Kraljevich
Founded 1999. Member: ATA. Accepts resumes. Translates mainly Spanish, French, German, Chinese, Japanese, Portuguese, Italian, Korean, Norwegian and Swedish. Mostly software, IT-Telecom, finance, travel and medical. Provides full suite of globalization services. Pool of 500 translators.

**Translation3**, 49 Union Park, #2, Boston, MA 02118
Phone: (617)482-2223 Fax: (617)482-2121
e-mail: jjtranslation3@translation3.com Website: www.translation3.com
Contact: Jacqueline M. Jacquiot Member: ATA

**The Translators,** PO Box 303, Topsfield, MA 01983
Phone: (978)887-9234 Fax: (978)887-6657
e-mail: trnslate@shore.net Web site: www.thetranslatorsinc.com

Contact: Jim Swift, Personnel Manager
Founded 1980. Accepts resumes. Translates all languages, mostly medical, patents, human resources, computer, sci-tech, legal, electronic and engineering. Unlimited translator pool.

**Translingua, Inc.**, 5457 Twin Knolls Rd., Columbia, MD 21045
Phone: (410)730-9700 Fax: (410)730-9736
e-mail: moneill@translingua.com Website: www.translingua.com
Contact: Mary J. O'Neill
Founded 1984. Member: ATA, NCATA, STC, CATI. Translates French, Italian, German, Spanish, Japanese, Chinese, Korean, Swedish, Danish, Portuguese, Russian, Hebrew, and Arabic from English. Emphasis on technical, scientific, medical, financial, software, packaging and labeling, marketing and advertising. Specialty in full-service graphics and high resolution double byte output. Prospective translators should have an area of expertise as well as a computer, email, modem, and fax. Resumes are screened, evaluated and databased. The company's translations, often large and multilingual, are aimed at publication and the end user. It provides services for the entire process from project management to printing. Maintains a pool of more than 1000 translators.

**Transperfect Translations International, Inc.**, 3 Park Ave., 28th Fl., New York, NY 10016 Phone: (212) 689-5555
Fax: (212)251-0981
e-mail: info@transperfect.com Website: www.transperfect.com
Contact: Information Member: ATA

**Transtek Associates, Inc.**, 599 North Avenue, Door 9, Wakefield, MA 01888 Phone: (781) 245-7980 Fax: (781)245-7993
e-mail: michele@transtekusa.com Website: www.transtekusa.com
Contact: Michele Phillips
Founded 1964. Member: ATA. Uses freelance translators and interpreters. Accepts unsolicited resumes.

**Tristan Translations**, 1130 Taylor St., San Francisco, CA 94108 Phone:(415)474-2611
Fax:(415)928-4755 e-mail: tristant@ix.netcom .com
Contact: Marc de Tristan, Jr., Owner.
Founded 1978. Accepts resumes. Translates Spanish, German, Chinese, Japanese, Portuguese, French, Italian, and numerous other languages, both from and into English. Emphasis on Patents, Technical Document, Proposals and RFQ, Discovery Document and Insurance Claim translation. Prospective translators should exhibit fluency in the English resume or phone contact, education and word processing and file transfer skills. Resumes are read with an eye to flaws, and if approved, entered into a database for future work. Maintains a pool of over 100 translators.

**Tru Lingua Language Systems, Inc.**, 2081 Business Center Drive, Irvine, CA 92626 Phone: (949)955-1151 Fax: (949)955-1153
e-mail: Trulingua@aol.com
Contact: Diana Knapstein
Founded 1984. Accepts resumes. Translates mainly Spanish, French, German, Dutch, Portuguese and Japanese. Mostly technical, medical and lega. Prospective translators should be ATA certified, ATA members, and possess wide experience. Maintains a pool of over 350 translators.

**Trustforte Language Services**, 271 Madison Ave., 3rd Fl., New York, NY 10016 Phone: (212)481-4980 Fax: (212)481-4972
e-mail: aschroeder@trustforte.com
Website: www.trustfortelanguages.com
Contact: Jackie Cordero
Founded 1992. Member: ATA. Accepts resumes. Works in most languages. Provides translators and interpreters to a variety of fields, from business to entertainment.

**turkishtranslation.com, MSR Consulting Ltd.**, 33 N. High St., Clinton, CT 06143 Phone: (860)669-2777 Fax: (909)363-9150
e-mail: info@turkishtranslation.com Website: www.
turkishtranslation.com
Contact: Asiye Yucel Member: ATA

## -U-

**Uniscape, Inc.**, 1292 Hammerwood Ave., Sunnyvale, CA 94089
Phone: (408)743-3500 Fax: (408)743-3600
Website: www.uniscape.com
Contact: Seda P. Mansour Member: ATA

**United International Services, Inc.**, 12701 W. Warren, Dearborn, MI 48126 Phone: (313)846-6903 Fax: ( 313)846-4278
Contact: Faye Awada Member: ATA

**United Nations Translators & Interpreters, Inc.**, 1515 E. Livingston St., Orlando, FL 32803 Phone: (407)894-6020 Fax: (407)894-6693
e-mail: unti@unti.com Website: www.unti.com
Contact: Fiona Como
Founded 1991. Member: ATA. Accepts resumes. Translates mainly Spanish, Creole, French, German, Arabic, Farsi, Italian, Portuguese and Vietnamese. Mostly legal, medical, technical and INS documents. Uses about 50 translators.

**Universal Dialog**, 4150 Murphy Canyon Road, Suite 210, San Diego, CA, 92109 Phone: (858) 273 9060 Fax: (858) 273 9062
e-mail: email@universaldialog.com Web site: www.universaldialog.com
Contact: Alexandra Briskin Member: ATA

**University Language Center, Inc.**, 1313 Fifth St. SE, Ste. 201, Minneapolis, MN 55414 Phone:(612)379-3574 Fax:(612)379-3832
e-mail: translation@ulanguage.com Website: ulanguage.com Contact: Therese Shafranski, Translation Department Manager
Founded 1986. Member: ATA. Accepts resumes. Translates Spanish, French, German, Italian, Portuguese, Russian, Chinese, Japanese and Hmong, as well as Turkish, Indonesian, Arabic and all Southeast Asian languages. Emphasis in all technical areas. The company handles all phases of production from translation to camera-ready art, including cultural assessment of the source documents. Maintains a pool of 250 translators.

**University Translators Services LLC,** 220 N. 5th Ave, Ann Arbor, MI 48104 Phone: (734)655-7295 Fax: (734)655-1345
e-mail: lfinch@univtrans.com Web Page: www.univtrans.com
Contact: Laurie Finch, President
Member: ATA. Founded in 1988. They do accept freelance and unsolicited resumes. The resumes are entered into their database under language, specialty and location. They require that you have 10+ years of experience, certification and/or ATA and/or Master's Degree in Translation/Interpretation. Their main language pairs are English to French, German, Spanish, Portuguese, Chinese, Japanese, Korean, Thai, Arabic, Urdu and Vietnamese. Some of tier subjects are manuals for automotive & manufacturing of all types, patents, immigration related documentation, consumer surveys, promotional brochures and video for sales, court interpreting, subtitling and voice over, website HTML pages and software localization. Their work load is about 50% written translation and 50% interpretation. They have 25 full time translators or 50 full and part time translators. University Translators Services is a woman owned agency operating in the capacity of an LLC.

**U.S. Translation Company**, 3701 Harrison Blvd., Ogden UT 84403
Phone: (801)393-5300 Fax: (801) 393-5500
e-mail: info@ustranslation.com Website: www.ustranslation.com
Contact: David Utrilla Member: ATA

## -V-

**Venturi Technology Partners,** 400-1 Totten Pond Rd., Waltham, MA 02451 Phone: (781)890-7007 Fax: (781)890-4433
e-mail: mklinger@ventwipartners.com

Web site: www.venturiglobalization.com
Contact: Michael L. Klinger
Founded: 1993. Member: ATA, NETA, STC. Accepts resumes. Translates mainly Japanese, French, Italian, German, Spanish, Korean, Chinese, Portuguese, Hebrew and Arabic. Mostly software, medical and pharmaceutical. Has a pool of 500 translators.

**Vital International Programs, Inc.**, 34514 Dequindre, Ste. C, Sterling Heights, MI 48310 Phone: (586) 795-2500 Fax: (586) 795-5763
e-mail: lnespolo@protranslating.com website: www.vitalinternational.com

**Voices for Health, Inc.**, 894 Fuller NE, #2, Grand Rapids, MI 49503
Phone: (616)458-8388 Fax: (616)458- 8322
e-mail: info@voicesforhealth.com Web site: www.voicesforhealth.com
Contact: Scott Van Til, Translations; Van Nguyen, Interpretation Coordinator.

Founded 1997. Member: ATA. Accepts resumes. Translates mainly Spanish, Vietnamese, Chinese and Arabic. Mostly healthcare and social services. Uses hundreds of linguists.

**Vormbrock Translations, Inc.**, 10415 Jockey Club Drive, Houston, TX 77065 Phone: (281)894-9722 Fax: (281)890-0062
e-mail: VTITrans@pdq.net Website: www.vormbrock.com
Member: ATA

## -W-

**WKI International Communications**, 27 W. 20th St., Ste. 402, New York, NY 10011 Phone: (212)255-6100 Fax: (212)255-8461
e-mail: smwoodruff@wkiintl.com Website: www.wkiintl.com
Contact: Susan Woodruff Member: ATA

**Welocalize.com**, 241 E. 4th St., Ste. 207, Frederick, MD 21701
Phone: (301)668-0330 Fax: (301)668-0335
e-mail: info@welocalize.com Website: www.welocalize.com
Contact: E. Smith Yewell Member: ATA

**Wizards Of The Coast, Inc.**, P.O. Box 707, Renton, WA 98057
Fax: (425)204-5806 Website: www.wizards.com
Contact: David Serra Member: ATA
**Word for Word, Inc.**, 325 W. Chickasaw Rd., Virginia Beach, VA 23462 Phone: (757)557-0131 Fax: (757)557-0186
e-mail: wrd4wrd@exis.net Contact: Curtis Hovey Member: ATA

**Word Magic Software**, 12220 Beechnut PMB 2026, Houston, TX, 77072 Phone: (281)564_3022 Fax: (281)568_2143
e_mail: info@wordmagicsoft.com Web Page: www.wordmagicsoft.com Contact: Kristha Serrano
Founded in 1989; Word Magic Software only translates English into Spanish. They translate any subject. They do not use freelance and they do not accept resumes. They have English-Spanish Translation Software, Dictionary, Thesaurus, Spell Checker, Verb Conjugator. They also offer translation services in both languages, English and Spanish.

**WORDNET, Inc.**, 282 Central St., Ste. 2, P.O. Box 976, Acton, MA 01720 Phone: (978)264-0600 Fax:(978)263-3839
e-mail: wordnet@wordnet.com Website: www.wordnet.com
Contact: lee Chadeayne
Founded 1985. Member: ATA, German-American Business Council. Uses freelance translators and interpreters. Accepts unsolicited resumes. Resumes are reviews and applicants are sent out forms to fill out, and are periodically tested and evaluated. Main languages translated are French, Spanish, German, Italian, Chinese, Japanese, and Korean. Main areas are technical, medical, machinery, legal, and business/marketing. The company specializes in translation, typesetting and printing, preparing brochures, catalogs, manuals, legal agreements and Web pages.They help companies get started in the international marketplace. Maintains a pool of some

2000 translators.

**Worldwide Translations, Inc.**, 2317 Fossil Canyon, Henderson, NV 89052 Phone: (800)293-0412 Fax:(800)536-6995
e-mail: wwtranslate@cs.com Web site: www.wwtranslations.com
Contact: Robert Sansing
Founded 1994. Member: ATA, RAPS, FDLI, DIA, NAJIT. Accepts resumes. Translates mainly French, Italian, German, Spanish, Dutch, Portuguese, Greek, Swedish, Japanese and Chinese. Emphasis on Medical, Machinery Manufacture and Computer Products translation. Prospective translators should be native_speaking ATA members with 5+ years technical translation experience and references. Resumes are responded to by telephone when work becomes available. The company is expert in the CE Mark and Medical Device areas and specializes in the translation of instructional manuals. They hold their translators to a high standard of accuracy. Maintains a pool of over 100 translators.

**The Write Stuff**, 11000 Lake City Way, NE, Seattle, WA 98125
Phone: (206)548-1111 Fax: (206)548-9116
e-mail: translations@writestuff.com Website: www.writestuff.com
Contact: Susan Hedding Member: ATA

**Wudang Research Association,** 2301 South Congress Ave., #1021 Boynton Beach, FL 33426 Phone: (561) 733-1417
e-mail: tmorgan@wudang.com Web site: www.wudang.com
Contact: Theresa M. Morgan

**-Z-**

**Zanzitek, LLC**, 475 Commonwealth Ave., Ste. 101, Boston, MA 02215
Phone: (617)236-7791 Fax: (617)236-7792
e-mail: antonio_gangemi@zanzitek.com
Contact: Sara M. Demeter

## FOREIGN TRANSLATION COMPANIES

**Argentina**
**Translationary,** Viamonte 524, 2º Ofc. 17, Buenos Aires, 1053 Argentina Phone: 54(11)43130088 Fax: 54 (11) 43115301
e-mail:info@translationary.com
Contact: Marcos von Haeften

**Australia**
**Pacific Rim Translation International Pty., Ltd.**, Level 10, 55 Swanton St., Melbourne, Victoria 3000, Australia
Phone: 61(3)96533012 Fax: 61(3)96548644
e-mail: apak@prti.com.au Website: www.prti.com.au
Contact: Audrey Pak

**Belgium**
Anthea Languages S.A., 8 Quai Godefroid Kurth, Liege, B4020 Belgium
Phone: 32(4)3444566 Fax: 32(4)3444335
e-mail: info@anthealanguages.com
Website:www.anthealanguages.com
Contact: Yves G. Vanneste

**Brazil**
**Amerikas Traducôes. Ltda.**, Av. Franklin Roosevelt 39, Ste. 1108, Rio de Janeiro, RJ, 20021-120 Brazil
Phone: 55(21)533-5821 Fax: 55(21)533-6853
e-mail: amerikas@tradutores.com
Contact: Leonardo R. Moraes

**Canada**
**All Languages Ltd.**, 421 Bloor St. E, Ste. 306, Toronto, Ontario
M4W 2T1 Canada Phone: (416)975-5000 Fax: (416)975-0505
e-mail: info@alllanguages.com Website: www.alllanguages.com
Contact: Paul M. Penzo

**The Bank of Nova Scotia**, 44 King St. W, Toronto, Ontario M5H 1H1 Canada Phone: (416)866-3354 e-mail: joanne.akai@scotiabank.com
Contact: Joanne Akai
**Global Translations & Interpreters Services, Inc.,** 277 Wellington St. W, Ste. 710, Toronto, Ontario M5V 3E4, Canada
Phone: (416)593-1444 Fax: (416)593-6344
e-mail: mailbox@globaltranslations.com
Website: www.globaltranslations.com
Contact: Tim Koressis

**HSN Linguistic Services Ltd.**, 5360 Canotek Rd., Unit 20, Gloucester, Ontario K1J 9ES, Canada
Phone: (613)748-1915 Fax: (613)748-5596
e-mail: dcyr@hsntraslation.com Website: www.hsntraslation.com
Contact: Diane Cyr

**in FRENCH only inc./in SPANISH too! Translations,** 25 Rockcastle Drive, Toronto, Ontario M9R 2V2, Canada
Phone: (416)248-5648 Fax: (416)614-3806
e-mail: translations@idirect.com Website: www.translations.ca
Contact: Kim Pines
**Multicorpora R&D Inc.**, 490 Saint Joseph Blvd., Ste. 102, Hull, Quebec, J8Y 1G3, Canada
Phone: (819)778-7070 Fax: (819)778-0801

e-mail: info@multicorpora.com   Website: www.multicorpora.com
Contact: Gerry Gervais

**Parenty Reitmeier Translation Services,** 123-B Marion St., Winnipeg,
Manitoba R2H 0T3, Canada
Phone: (204)237-3737   Fax: (204)237-9997
e-mail: Joanne@parenty.mb.ca   Web site: www.parentyreitmeier.com
Contact: Joanne Rasmussen
Founded 1992. Member: ATA, STC, SAE, LISA. Accepts resumes. Requires translation into mother tongue and knowledge of Trados. Main languages are French, Spanish, Portuguese, German, Italian, Dutch, Danish, Norwegian, Swedish and Finnish.Mostly mechanical, medical and legal. Maintains pool of 90 translators.

**Shoreline Translations, Inc.**, 100 Waverley St., #103, Ottawa, Ontario K2P 0V2, Canada   Phone: (613)237-3503
Fax: (613)237-3503
Contact: Gordon R. McLeod

**Transcript Communications, Inc.**, 625 Ave. du President Kennedy, Bureau 800, Montreal, Quebec H3A 1K2, Canada
Phone: (514)874-9134   Fax: (514)874-9192
e-mail: info@comtranscript.com   Website: www.comtranscript.com
Contact: Wilma Scappaticci

**China**

**Beijing E-C Translation & Localization Co., Ltd.,** P. O. Box 9213, Ste. 3001-3004, Hui Bao, Long Commerce Center, Beijing, Capital, 100076, China
Phone: 86(10)67987599   Fax: 86(10)67987619
e-mail: info@e-cchina.com   Web site: www.e-cchina.com
Contact: James Wei

**Transco Technology Co., Ltd.**
B406 Grand Pacific Garden Mansion, 8 Guanghua Road, Beijing 10026, China
Phone: (8610) 6581 9699  Fax: (8610) 6581 9799
e-mail: info@Transco.com.cn   Web site: www.Transco.com.cn
Contact: Vic Dickson
Founded 1998. Member: ATA, LISA. Accepts resumes. Translates only Chinese into and from English, both traditional and simplified. Mostly technical, software. Has more than 100 in-house staff.

**Denmark**

**eb Graphics Design**, Boserupvej 13, Farum, Denmark
Phone: 45 44 99 66 36   Fax: 45 44 99 66 37
e-mail: dkgraph01@attglobal.net
Website: www.users.cybercity.dl/~dko1501/
Contact: Boris Christensen
Founded 1993. Member: ATA. Accepts resumes. Translates Swedish into Danish and English into Danish. Mostly IT, Technical, marketing and automotive. Has 6 translators.

**Network Communications, A/S**, P.O. Box 2034, Hobrovej 134, Randers, DK-8900, Denmark
Phone: 45(86)407600   Fax: 45(86)424311
e-mail: network@netcomms.dk   Website: www.netcomms.dk
Contact: Robin Brown

**France**

**Medialocate**, 31 Rue Tourat, Bordeaux, 33000, France
Phone: 33(5)56822828   Fax: 3(3)556811818

e-mail: info@medialocate.com Website: www.medialocate.com
Contact: James A. Anderson

**Germany**

**Fachübersetzungen C.P. MacKusick**, Im Eck 4, Niederweiler, D-55491, Germany Phone: 0049(6543)6062 Fax: 0049(6543)6286
e-mail: cpm@mackusick.de Website: www.mackusick.de
Contact: Christine P. MacKusick

**Localize-IT Communication Services GmbH**, Lohenstr. 8, 82166 Graefelfing, Germany Phone: 49(0)898786-0 Fax: 49(0)898786-33
e-mail: info@Localize-it.de Website: www.Localize-it.com
Contact: Rolf W. Blum
Founded 1999. Member: ATA, BDUE, STC, LISA. Accepts resumes. Translates English and German into all European language. Mostly IT, telecom and software. Maintains pool of 120 translators.

**SAP AG**, Postfach 1461, Walldorf, 69185, Germany
Phone: 49(6227)741830 Fax: 49(6227)744260
e-mail: hanno.holzheuser@sap.com Website: www.sap.com
Contact: Hanno Holzheuser

**Scholl Translations International**, Nuen Morgen 1, Remseck, 71686, Germany Phone: 49(7146)821067 Fax: 49(7146)3780
e-mail: scholl@aol.com Website: www.scholl-translations.com
Contact: U.L. Scholl-Ogholoh

**SciTech Communications GmbH**, Im Weiher 12, Heidelberg, D-69121, Germany Phone: 49(6221)905040 Fax: 49(6221)161935
e-mail: info@scitech.de Website: www.scitech.de
Contact: Brigit Stäudel
Founded 1994. Member: ATA. Accepts resumes. Main language pairs are German into English, French, Italian, Spanish and Portuguese. Mostly medical, technical and scientific. Pool of about 50 translators.

**Siemens Language Services**, Steinstr. 14, Velbert, 42553, Germany
Phone: 49(5251)8-11558 Fax: 49(5251)2053-504002
e-mail: ilona.volmer@mch20.sbs.de
Website: www.siemens.com/language_services
Contact: Helen Volmer

**XTRA Translation Services**, Calwer Str. 7, Boeblingen, 71034, Germany Phone: 49(7031)2136653 Fax: 49(7031)2136677
e-mail: stefan.lampert@xtra-services.com
Website: www.xtra-services.com
Contact: Stefan Lampert

**Hong Kong**

**Mutilingual Translation Services**, 8/F, Sing Hing Commercial Bldg., 139, Wing Lok St., Sheung Wan, Hong Kong, Hong Kong
Phone: (852)25819099 Fax: (852)25819066
e-mail: syhkmts@netvigator.com Website: www.multilingual.com.hk
Contact: Stephen Viu

**India**

**International Academy of Foreign Languages**, S-351 Greater Kailash Part-I, New Delhi, 110048, India
Phone: 91(11)6475810 Fax: 91(11)6235557

e-mail: iafl@nde.vsnl.net.in Website: www.iafltrans.com
Contact: Narender Parwanda
Founded 1989. Member: ATA. Does not accept resumes. Translates mainly Hindi, Urdu, Bengali, Gujarati, Arabic, Punjabi, Tamil, Nepali, Marathi, Dari, Persian and Pushtu. Mostly business, telecommunications, medical, legal and IT. Has a pool of 800 translators.

**Ireland**
**Alchemy Software Development**, Harcourt Business Centre, Block 2, Harcourt Street, Dublin 2, Ireland
Phone: +353-1-708-2800 e-mail : info@AlchemySoftware.ie
Web Site : www.AlchemySoftware.ie
Contact: Anthony G. Powch

**Italy**
**Interlanguage S.R.L.**, Strada Scaglia Est 134, Modena, MO 41100, Italy
Phone: 39(059)344720 Fax: 39(059)344300
e-mail: info@interlanguage.it Website: www.interlanguage.it
Contact: Susanna Ferretti
Founded 1986. Member: ATA. Accepts resumes. Main languages are Italian, German, French, Spanish, Portuguese and Dutch. Mostly mechanics, electronics, textiles, ads, marketing, legal, finance, economics and tourism. Has pool of about 500 translators.

**Lexikon**, Via Carlo Cattaneo 21, Napoli, 80128, Italy
Phone: 39(081)5586768 Fax: 39(081)5586737
e-mail: info@lexikon.it Website: www.lexikon.it

**Lexis Srl**, Via Dario Campana 56/A, Rimini, 47900, Italy
Phone: (39)0541790190 Fax: (39)0541790685
e-mail: lexis.rimini@lexisitalia.com Website: www.lexisitalia.com
Contact: Roberto Ganzerli

**Japan**
**Techlingua, Inc.**, 10-3-206, Denen-Chofu 1-chome, Tokyo, 145-0071, Ota-ku, Japan Phone: 81(3)37225211
Fax: 81(3)37215223
Contact: Atsushi Tomii

**TranNet.K.K.**, 26-40 Shinjuku, 7–Chome, Shinjuku-Ku, Tokyo, 160-0022, Japan Phone: 81(3)52875881
Fax: 81(3)52875882
e-mail: hamaji@trannet.co.jp Website: www.alc.co.jp/trannet
Contact: Michio Hamaji

**Malta**
**International Translation Agency LTD Malta**, "Ajirce"/5, Testaferrata St., Msida, MSD 02, Malta
Phone: (356)322404 Fax: (356)319008
e-mail: corporate@translatedotcom.com
Website: www.translatedotcom.com
Contact: Rachid Titouah

**Mexico**
**Comunicar Servicios Profesionales de Traducción & Interpretación**, Joaquin Romo 109-103, Colonia Miguel Hidalgo, Mexico D.F. 14260, Mexico Phone: (5)6060389 Fax: (5)6650268
e-mail: comunica@avantel.net Contact: Maria Elena Cruces Ramirez

**Netherlands**
**Alchemy Software Development**, Harcourt Business Center, Bloch 2 Harcourt St., Dublin 2, The Netherlands Phone: (353)170-8280

Fax: (353)170-8280 e-mail: tonyod@alchemysoftware.com
Website: www.alchemysoftware.com Contact: Anthony G. Powch

**WYO Translation Agency**, P.O. Box 292, Emmasingel 51, Weert, 6001BA, The Netherlands
Phone: 31(495)537334 Fax: 31(495)543219
Website: www.wyo.nl

**Peru**
**INTERCONTACT - PERU**, Gral. Borgoño 518, Lima, 18 Peru
Phone: 51(1)4474157 Fax: (51(1)4474157
e-mail: interc6@attglobal.net Website: www.intercontactperu.com
Contact: Claudia Delgado Nachtigall

**Portugal**
**Cial Lingua Service International**, Avenue República, 41-8 , Lisbon, 1050 Portugal Phone: 351(1)7937610 Fax: 351(1)7960783
e-mail: cialis@mail.telepac.pt

**Russia**
**Delos O.O.O.**, 10-14, Nagatinskaya Naberezhnaya, Moscow, 115533 Russia Phone: 007-0959552530 Fax: 007-0959552530
e-mail: russianize@delos.ru Website: www.delos.ru
Contact: Anna Evgrafova
Founded 1990. Member: ATA, LISA. Accepts resumes. Main languages are Russian, German, French, Spanish, Japanese, Portuguese and Chinese. Mostly petroleum engineering, electric engineering, telecom-munications and IT. Has a pool of 200 translators.

**Singapore**
**Getlocalized.Com**, 46a & 48a Bukit Pasoh Rd., Singapore, 089858 Singapore Phone: (65)2200633 Fax: (65)3237097
e-mail: deepali@teamworks.com.sg Website: www.getlocalized.com
Contact: Deepali Chaturvedi

**Spain**
**Hermes Traducciones Y Servicios Lingüísticos**, Ronda de Poniente,
6-2 E, Centro Empresarial "Euronova", Tres Cantos, Madrid 28760, Spain Phone: 34(91)8036294 Fax: 34(91)8035300
e-mail: hermestr@hermes.com Website: www.hermestrans.com
Contact: Juan José Arevalillo
Founded 1991. Member: ATA, LISA, ACT. Accepts resumes. Translates mainly Spanish from and into other European languages. Mostly computing, localization, legal, medical, finance and business. Has 20 in-house translators and 25 off-site.

**Interglossa, S.C.P.**, C/Rosselló 34, 2 -2 , Barcelona, 08029, Spain
Phone: 34(93)5396910 Fax: 34(93)5396911
e-mail: interglossa@interglossa.com Website: www.interglossa.com
Contact: Sonia Carrera Martinez Member: ATA

**Translationary,** Corsega 281, 08008, Barcelona Phone 34 932176822,
Web site: www.translationary.com
Contact: Marcos von Haeften

**Switzerland**
**CLS Corporate Language Services AG**, Dianastrasse 6, P.O. Box 1003, Zurich, 8039 Switzerland Phone: 41(1)2066850 Fax: 41(1)2066890
e-mail: cls@cls.ch Website: www.cls.ch

Contact: Doris Marty-Albisser

**Taiwan**

**American Translation Link (AT-Link),** 8F-12, 2 Fuhsing North Rd., Taipei, 104 Taiwan
Phone: 886(2)27763577 Fax: (419)793-1279
e-mail: mwang@american-translation.com
Website: www.american-translation.com Contact: Muriel Wang

**United Arab Emirates**

**Eman Translation Services**, Beniyas Square, Shaikha Maryam Bldg., 1st Fl., Office 104, Dubai, 27750 United Arab Emirates
Phone: 00971(4)2247066 Fax: 00971(4)2247944
e-mail: ets@emirates.net.ae
Contact: Omer Bashier
Founded 1995. Accepts resumes. Translates mainly Arabic, French, German, Italian, Spanish, Farsi, Hindi, Chinese and Turkish. Mostly legal. Has pool of 10 and uses freelancers.

**United Kingdom**

**Chambers Harrap Publishers Ltd.**, 7 Hopetoun Crescent, Edinburgh
EH7 4AY, United Kingdom
Phone: +44(0)131 556 5929 Fax: +44(0)131 556 5313
e-mail: admin@chambersharrap.co.uk
Website: www.chambersharrap.co.uk
Contact: Administrator
Founded 1994 (Chambers - 1890; Harrap - 1901). Member: ATA. Accepts resumes. Requires excellent language skills and experience of dictionary translation. Translates mainly English into French, Spanish, German, Italian and Portuguese. Mostly dictionaries and language guides, including slang, business and IT dictionaries. Uses 20-50 translators.

**CTT Languages**, Fieldgate, Coltstaple Lane, Horsham, RH13 7BB, United Kingdom Phone: 44(7000)005006 Fax: 44(7000)005007
e-mail: info@ctt-languages.co.uk Website: www.ctt-languages.co.uk
Contact: Tristan Loraine

**The Language Technology Centre, Ltd.**, 5-7 Kingston Hill, Kingston Upon Thames, Surrey, KT2 7PW, United Kingdom
Phone: 44(208)5492359 Fax: 44(208)9746994
e-mail: asirjean@langtech.co.uk Website: www.langtech.co.uk
Contact: Adriane E.M. Rinsche

**SDL International**, Butler House, Market Street, Maidenhead, Berkshire SL6 8AA, United Kingdom
e-mail: cstoldt@sdlintl.com Website: www.sdlintl.com
Contact: Vendor Management Group

**TECHNOTRANS**, Ridgeside Farm, The Ridge, Corsham, Wiltshire SN13 9PL, United Kingdom, Phone: 44(0)1225 811 891 Fax: 44(0)1225 811 416
e-mail: tmoa@ukgateway.net
Contact: Thomas Moser

## APPENDIX F: COMPUTERS, TRANSLATION, AND THE INTERNET

Digital technology as it relates to translation and to almost anything else in today's world is in a constant state of change. In the nearly three years since this handbook was last revised, computers have become more dominant in the translation craft. More work is now being transmitted electronically by e-mail attachment rather than by fax. The Internet has become a routine tool for translators – from work search to word search. And a growing number of translators has become involved in the translation of such computer-based material as websites, a process now generally referred to as localization. All this has resulted in this newly revised and expanded chapter that looks at all the above developments and how they benefit or fail to benefit translators.

Once you have read this chapter you will be glad to find out that one thing has not changed, which should come as no surprise: translation continues to be a human, rather than a machine function. Computers are no closer now to replacing human translation than they were three years ago, or at any other time in the past. Notwithstanding the great benefits translators are deriving from the digital revolution, computers continue to be the tools, rather than the decision-makers of the translation process.

### Computers and Related Equipment

As was mentioned before, only a few years ago a translator would use a pen or a typewriter to translate. In 1980, for example, the ultimate text-producing tool in the world was the IBM Selectric electric typewriter, which we thought we would proudly bequeath to our children and grandchildren. All of this changed forever with the birth of the word processor, and more specifically, the PC, or Personal Computer, which is getting better every year, as if it were a magical tool with boundless possibilities. Certainly the PC has changed the lives of translators, increasing their productivity and profitability three- and fourfold, and enabling them to receive and transmit work, look for answers to linguistic questions, communicate around the world, and take advantage of computer-assisted tools (see below) that in certain cases can save a great deal of time and effort.

#### *Bare Minimum Hardware and the Wish List*

The electronic age offers a great deal more than the word-processor. There is the fax, modem, optical scanner, e-mail, various types of translation software such as translation memory, and last but not least, the Internet. No doubt, it all seems quite overwhelming. Which is the best tool? How much should I spend? How much do I need?

Perhaps the best way to start is by asking two questions: What is the bare minimum a translator needs to get started, and, if money were no object, what would be my wish list of electronic equipment?

The first thing you need to get is a good, current personal computer. This is a must. The question is whether to get a desktop PC, or a portable notebook? The desktop PC is bigger,

heavier, has a larger, easier-to-read screen, and an easier-to-use keyboard. The notebook, on the other hand, only weighs a few pounds, can fit in your briefcase, can be used anywhere (it has a rechargeable battery that gives you several hours of use), and, like a toothbrush, becomes a truly personal item. This book is being revised on a three-year-old IBM ThinkPad notebook. Though thin (1.8 inches) and flimsy-looking, it is a real powerhouse. The base price was $1,699.00. For $99.98 I upgraded the memory from 32MB RAM (see glossary in the back of the book) to 64MB. For $225.98 I got a second battery for more cordless computing hours while traveling. For $237.98 I got a 3-year warrantee for parts and service. It has a 266MHz Intel Pentium II processor, 3.2GB of hard drive space (upgradable to 6.4GB), a 56K modem, a 3.5 inch disk drive, and a CD-ROM drive which at the moment hosts a disk containing the entire Encyclopedia Britannica. The color monitor, a 12-inch SVGA, has good, sharp resolution. It operates on Microsoft Windows® 98. I use it mainly for word-processing, for e-mail, to surf the net, occasionally for graphics, and sometimes to hear music. At the moment it has some 25 programs, including WordPerfect 6.0 for Windows, MS Word, Lotus Notes, as well as my Internet provider, to mention only a few.

To me as a translator and a writer, this notebook is the best of all possible worlds. On the other hand, many translators prefer a desktop PC for all sorts of reasons, not all of which are known to me. Since I have access to both, it's hard for me to judge. My suggestion to you is to check around and try both, and make your own decision. But again, a translator without a computer in this day and age is like a painter without brushes. One more thing: The standard computer for translators is the IBM or IBM-compatible. The Macintosh, favored by graphics people, is not nearly as widely used in our circles, so we will concentrate here on the former.

The above configuration of my notebook computer, which one can also get in a desktop PC (except for the batteries), is quite close to what a translator would consider a "wish list" configuration. Keep in mind that there is a vast difference between storing text and storing graphics on a hard drive. One hundred pages of text take less disk space that one or two pages of graphics. If your translation work entails extensive graphics, you need a bigger hard drive and a faster computer, and the cost can go up 50%-100%. Most translators, however, do not have such a need. Instead, they can store data on their hard drive, and when it gets too crowded, they transfer files to a disk.

The other item that's a must is a printer. Although you can deliver text on disk or by e-mail, there are many good reasons why you need a printer. First, there is still a widespread requirement for hard copy. Second, you may want to print drafts to check your translation, and third, you need a printer for correspondence, for printing your resume, and certainly for printing an invoice. We recommend the Hewlett Packard family of printers, particularly the LaserJets. Depending on the volume, you can start with a smaller model and go up to the HP 4+ or a newer model, which is a bit faster and better.

The next item that's a must is the facsimile machine, popularly known as the fax. These days information travels very fast, and a sure way to get translation assignments is via the fax. Once you have translated a document, the fastest way to send it back is as an e-mail attachment. In other words, the basic translator tools today are the computer, the printer, the fax and the modem.

Another item you may want to look into is the optical scanner, starting with a recent model of the HP ScanJet family. Be sure to get it with the OCR, or Optical Character Reader. This optional piece of equipment provides two valuable functions—you can scan text from a page into a disk, which can be a great timesaving shortcut, and you can scan graphics, such as tables and photographs, into your text file.

What about the cost? You can easily spend around $5,000 on the above four items, if you go directly to the top of the line. But you don't have to start at the top of the line. You can start a couple of notches below the top, and still be able to give yourself a decent start.

You could, if you really want to watch your pennies, take advantage of the fact that computers are changing so fast, and look in the paper for a year or two old second-hand computer, but not older. You should be able to find a good one for $400-$800. You can do the same with the printer, by getting a second-hand one for about $100, or a new one for about $300-$400. A good modem (at least a 28.8 or higher) can be found for around $100, although you could spend $300-$400. A plain paper fax machine (thermal paper is out) can be found for around $200-$400, or you could start out by using a local service, like Kinko's. In short, you could get started with the basic equipment for as little as $600-$700 if you had to, and go on from there. As you prosper, you can start upgrading.

### *Other Useful Kinds of Software*

You can use your word-processing software for doing record-keeping and invoicing as well, but if your operation becomes more involved you may want to consider a database program, such as Excel, for record-keeping (and also for other databases, such as glossaries), and some basic invoicing program, which only runs $20-$30.

To protect your computer against computer viruses—the dreaded new computer age affliction—you may want to get a program such as Norton AntiVirus. To be able to retrieve lost text, you need the Norton Utilities program. Both are excellent safety measures. Another safety measure is the constant backing up of all your files. This can be done on the hard drive or on an external medium such as floppy disk or CD disk. Computers are great when they work, but when they fail they can cause you serious losses, which you cannot afford.

For word-processing, translators uses mainly Microsoft Word, but also WordPerfect, the old favorite.

### *Foreign Language Software*

English-language word-processing is the most advanced in the world. Great strides have been made in programs for other languages, but there is still a long way to go. Some languages, such as Russian, Chinese, Japanese, Arabic and Hebrew are simply too complex in either their script or their noun and verb forms or both to lend themselves to, say, spell-check as readily as English. So don't expect to "cruise" as easily in those languages as you do in English. However, if you translate text from English into almost any other language, you are expected these days to deliver the text on electronic media, which means getting involved in word-processing in that language (see Appendix 3, Foreign Language Software Sources).

As a translator from English into a foreign language, you need software that accommodates not only your target-language, but also the source-language, namely, English. Sometimes you'll need to include English text in the body of your Chinese or Arabic text. Also, you have to make sure your foreign language software is compatible with English-language software, so that it can interface with your client's equipment. Therefore, we are focusing here on American-made foreign language software, rather than foreign-made.

### *Foreign Language Software Sources*

In recent years the leading source for European languages software was WordPerfect. Its language modules covered a large variety of languages, and there were frequent upgrades. The WordPerfect foreign language modules are still used by many translators, but the trend is shifting to the localized products of Microsoft. These products use the Unicode system which makes Microsoft's English word processing compatible with its foreign versions, enabling the user to use English and foreign word processing in the same document with relative ease. Microsoft's foreign language word processing is now part of its package of English word processing, which eliminates the high cost only a few years ago of buying foreign language modules separately.

## Machine Translation Vs. Human Translation

Machine Translation, or MT, is the term used to describe trans-lation performed by a computer software program, as an alter-native to human translation (HT), performed by a human translator. Machine Translation belongs in the area of artificial intelligence. Artificial intelligence is the branch of computer science that deals with using computers to simulate human thinking. It looks to create programs that can solve problems *creatively,* rather than merely respond to commands. In other words, to operate just like the human brain.

In the late 1950s people in organizations such as the U.S. Air Force believed that computers would soon be programmed to accept human language input and translate it into English or into any other language. During the following 50 years, millions of dollars were spent by the Air Force and by other U.S. Government bodies and by big business in the hope of having computers take over the human function of translation. So far, the results have been quite limited, for two main reasons: (a) while computers have a seemingly unlimited capacity for processing data, they are a long way from having the capacity to think creatively like human beings; and (b) human language is not merely a collection of signs and symbols that can be easily programmed, manipulated, and computerized. This is true of human language used not only in poetry and philosophy, but also in technical subjects, in which language expresses thought processes far more complicated than merely "one plus one equals two."

Many people today maintain that computers will soon replace translators. Most of those people are not translation experts. In fact, hardly any of them are. Some point to the fact that computers have already replaced typists and secretaries and reduced the work force of many companies. All this reminds me of a remark by George Bernard Shaw, according to which a monkey could write *Hamlet* if it managed to hit all the right keys on the typewriter. Very few translators can lay claim to creating literary works on the order of *Hamlet*, but lumping translators with typists and office support staff is missing the whole point of translation. As long as language continues to communicate more than the immediate literal meaning of words, as long as there are shades of meaning that keep changing all the time, as long as people have to make value judgments about the meaning and intent of a text, one will continue to need human translators to get the job done.

In recent years several companies in the U.S. and around the world have produced software designed to translate from one language into another. This software varies from a very basic word finder for the tourist, to complex programs for translating technical and scientific data. Some of the latter range in price from as low as $250 to as high as $250,000, and have been sold to governments and international organizations. One important lesson, however, has been learned by both the makers of those programs and their consumers. Machine translation does not replace human translation. At best, the former can achieve around 60 percent accuracy, when the goal is as close to 100 percent as possible. Consequently, the expectations regarding MT have been modified, and it is now recognized that to achieve full accuracy such translations must be post-edited by a human translator.

All of the above notwithstanding, Machine Translation does have its uses. Certain limited language environments do allow for machine translation. One example is the Canadian weather bureau, which transmits weather reports in both English and French. The number of words involved in the daily weather report is very limited, and can be easily programmed into a computer for translation from one language into another. Another example is official forms which contain simple basic questions. An organization such as NATO can have forms put out in ten different languages and set up a program to automatically translate each form into those languages. A third example is the Caterpillar company in Illinois that sells its agricultural machinery around the world and maintains operation manuals in various languages. This company has invested millions in its in-house translation software which allows it to update and modify its technical literature in a cost-effective way. In all of the above examples the software was customized for one particular work environment where repetition is the common denominator.

Another use of machine translation is for processing a large body of a foreign language text to find out what the gist of it is, rather than to achieve a fully accurate translation, in order to decide whether on not to select parts of it for accurate (viz., human) translation. This process is only partially reliable.

Translators for the most part are not fond of post-editing machine translation. Often the pay is not adequate, and the work can be harder and more time consuming than translating directly from the original. This certainly applies to freelancers, but also to in-house translators who are on a salary.

At the present time the ones who benefit the most from machine translation are not those who buy such services, but rather the companies who develop and manufacture the software and the translators who work on those machine translation projects either as developers of the programs or editors of the machine-translated text. In other words, machine translation has not made translation cheaper for the average consumer of translation services, and therefore does not pose a real threat to translators.

**Translation Memory**

One computer tool commonly used today in the area of computer-assisted-translation (CAT) is called translation memory. Here sentences and other parts of translated texts are stored and can be used again when the same or similar translation is required. This tool is best applied to major projects, such as automotive operation manuals that are updated or modified on a regular basis, whereby most of the text remains the same while certain sentences and/or paragraphs are changed.

While this tool has its practical uses, it has been hyped beyond its actual application and has been promoted as a universal aid for translators in nearly all types of translation. Here one should be careful not to invest in this kind of software unless one has a clear ongoing use for it. This applies both to individual translators and to translation companies, since in both cases only a small percentage of the work done is of the above-described kind.

Furthermore, as in the case of machine translation and localization (see below), here too the tools are far from able to accomplish their stated goals, and are still being improved upon. Translation memory is certainly not human memory, and while it does work part of the time, human memory remains irreplaceable.

**Localization**

Localization is defined as

the process of creating or adapting a product to a specific locale, i.e., to the language, cultural context, conventions and market requirements of a specific target market. With a properly localized product a user can interact with this product using his or her own language and cultural conventions. It also means that all user-visible text strings and all user documentation (printed and electronic) use the language and cultural conventions of the user. Finally, the properly localized product meets all regulatory and other requirements of the user's country or region.

Clearly, this definition takes us out of the strict realm of translation into the domain of computer programming and international business. It alludes primarily to the localization of websites (as well as software) in other languages and cultures. Two other terms often used in conjunction with localization are internationalization and globalization. The first refers to the preparation of computer text to be used in localization in such a way that it meets the requirements of the target language and culture. Globalization generally refers to both processes together, namely, internationalization and localization.

With the fast proliferation of websites and the rapid growth of many kinds of computer software, a growing number of translation companies have ventured into the field of localization, and more than a few computer hardware- and software-producing companies (including giants like IBM and Microsoft) have turned to the field of translation as a function of localization.

Thus, localization has been presenting translators with new opportunities and some difficult questions. On the one hand, there is a huge volume of text these days in website and software development that necessitates multilingual translation. On the other hand, for a translator to become involved in localization a specialized knowledge of computers is usually required, since website and software localization requires not only language translation but also adaptation of computer commands to the requirements of the target language. Hence, a translator may want to carefully consider how far he or she may wish to become involved in technical computer work that requires skills and training beyond the scope of actual translation work.

It should be mentioned that localization in the sense of translating a text and adapting it to another culture existed long before the computer age. Thus, for example, an American advertisement company in the pre-computer era that planned an international ad campaign for a company such as Coca Cola, had to study the cultures of other countries and customize the ads not only in terms of the target language, but also the cultural conventions, preferences, taboos etc. of the target country. Furthermore, the act of translating itself is in a sense a form of localization, since language does not exist separately from its culture.

Website and software localization has been around now for several years. It relies heavily not only on human translation but also on machine and machine-assisted translation tools, such as translation software and translation memory. Given the limitations of these tools, the often unrealistic expectations of the marketplace and the eagerness to process a large volume of material in record time, localization has been experiencing many problems, and the goals its pursuers have set for themselves are yet to be realized. One should keep all of this in mind before getting involved in this area of translation.

## The Uses of the Internet for Translators

The translation field has become increasingly "wired," witnessing a proliferation of sites relating to professional activities, job-hunting, commercial products, and online reference mate-rials for translators. It is not an exaggeration to say that trans-lators do themselves (and potentially their clients) quite a disservice by ignoring the virtual translation community.

This section will introduce you to a selection of highly-regarded and well-maintained sites of use to translators. It assumes basic Web literacy. Of course, the Internet's ever-changing nature guarantees that certain websites will decline or disappear, while new ones will emerge by the time this book becomes available. So please be aware that you will probably have to do some updating of the following information on your own.

### *Where We Are on the Web*

First, let us invite you to Schreiber Publishing's website. Our address: **schreiberpublishing.com**. Its objective is to provide reference literature, training materials, and useful information for translators.

### *Professional Activities*

Translators wishing to learn about the state of their profession will benefit from a visit to the American Translators Association's
site, **www.atanet.org**. I discuss the ATA in greater detail in the chapter on Translators' Organizations; its Website includes information on the Association's formal activities such as conferences, publications and accreditation procedures. Even if you are not an ATA member, the site is useful because it can guide you to other translation-related sites.

Another major website of interest to translators is the site of the
international umbrella organization of the world's translator associations, the International Federation of Translators, found on **www.fit-ift.org**.

*Aquarius*, at **www.aquarius.net.** Claims to be "the world's language network." This commercial website lists translation agencies seeking translators and interpreters who, in turn, can post resumes to make their services known. It also links to other translation sites.

### *Networking with Other Translators*

An extremely popular program on the Internet for translators has been the *Language Forum* of Compuserve, popularly known as FLEFO (Foreign Language Education Forum). You have to subscribe to this forum to be able to participate. You enter FLEFO in the keyword box and you find yourself in a virtual forum full of translators from around the world, who post messages and get answers to almost any question a translator may ask, from the cost of a dictionary, to the meaning of a word, to a social get-together. FLEFO can also link you to translation wesites.

Another online forum for translators is the newsgroup: subscribers post messages and receive answers (say, to a specialized translation query). A newsgroup for translators is sci.lang. translation.

### *Reference Materials*

*The Translator's Home Companion* at **www.rahul.net/lai/ companion.html**, provides Links to glossaries, dictionaries, translation publications, and other translators.

*The Human Languages Page* at **www.june29.com/IDP** provides links to other translation-related sites, including some listed here.

*Language Today*, an online publication (also available in print; see Bibliography appendix) covering language technology, translation and interpreting: **logos.it/language_today**

### *Online Dictionary Services*

*Eurodicautom* at **www.europa.eu.int/eurodicautom** is a very useful service, Eurodicautom handles European languages such as Spanish, Portuguese, French, German, Italian, English, Danish and Dutch. Includes many specialized dictionaries in non-technical, legal and technical areas. Terms are both translated and defined.

*Online Dictionaries* at **www.yourdictionary.com** covers a far greater range of languages than the above entry. It provides links to dictionaries and translations in many specializations.

### *Glossaries*

There are many mediocre glossaries out there in cyberspace, so use caution with this type of online resource. Here are some better ones:

**www.refer.fr/termisti/liste.htm**

**www.yahoo.com/references/dictionaries**

U.S. Government agencies provide some very useful glossaries. For example:

**www.epa.gov** (for environmental terminology).

### *Finding Cultural Information*

A quick way to access cultural and historical information on other countries is via The Electronic Embassy at **www.embassy.org.** This service provides links to embassy and/or United Nations home pages of many nations. Most countries' pages include links to cultural resources such as online newspapers, libraries, and so on. You may have to do some digging to find the information you're after, but if it exists online, you will probably find it by starting here. Also the foreign ministries of various countries are a good source for all sorts of information related to that particular country.

### *Shopping for Dictionaries*

A prime source for dictionaries is i.b.d. Ltd.'s website is:
**www.ibdltd.com**.

Another site under construction is: **www.schoenhofs.com**.

Major virtual bookstores also have good selections of dictionaries (see box). Examples:

**www.barnesandnoble.com**
**www.amazon.com**
**www.borders.com**

You may also wish to consult these websites of major dictionary publishers:

Elsevier at **www.elsevier.com**
Routledge at **www.routledge.com**
McGraw-Hill at **www.mcgraw-hill.com**

### *Machine Translation*

If you want to experience some machine translation, try these two sites:
**www.babelfish.com/Languages/English/EnglishMachine.shtml**
**http://babelfish.altavista.com**

### *Work Sources on the Internet*

A European-based website that offers work sources and a newsletter with work information for translators is:
**www.transtree.com**
Three websites offer the capability to communicate with other freelancers and find out about the payment practices of translation agencies. For the most part they are free, but you have to join to be able to use them:

**www.trwenterprises.com/payment_practices.htm**
**www.topica.com/lists/transpayment/**
**www.tcrlist.com/**

**Order Form**

**Fax** order to 443-920-3450,
or **e-mail** to SchreiberPublishing@comcast.net,
or **mail** to: **Schreiber Publishing**, PO Box 4193 Rockville, MD 20849 USA
or **call** toll free 1-800-296-1961 (in Maryland 301-725-3906)
or visit our website: **www.SchreiberLanguage.com**

____ copies of ***The Translator's Handbook*** 8th Revised Ed. $25.95 $ ____

____ copies of ***American English Compendium*** 2nd Revised Ed. List price: $24.95 You pay: $22.46 $ ____

____ copies of ***Spanish Business Dictionary*** 3rd Edition. $24.95 $ ____

____ copies of ***Multicultural Spanish Dictionary, 2nd Ed*** $24.95 $ ____

____ copies of ***Translator Self-Training*** $69.00 Circle language(s):

Spanish French German Russian Japanese Chinese Portuguese Italian Arabic Hebrew $ ____

____ copies of ***Translator Self-Training - Spanish Medical*** $69.00 $ ____

____ copies of ***Translator Self-Training - Spanish Legal*** $69.00 $ ____

sub-total $ ____

Maryland residents add 6% sales tax to sub-total $ ____

In the U.S. add $4.50 for shipping/handling per single copy and $2.00 for each additional book.
Overseas add US$9 for one book, and $5 for each additional book (for books priced under $50),
or $18 per book priced over $50 $____

Order total $ ======

Please charge my Visa, MasterCard; Check or money order enclosed.

Name ________________________ Phone ________________ E-mail ________________________

Addrcss ________________________ City ____________ Statc____ Zip ______

Card No. ________ ________ ________ ________ Exp. date (month) ___ (year) ___